Memoirs of a Polar Bear

ALSO BY YOKO TAWADA

The Bridegroom Was a Dog
Facing the Bridge
The Naked Eye
Where Europe Begins

Memoirs of a Polar Bear

•

YOKO TAWADA

Translated from the German by Susan Bernofsky

Portobello
BOOKS

First published in Great Britain by Portobello Books as an ebook in 2016 and in print in 2017

Portobello Books
12 Addison Avenue
London
W11 4QR

First published in the United States in 2016 by New Directions, New York.

Originally published in German by Claudia Gehrke Konkursbuch in 2014 as *Etüden im Schnee*

This is a work of fiction. All of the characters, organizations, and events portrayed in this novel either are products of the author's imagination or are used fictitiously.

A CIP catalogue record for this book is available from the British Library.

1 3 5 7 9 10 8 6 4 2

ISBN 978 1 84627 631 6 (trade paperback)
ISBN 978 1 84627 633 0 (ebook)

Design by Erik Rieselbach

Offset by Avon DataSet Limited, Bidford on Avon, B50 4JH

Printed and bound by CPI Group (UK) Ltd, Croydon, CR0 4YY

www.portobellobooks.com

MIX
Paper from
responsible sources
FSC® C020471

I

THE GRANDMOTHER:
AN EVOLUTIONARY THEORY

SOMEONE TICKLED ME BEHIND MY EARS, UNDER MY ARMS. I curled up, becoming a full moon, and rolled on the floor. I may also have emitted a few hoarse shrieks. Then I lifted my rump to the sky and slid my head below my belly. Now I was a sickle moon, still too young to imagine any danger. Innocent, I opened my anus to the cosmos and felt it in my bowels. Everyone would have laughed if I'd used the word "cosmos" in those days: I was still so small, so lacking in knowledge, so newly in the world. Without my fluffy pelt, I'd have been scarcely more than an embryo. I couldn't walk very well yet, though my paw-hands had already developed the strength to grasp and hold. Every stumble moved me forward, but could you call that walking? Fog shrouded my field of vision, and my ears were echo chambers. Everything I saw and heard lacked contours. My life force resided, for the most part, in my claw-fingers and tongue.

My tongue could still remember the taste of my mother's milk. I took the man's index finger into my mouth and sucked on it, that calmed me. The hairs growing out of the backs of his fingers were like shoe brush bristles. The finger wriggled into my mouth, poking around. Then the man prodded me in the chest, challenging me to wrestle.

Exhausted from playtime, I placed both my paw-hands flat

on the ground with my chin on top—my favorite position for awaiting the next meal. Half asleep, I licked my lips, and the flavor of honey returned to me even though I'd only tasted it a single time.

One day the man attached strange objects to my feet. I tried to shake them off but couldn't. My bare paw-hands hurt, it felt as if the floor were stabbing them from below. I raised my right hand and then the left but couldn't keep my balance and fell back down. Touching the ground made the pain return. I pushed off from the ground, my torso stretched far up and back, and for several seconds I stood upright. When I exhaled, I fell back down again, this time on my left paw-hand. It hurt, so I pushed the floor away from me again. After several more attempts, I was able to balance on two legs.

Writing: a spooky activity. Staring at the sentence I've just written makes me dizzy. Where am I at this moment? I'm in my story—gone. To come back, I drag my eyes away from the manuscript and let my gaze drift toward the window until finally I'm here again, in the present. But where is *here*, when is *now*?

The night has already reached its point of greatest depth. I stand at the window of my hotel room, looking down at the square below that reminds me of a theater stage, maybe because of the circular light cast by a streetlamp. A cat bisects the circle with its supple stride. A transparent silence settles over the neighborhood.

I'd taken part in a congress that day, and afterward all the participants were invited to a sumptuous feast. When I returned to my hotel room at night, I had a bear's thirst and greedily drank water straight from the tap. But the taste of oily anchovies refused to leave me. In the mirror I saw my red-smeared lips, a masterpiece of the beets. I'd never eaten root vegetables voluntarily, but when a beet came swimming in my bowl of borscht, I immediately wanted to kiss it. Bobbing amid the lovely dots of fat floating on top—which at once awoke my appetite for meat—the beet was irresistible.

The springs creak beneath my bearish weight as I sit on the hotel sofa thinking how uninteresting the conference had been yet again, but that it had unexpectedly led me back to my childhood. The topic of today's discussion was The Significance of Bicycles in the National Economy.

Anyone, especially an artist, can only assume it's a trap to be invited to a conference. For this reason, most of the participants refused to say anything at all unless forced. But I willingly piped up—confidently, elegantly, unself-consciously, unceremoniously sticking my right paw high in the air. All the other participants in the assembly hall looked over at me. I was used to attracting an audience's attention.

My round, soft upper body is encased in sumptuous white fur. When I press my raised right arm and rib cage slightly forward, hypnotically shimmering particles of light are released into the air. Yes, I was at the center of everything, while the tables, walls and even the people in the audience gradually faded and withdrew into the background. My fur's gleaming white hue is unlike any ordinary white. It's translucent, permitting the sunlight to reach my skin through the fur, and the light is carefully stored beneath my skin. This is the color my ancestors acquired, allowing them to survive in the Arctic Circle.

To make your opinion known, you have to first be seen by the session leader. This doesn't happen unless you raise your hand quickly—more quickly than all the others. Almost no one can get his hand up in the air at a conference faster than me. "You seem fond of sharing your opinions": I was once treated to this ironic bit of commentary. I parried with a simple response: "That's how democracy works, isn't it?" But that day I discovered it wasn't free will thrusting my paw-hand into the air like that, it was a sort of reflex. I felt this realization like a stab in the chest. I tried to put aside the pain and get back into my groove, a four-part rhythm: The first beat was the session leader's restrained "Go ahead." The second was the word "I," which I slammed down on the table in front of me. On the third beat, all the listeners swallowed, and on the fourth I took a daring step, clearly enunciating the word "think." To give it some swing, I naturally stressed the second and fourth beats.

I had no intention of dancing, but my hips began waggling back and forth on the chair. The chair immediately chimed in, contributing cheerful creaks. Each stressed syllable was like a tambourine underscoring the rhythms of my speech. As if bewitched, the audience listened, forgetting their duties, their vanity, themselves. The men's lips hung limply open, their teeth gleaming a creamy white, and from the tips of their tongues dripped something like liquefied carnality in saliva form.

"I think the bicycle is beyond all doubt the most excellent invention in the history of civilization. The bicycle is the flower of the circus stage, the hero of every environmental policy. In the near future, bicycles will conquer all the world's major cities. And not just that: every household will have its own generator attached to a bicycle. You'll be able to get fit and produce electricity at the same time. You can also get on your bicycle to pay your friends a spontaneous visit instead of first calling them on your cell phone or sending an e-mail. When we learn to utilize the multifunctional capacity of the bicycle, many electronic devices will eventually become superfluous."

I saw dark clouds gathering on several of the faces. Putting even more power into my voice, I continued: "We will ride to the river on our bikes to do our laundry. We'll ride our bikes to the forest to collect firewood. We won't need washing machines anymore, and we won't have to rely on electricity or gas to heat our apartments or cook our meals." Several faces were amused by these fanciful proposals, displaying unobtrusive laugh creases, while others turned gray as stone. Not a problem, I cheered myself on, don't let them intimidate you. Pay no attention to these bores. Relax! Ignore this fake audience, imagine yourself standing before hundreds of ecstatic faces and keep talking. It's a circus. Every conference is a circus.

The chairman coughed dismissively, as if to show he had no intention whatever of dancing to my tune. Then he exchanged a knowing glance with a bearded official seated beside him. I remembered that the two men had entered the room side by side. That official, thin as a nail, wore a matte black suit even though he wasn't at a funeral. He began to speak without first asking permission: "Rejecting automobiles and worshipping bicycles: this is a sentimental, decadent cult already familiar to us from Western countries. The Netherlands is a good example. But supporting machine culture is a matter of the utmost urgency. We must provide rational connections between places of employment and residential areas. Bicycles create the illusion that one might ride anywhere one likes at any time. A bicycle culture could exert a problematic influence on our society." I raised my hand to contradict this line of argument. But the session leader ignored me and announced the lunch break. I left the room without a word to anyone and dashed out of the building like a schoolchild running onto the playground.

As a child, I was always the very first to run out of the classroom at recess, even when I was still in preschool. I would make a beeline for the far corner of the playground and act as if this tiny patch of earth held special significance for me. In reality, it was nothing but a shady, damp spot under a fig tree where brazen neighbors would sometimes secretly deposit their trash. No other child ever approached the spot, which was fine with me. Once one of my schoolmates hid behind the fig tree so he could sneak up on me as a joke. I threw him over my shoulder. It was an instinctual act of self-defense, I didn't mean him any harm, but given my powerful build, he went flying through the air.

Behind my back, the other children called me "snout face"

and "snow baby," as I later learned. Someone tattled, otherwise I would never have heard these nicknames. My informant pretended to be on my side, but perhaps it filled her childish heart with pleasure to see my feelings hurt. Until then, I'd never asked myself what I looked like in my classmates' eyes. The shape of my nose, the color of my fur made me stand out from the majority—it took hearing these nicknames to bring this home to me.

Next to the conference center was a tranquil park with white benches. I picked a bench in the shade. There was a plashing sound behind me, presumably a brook. The willow trees, elegant, cunning, and overcome with ennui, kept poking their thin fingers into the water, perhaps hoping it would play with them. Pale green shoots punctuated their branches. The earth beneath the soles of my feet crumbled, it wasn't a mole at work, just the crocuses. The more impudent among them were doing imitations of the Tower of Pisa. The inside of my ear itched. No digging around in there! This was a rule I never broke, at least not back when I was still working at the circus. But the itching in my ear wasn't caused by wax, it was because of the pollen and the songs of the birds that kept pecking out sixteenth notes in the air. Rosy spring with its unannounced arrival caught me unawares. What sort of trick had it employed to reach Kiev so quickly and surreptitiously, with such a large delegation of birds and flowers? Had it secretly been preparing its invasion weeks in advance? And was I the only one who hadn't noticed, being preoccupied with winter, which had taken charge of my consciousness? I hate making small talk about the weather, so I often miss forecasts of major changes. Even the Prague Spring came as a complete surprise to me. When the name "Prague" occurred to me just now, the beating of my heart became palpable. Who knows, perhaps an even greater change in the weather is about to surprise me, and I'll be the only one here who didn't have the faintest idea what was coming!

The frozen earth melted and muddily wept. A slug of mucus crawled out of my itchy nasal passages, and tears pearled from the swollen membranes around my eyes. In a word: spring is the season of mourning. Some people say spring makes them young again. But a person who gets younger returns to childhood, a return not without its indignities. As long as I could feel pride at being the first to share my opinion at every conference, I was content. I didn't waste time thinking about where this rapid hand gesture of mine had come from.

I had no particular urge to know things, but the spilled milk of knowledge refused to flow back into the glass. And as the milk's sweet scent rose from the tablecloth, I wept for my spring. Childhood, that bitter honey, stung my tongue. It had always been Ivan who prepared my food. I had no memory of my mother. Where had she gone?

Back then I didn't know yet what to call that part of my body. The painful tingling disappeared when I pulled away, it was really just a reflex. But it wasn't possible for me to keep my balance long. I would fall back down again. And the moment my paw-hands came into contact with the ground again, the pain returned.

I'd hear Ivan shout "Ouch!" whenever he scraped his shin or a wasp stung him. So I understood that the expression "ouch" was connected with a particular feeling someone was having. I'd always thought it was the floor feeling pain—not me—so it was the floor that had to change—not me—to make the pain go away. How I struggled until finally I learned to stand upright!

After the official dinner, I came back to my hotel room and wrote up to this point. Writing wasn't a familiar activity to me—

weariness crashed down on my head, and I fell asleep at the desk. Waking up the next morning, I could feel that I'd grown old overnight. Now the second half of life is beginning. On a long-distance run, this would be the midpoint, the moment to turn around, to go back the way I'd come, the starting line my goal. The place where the pain began is where it will end.

Ivan would pluck a morsel of sardine from a can, grind it up in a mortar, add a shot of milk and place it in front of me. A custom-made repast. When I deposited a modest excretion, he'd immediately come running with his dustpan and brush to tidy up. He never scolded me; not even the faintest groan crossed his lips. For Ivan, cleanliness was always a priority. Every day he'd arrive with a dangling long hose and a special brush to clean the floor. Sometimes he'd point the hose at me. There was nothing I liked more than being sprayed down with ice-cold water.

Not often but occasionally Ivan would find himself without a task to perform. He'd sit down on the floor, put his guitar on his lap, pluck its strings with his fingers, and sing. A melancholy tune from some damp back alleyway would turn into a rhythmical dance number before finally plunging into an abyss of endless lament. All ears, I felt something awaken within me, perhaps my first longing for far-off lands. Distant places I'd never seen were drawing me to them, and I found myself torn between there and here.

Sometimes by chance our eyes met, and an instant later I would be in his arms. He would press my head into the crook of his neck, rubbing his cheek against mine. He tickled me, rolled my body back and forth on the floor, and threw himself on top of me.

Since returning from Kiev, I'd done nothing but sit in my room in Moscow, scratching away at my text without respite. My head bent over the letter paper I'd taken from the hotel without asking. I kept painting over the same period of my childhood again and again, I couldn't seem to get beyond it. My memories came and went like waves at the beach. Each wave resembled the one before, but no two were identical. I had no choice but to portray the same scene several times, without being able to say which description was definitive.

For a long time, I didn't know anything: I sat in my cage, always onstage, never an audience member. If I'd gone out now and then, I would've seen the stove that had been installed under the cage. I'd have seen Ivan putting firewood in the stove and lighting it. I might even have seen the gramophone with its giant black tulip on a stand behind the cage. When the floor of the cage got hot, Ivan would drop the needle on the record. As a fanfare split the air like a fist shattering a pane of glass, the palms of my paw-hands felt a searing pain. I stood up, and the pain disappeared.

For days and weeks, the same game would be repeated. In the end, I'd stand up automatically whenever I heard the fanfare. "Standing" wasn't yet a concept for me, but it was clear what freed me from the pain, and this knowledge was burned into my brain together with Ivan's command "Stand up!" and the stick he would hold aloft.

I learned expressions like "Stand up," "Good," and "One more time." I suspect that the strange objects attached to my feet were specially made shoes impermeable to heat. As long as I was standing up on my back legs, it didn't hurt, no matter how the floor glowed with heat.

After the fanfare had come to an end and I was standing steadily on two legs, it was time for the sugar cubes. First Ivan would carefully say the word "sugar cube," and then he would put one in my snout-mouth. "Sugar cube" became my first word for the sweet pleasure that would melt on my tongue after the fanfare and the standing up.

•

Suddenly Ivan stood beside me, looking down at my text from above. "Ivan! How are you? How have you fared since the old days?" These are the questions I wanted to ask, but my voice failed me. As I breathed deeply in and out several times, Ivan's figure silently vanished. He left behind his familiar body heat and a faint burning sensation on my skin. I found it hard to go on breathing normally. Ivan, dead within me for so many years, came back to life because I was writing about him. An invisible eagle clutched my heart in its talons, I couldn't keep breathing, and it occurred to me that I should immediately drink some of that transparent holy water to rid myself of the unbearable pressure. At the time, it was difficult to get good vodka in the city, since most of it was exported as bait for foreign currencies. The superintendent of my shabby apartment building was proud of her connections and the occasional luxury products they netted her. I knew she sometimes had a bottle tucked away in her cupboard.

I hurried out of my apartment, rolled down the stairs, and ambushed the concierge, asking whether she happened to have any of that elixir in her apartment. A peculiar smile appeared on her face, resembling Sumerian cuneiform writing. Indecently rubbing her index finger and thumb together, she asked: "Have you perhaps received some …" Irritated, I replied: "No! I don't have any foreign currency on me!" Now that I'd exposed her sweet, titillating secret, which she'd wanted to share with me surreptitiously, with my use of the loveless, insipid designation "foreign currency," she felt insulted and turned her back on me. Quick, get her in a chatty mood!

"You have a new hairstyle. It looks great on you."

"Oh, do you mean this disgusting mop? I slept on it wrong last night."

"And your new shoes? They're marvelous."

"What, these shoes? You noticed them? I didn't buy them new. A gift from my relatives—I like them."

Although my compliments were obviously just awkward attempts at flattery, the superintendent was willing to acknowledge my good intentions. Like a fat, hairy worm, her gaze crept back toward me.

"You hardly ever drink. Why are you suddenly so interested in my vodka?"

"I was remembering my childhood—even though honestly I'd forgotten all about it for years—and now I find it oppressive. I'm having trouble breathing."

"Did you remember something unpleasant?"

"No. I mean, I don't know yet whether it will be unpleasant or not. For the moment it's just a breathing problem."

"You shouldn't drink to forget. Otherwise you'll end up like that poor district magistrate who used to live above you."

I remembered the day when something heavy crashed down on the cobblestones in front of the building, sounding much heavier than a man's body. I heard the sound once more and was covered in goosebumps.

"You ought to keep a journal if you're interested in stockpiling your experiences."

Her suggestion surprised me—it was so intellectual, it didn't sound like her. I prodded a bit, and she admitted that last week she'd read *Sarashina Nikki*, a masterpiece of Japanese diary literature from the Middle Ages, in Russian translation. Her good connections had made it possible for her—despite the modest edition of fifty thousand copies that had sold out in advance via subscription—to get her hands on a copy. The pride she took in being socially so well connected was no doubt the only reason she'd read the book.

"You must have the courage to write, like the author of this diary!"

"But I thought a diary was for recording the day's events. I want to write to call back to mind something I can no longer remember."

The superintendent listened to me and then casually made one more suggestion: "So write an autobiography!"

There were reasons why I had given up my stage career to spend my valuable time at paralyzingly boring conferences. Back when I was still the shining star of our circus, we were asked to put together an evening's program with a dance company from Cuba. Originally the idea had been for us to take turns performing without truly producing a synthesis. But our collaboration developed in an unforeseen direction. I fell in love with the South American style of dancing and wanted to master it and incorporate it into my repertoire. I had them give me a crash course in Latin American dances and rehearsed assiduously. Too assiduously. After hours and days spent vigorously shaking my hips, my knees were in such bad shape that I was incapable of performing acrobatics of any sort. I was unfit for circus work. Ordinarily they would have just shot me, but I got lucky and was assigned a desk job in the circus's administrative offices.

I never dreamed I had a gift for office work. But the personnel office left no talents of their workers unexplored if they could be employed and exploited to the circus's advantage. I would even go so far as to say I was a born office manager. My nose could sniff out the difference between important and unimportant bills. My inner clock was always right on schedule—I could be punctual without so much as glancing at a watch. When it was time to calculate a paycheck, I never had to wrestle with numbers, for I could read in people's faces what wages they should receive. If I wanted, I could get my boss to approve any project at all, regardless of how utopian it sounded. My mouth mastered the art of premasticating difficult-to-digest material and then communicating a persuasive plan.

There was plenty for me to look after in the service of our circus and the ballet: the preparations for foreign tours, publicity, advertisements for job openings, all the usual administrative paperwork—and, chiefly, attending conferences.

I was perfectly content with my new life until I began to write my autobiography. Suddenly I lost all desire for conference-going. When I sat in my room licking the tip of my pencil, I wanted to go on licking it all winter long, not seeing anyone, just working on my autobiography. Writing isn't particularly different from hibernation. Perhaps I made a drowsy impression, but in the bear's den of my brain, I was giving birth to my own childhood and secretly attending to its upbringing.

I was sucking absentmindedly on my pencil when a telegram arrived with the news that I was to participate in a panel discussion the next day. The topic would be Working Conditions Among Artists.

Panel discussions are like rabbits—usually what happens during such a session is that further sessions are declared necessary—and if nothing is done to prevent this, they multiply so quickly and become so numerous that it is no longer possible to provide a sufficient number of participants, even if we all devote most of each day to these sessions. We've got to think of a way to end this proliferation of panel discussions. Otherwise our bottoms will be squashed flat from all the sitting, and all our organizations and institutions will collapse beneath the weight of our derrieres. There are ever larger contingents of people who use their heads primarily to think up plausible excuses for why they can't possibly show up for the next panel discussion. The excuse virus has been spreading faster than a dangerous flu. And then everyone's real and fictitious relatives are all having to die several times over, so that their funerals can serve to excuse absences. I have no relatives I can condemn to fictional death. My physical makeup makes me immune to influenzas of every sort, and so I'm left without excuses. Time passed, and I kept getting lost in the pages of my appointment book, which had been attacked by a mildew of obligations.

Besides the sessions and conferences, I had to attend formal receptions, look after the official guests of the circus, and take part in business luncheons and dinners. These duties made me ever plumper, and this was the only positive development in my new life. Instead of dancing on the stage, I sat in comfortable chairs in conference rooms, and afterward soiled my fingers with oily pierogi, ate heavy borscht, shoveled glistening black caviar into my mouth, and accumulated a fortune in body fat.

I might have gone on living like that if spring hadn't caught me unawares and shaken me to my core. Now I lay there like a person who's fallen from a tall ladder. When I climb up to the roof to check the tiles in early spring, I'm not thinking that the house might suddenly cave in beneath me; a flawlessly structured republic, a heroic self-portrait in bronze, a stable mood, without ups and downs, a regular life rhythm: suddenly it was all on the brink of collapse, and I hadn't suspected anything. There's no point sitting patiently in a sinking ship, it's better to jump in the ocean and make use of your limbs. It was the first time I'd ever turned down a conference invitation. I was afraid of being annihilated on account of saying no: those who refuse to fulfill their duties lose their right to exist. But my desire to go on writing my autobiography was by that point already three times the size of my fear of having my existence destroyed.

It felt strange to be writing an autobiography. In the past, I'd used language primarily for exporting an opinion. Now language remained at my side, touching soft spots within me. It felt as if I were doing something forbidden. I was ashamed of what I was doing and didn't want anyone to read the story of my life. But when I saw the pages swarming with letters,

I felt an urge to show them to someone. Perhaps the pride I felt was like that of a toddler eager to show off a stinky masterpiece. Once I dropped in on the superintendent just as her granddaughter was showing the grown-ups her freshly produced brown dumpling. It was still steaming. At the time I was shocked, but now I can understand the little girl's pride. That excrement was the first thing the child had ever produced without outside help, and there was no reason to take offense at the pride she displayed.

But to whom should I show my work? There was something shady about the superintendent. Admittedly the friendship she showed me was to a considerable extent sincere, but it was her job to spy on the building's inhabitants. I had no parents, and my colleagues were out of the question, since they all avoided me whenever possible. I had no friends.

Then I remembered a man they called "Sea Lion." He was the editor of a literary journal. When my stage career was still in full bloom, he had been one of my fans and would often visit me backstage with a lavish bouquet of flowers.

Sea Lion looked more like a seal than a sea lion, but his nickname was Sea Lion, so that's what I'll have to call him, since over the years I've lost track of his real name. Supposedly he came down with a raging fever the first time he saw me onstage. He claimed to be hopelessly in love with me. After he'd visited me backstage who knows how many times, he confessed his desire to share my pillow. But he already knew that nature had made our bodies incompatible.

I, too, was convinced on first glance that our bodies could never conjoin in sexual union: his was moist and slippery, while mine was dry and rough. Everything in the region surrounding his beard was splendidly built, while the tips of his four limbs looked pathetically weak. By contrast, my own life force was concentrated in my fingertips. He had been bald since birth, while I was thickly furred everywhere from my head to my most intimate zone. We would never have made a good couple. Nevertheless we once wound up kissing. It felt as if a tiny fish were wriggling around in my mouth. Sea Lion had an ungainly row of teeth, but that bothered me least of all, since I instantly recognized his true masculinity in the fact that he had no cavities. This I truly appreciated. When I asked why he didn't have any rotten teeth, he replied that he never ate sweets. I, on the other hand, found them irresistible. What would I use as a metaphor for the best part of my life if there were no longer any sweets?

I hadn't seen him in quite some time, though he kept in touch: now and then he would send me his latest catalog, in which his office address was printed. I plucked up my courage and decided to pay him a surprise visit without contacting him in advance.

The offices of his firm, which was called North Star Publishing, were located at the southern edge of town. From the outside there was no indication that anything like a publishing house might be located here in this building. A young man stood in the lobby, smoking a cigarette. Sternly, he asked what business I had there. I had scarcely gotten out the words "Sea Lion" before he told me to follow him, walking ahead of me like a robot down the hall. To either side, peeling wallpaper hung down like burned skin. We penetrated ever deeper into the building's interior, and at the end of the hallway reached a green door behind which was a room with no windows. The ceiling was low, and the manuscripts piled up in enormous stacks were yellowed.

Sea Lion looked at me and flinched as if I'd slapped him in the face. "What are you doing here?" he asked coldly. Only at that moment did it occur to me that there is nothing in the world more dangerous than a former fan. Too late. I—a miserable former circus star—stood there defenseless before the bloodthirsty publisher, clasping my virginal work. Many times in the past I had danced atop a gigantic ball, ridden a stunt tricycle and a circus motorcycle. But publishing an autobiography was a far more dangerous acrobatic feat.

Carefully I opened my bag, took out the sheets of letter paper covered with writing, and placed them on the desk without a word. His gaze lingered quizzically upon my nose. When he glimpsed the written characters in my manuscript, he adjusted his glasses and began to read. His glasses had round lenses, and he read with his back bent over the manuscript. He read the first page, then the second. The more he read, the more delightedly his eyes gleamed, or maybe I just imagined that. After he had read through several pages, he stroked his beard and opened his nostrils very wide. "You wrote this?" he asked, his voice trembling. I nodded. He knit his brows, then set an expression of weariness on his face like a mask. "I'll keep the manuscript here. Honestly I'm somewhat disappointed that it's so short. Perhaps you'd like to keep writing and bring me more next week."

I said nothing, and my silence appeared to make him cocky. "And can I say one more thing? Don't you have any better paper to use? Did you steal this from a hotel? Poor thing! Take mine, if you like." He presented me with a stack of Swiss letter paper with the Alps as a watermark, adding a notepad and a Mont Blanc fountain pen.

I hurried home and wrote on a sheet of this freshly acquired fancy paper: "When I stood on two legs, I already came up to Ivan's navel." I scraped the metal point of the fountain pen across the paper's delicate plant fiber structure. It felt just as good as scratching my itchy back.

One day Ivan appeared riding a strange contraption. He rode in a circle a few times, got off, and then pressed the object, which he called a "tricycle," between my legs. I bit at the handle of this new vehicle, made of a material that was even harder than the grayish bread Ivan sometimes threw me, fell off, and sat down on the floor to inspect the tricycle. Ivan let me play for a while, then placed the thing between my legs again. This time I remained sitting in the saddle and was given a sugar cube as a reward. The next day, Ivan placed my feet on the pedals. I pressed into them as he indicated with his hand, and the tricycle rolled forward a little way. Then I was given a sugar cube. I pedaled and got sugar. More pedaling, more sugar. I didn't want to stop, but after a while Ivan took the tricycle away from me and went home. The next day, our game was repeated, and on the days after that, until one day I began to climb onto the tricycle of my own free will. The riding lessons didn't seem hard once I'd grasped the basic principles.

I did also have one awful tricycle experience. One morning Ivan showed up reeking—a nauseating mixture of perfume and vodka. Feeling crushed and betrayed, I hurled the tricycle at him, but he skillfully ducked out of the way and started shouting at me, his arms whirling through the air like a pair of wheels. This time there was no sugar for me; he pulled out his whip. Even after this, it was a long time before I understood that there were three sorts of actions. Performing actions in the first category got me sugar. The second category got me nothing: neither sugar nor a whipping. For third-category actions, I was copiously rewarded with lashes. I would sort new actions into these three categories the way a postal clerk sorts letters.

With this, I concluded the new section of my autobiography and brought my manuscript to Sea Lion. Outside a brisk wind was blowing, but inside his publishing house the air was stuffy, it smelled like the cold smoke of Soviet cigarettes. On his desk I saw plates filled with bones, probably the bones of chicken wings, and behind them sat Sea Lion, skillfully operating his toothpick like the beak of a little bird. As dessert, I served him my manuscript with its thickly clustered letters.

He gobbled it right up, gave a hoarse cough, yawned, and said: "This is much too short. Write more."

His arrogance set my teeth on edge. "How much I write is my business—not yours. What's in it for me if I write more?" My erstwhile circus star pride had suddenly returned. Sea Lion was nonplussed, apparently he hadn't reckoned with my making any demands. With nervous fingers he opened one of the drawers, pulled out a bar of chocolate, handed it to me and added a bit of commentary: "This is an excellent product of the GDR. I don't eat sweets, so you can have it."

I didn't believe a word he was saying, since the color of the packaging that sheathed the chocolate like metallic armor gleamed in a way that didn't look East German. No doubt Sea Lion had gotten hold of the chocolate through his West German connections. I could report you! But I gave no sign of having seen through him and instead broke the chocolate bar in half, wrapper and all. An attractive, pearly black cocoa skin was revealed. But unfortunately I found the taste rather too bitter. "You'll get more if you keep writing. Though to be honest, I'm not even sure you have anything more to say." Sea Lion put the Busy Publisher mask back on his face and let his mind crawl into his paperwork.

Irritated by his cheap provocation, I rushed home and hurled myself at my desk. Annoyance is an easily combustible power source that can be extremely useful in the production of a text. It gives you energy you'd have to generate elsewhere. Rage is a sort of fuel that can't be found in the forest. For this reason I'm grateful to anyone who enrages me. Apparently I was writing with too much force in my fingers. The point of my fountain pen gave out under the pressure and bent. The mountain-blue Mont Blanc blood spilled out, staining my white belly. It was a mistake to have taken off all my clothes because of the heat. An author should never sit down at her desk naked. I washed, but the ink stain remained.

•

I learned to wear a girly, lace-trimmed skirt—or rather, to endure it. At least I stopped ripping it off when they put it on me. I also let them adorn my head with large bows. Ivan said I had to put up with them since I was a girl. I couldn't swallow his argument, though I was capable of swallowing his sugar cubes ad infinitum. Various bits of fabric were tied around my head, and this too bothered me less and less, and even the terrifying spotlight beams stopped confusing me. I never lost my composure, even when I beheld a seething mass of people before me. The fanfare announced my arrival, and I would ride my tricycle steed onto the brightly lit stage. A lace-trimmed skirt encircled my hips, and atop my head fluttered a large bow. I got down off the tricycle, held out my right paw-hand to Ivan for a handshake, then I clambered onto a ball and balanced on top of it for a while. Amid the thunderous applause, I would catch a glimpse of sugar in the palm of Ivan's hand, bubbling up like water from a spring. The sweetness on my tongue and the billowing clouds of joy rising up from the pores of the spectators intoxicated me.

In one week's time I succeeded, with some difficulty, in writing up to here, then went to visit Sea Lion again. He greedily read through my manuscript, never forgetting to keep an indifferent expression on his face. When he reached the end, he delivered a brusque bit of commentary: "If we ever happen to have a gap in our production schedule, we can publish your text." Then he once again placed a bar of Western chocolate in my paw-hand and quickly turned away, as if to conceal his thoughts from me. "As a matter of principle, we do not pay our authors honoraria. If you need money, try getting accepted into the Writers' Union."

•

One day I flew to Riga to participate in a conference. Right away I noticed that several of the participants kept glancing surreptitiously in my direction—not out of distrust, which I was used to, but differently. Something was wrong with the air I was breathing, or had I missed something? During the break between two sessions, the conference-goers gathered in little whispering groups. When I approached one of these groups, they quickly switched into Latvian, and I couldn't understand a thing. I fled to the corridor and stood at the window. A man wearing glasses came up to me with a chummy air and disclosed: "I've read your work!" Another man, overhearing this, came to join us, faintly blushing. "I find what you write so fascinating. I'm so looking forward to the next installment." A woman who appeared to be his wife sidled up to him, smiling at me and whispering to her husband: "What a stroke of luck, getting to chat with the author in person." In no time, a hedge of people had sprouted all around me. It gradually dawned on me that Sea Lion had already printed my autobiography in his magazine without informing me. I found this unforgiveable.

The conference ended earlier than expected, and all I wanted to do was run down to the bookstore in the main shopping district to ask for a copy of the magazine. The salesman said that the issue was sold out, assuming I was referring to the journal's most recent issue, the one everybody was talking about. Surveying me from my forehead to my knees, he gave me a tip: "In the theater across the street they put on Chekhov's *The Seagull* every night. The actor who plays the role of Treplev just bought a copy of the magazine. He'll be on tonight."

I hurried from the bookstore over to the theater and knocked so violently on the glass door, which was locked, that a crack appeared in it. Fortunately no one witnessed this, with one exception: a young man with a contorted face on a poster. He winked at me with his right eye. No one but me saw this.

There was a park right next door. I drank a cup of kvass and passed some time with the help of the newspapers pinned up on the exterior of the kiosk like wallpaper. Exactly one hour before the start of the performance I returned to the theater. "I have to speak with Treplev," I told the woman at the ticket counter. "The performance begins in one hour. You can't speak with any of the actors now." A blunt refusal without any folderol. I couldn't think of anything better to do, so I bought a ticket for the performance, went back to the park, and drank another cup of kvass. An hour went by, and I proudly entered the theater through the big door in front and took my seat in the audience. All of this was a novelty. My work at the circus had occupied my entire being, and I had never managed to go visit some other stage, and certainly not from the perspective of an audience member. Besides, the theater world was separated from the world of the circus by as thick a wall as the one dividing East and West. It was a grave error, however, on my part to reject the theater the way a child disdains a particular vegetable without ever having tried it. There were many things I could have learned from the theater, for example how to vary the tempo in the course of a program, or how to combine melancholy and humor. If I had understood this back when I was still performing on the circus stage, I would have allowed myself frequent outings to the theater.

The performance was delectable. The part I found the most appetizing was the dead seagull on the stage.

When the play was over, I slipped backstage to the dressing room, where it stank of powder. In front of the mirrors fastened side by side along the wall, various colorful cosmetics lay strewn about. The actors hadn't yet returned. I discovered the magazine I was looking for, picked it up, and flipped hastily through its pages until I found the piece I had written. It was even adorned with a title. I couldn't remember having given it a title or being asked to give it one. It was no doubt Sea Lion who had dreamed up the cheesy headline: "Thunderous Applause for My Tears." In his impudence, he had added: "Part One." Without asking the author's permission, he was advertising the next installment! Apparently his high-handedness knew no bounds.

I heard a miscellany of sounds in the corridor, then smelled actors' sweat, intermingled with the scent of roses. Actresses and actors alike twitched their hips when they saw me standing in the middle of their dressing room. I held up the magazine and announced: "I am the author of 'Thunderous Applause for My Tears'!" It sounded like a clumsy excuse but nonetheless it was effective: the shock disappeared from the actors' petrified faces and was replaced with the glow of reverence. This change took place first around the mouth, gradually rising up to reach the forehead. Their eyelashes began to flutter coquettishly. Please, please, please, do take a seat! They offered me a scrawny little footstool. The moment I shifted part of my weight onto it, the thing began to creak violently, threatening collapse. I decided I could do without a seat. "May I ask for your autograph?" It was Treplev who asked this. His body odor was composed of soap, sweat, and sperm.

That evening I flew back to Moscow and, ensconced in familiar bed-smell, realized that now I had become an author, a career development that could no longer be reversed. Sleep eluded me, even a bowl of warm milk with honey didn't help. As a child I was constantly under pressure and always had to go to bed early so I could get up again at the crack of dawn to start my training. There had been a phase before my childhood began, one in which no clock ever ticked. I gazed at the moon, felt the sun's rays on my fur, and observed the gradual alternation of bright and dark, a series of tiny shifts. Falling asleep and getting up were not my own private concerns, they were the work of Nature. When my childhood began, Nature came to an end. Now I want to find out what happened to me before childhood.

I lay in my familiar bed and stared at the ceiling, where I discovered a prawn that in truth was only a stain. The narrow face of Treplev appeared, although it bore no similarity to the prawn. In the days, weeks, months, and years to come, he will act upon the stage, fall in love, and sooner or later die. And me? I'll die before him. And Sea Lion? He'll die even before me. After the death of all living creatures, all our unfulfilled wishes and unspoken words will go on drifting in the strato-sphere, they will combine with one another and linger upon the earth like fog. What will this fog look like in the eyes of the living? Will they fail to remember the dead and instead indulge in banal meteorological conversations like: "It's foggy today, don't you think?"

When I woke up, it was almost noon. I surprised Sea Lion at his desk. "Please give me the current issue of your journal!"

"We don't have any copies left. Sold out!"

"You printed my autobiography."

"That's certainly possible."

"Why didn't you send me a contributor's copy?"

"You know how the mail gets censored these days. I meant to hand-deliver a copy to you, but you can see how busy I am, and the copy I set aside for you disappeared somehow. You don't have to read the text again. You know what you wrote, don't you?" Not a drop of guilt showed in his face. And why should it? He was right: I didn't have to read my own text.

"By the way, make sure you turn in the second installment by the beginning of next month at the latest. Don't miss the deadline!" he said and cleared his throat.

"Why did you announce it as a series without asking me first?"

"What a shame it would be if a life story as gripping as

yours remained incomplete!" His flattering remark briefly soothed me, but then I remembered that he'd done something unforgiveable.

"You know perfectly well that it is part of my physical constitution to be incapable of tears. Why the inane title?"

Sea Lion rubbed his hands together as if choosing the right dough to knead into a new loaf of falsehoods. I stayed on the offensive. "Don't just randomly title the thing on a whim! At least give some thought to the meaning of the words. Tears belong to human sentimentality. To me, ice and snow are everything. You can't just thaw them out and turn them into tears."

Sea Lion grinned and wagged his beard. Apparently it had just occurred to him how he could turn matters to his advantage. "You hear the word 'tears,' and right away you assume it's *your* tears that are meant. But the world doesn't revolve around you. It's not you who should be shedding tears, it's the reader. Instead of crying, you should be meeting your deadline."

I let myself be intimidated by his insolent words, which left me feeling like an eared seal with regressed limbs despite the fact that I possessed a powerful gripping and running mechanism that made me a formidable opponent. Sea Lion spit his final words in my direction: "Are you done reciting your lines? Then go home! I've got work to do."

Instead of slapping his face, I stuck out my tongue at him, which was recalling a certain sweet flavor. "By the way, that West chocolate you gave me wasn't half bad. Do you have connections in the West?" Sea Lion, breaking character, pulled a bar of chocolate from his desk drawer with nervous fingers and tossed it to me.

As soon as I shut the door of my apartment behind me, I sat down at my desk. I was still furious, and the desire to write clamped down on my ankle like a trap, refusing to release me. Even as far back as the Middle Ages, there were men like Sea Lion who placed traps in the woods to catch bears alive. They would put flowers on a bear and make him dance in the street. The masses delighted in these performances, and would applaud and throw coins. Knights and artisans, perhaps, viewed the bear with contempt, seeing him as a street entertainer flirting with the crowd—flattering, submissive, and dependent. The bear, meanwhile, had quite different goals in mind: he wanted to enter into a state of ecstasy along with his audience, or else use his dancing and music to commune with spirits and ghosts. He didn't know who the masses were or what it meant to flirt.

Already as a child I'd started performing every day, but I never learned what other acts were being presented. Sometimes I heard a lion roar, but I never saw a lion performing onstage.

In addition to Ivan, several other people worked for me. One of them brought me ice cubes and scattered them on the floor, another cleared away my dishes. When I was asleep, they would converse in hushed tones and creep around on tiptoe so as not to wake me. This made me laugh, because even when I was sleeping, I could always tell right away if a tiny little mouse at the far end of the room started polishing her snout with her velvet gloves. The bodies of Ivan and the other men had such a strong smell that even in sleep my nose couldn't possibly overlook their presence.

My sense of smell was the most reliable of all my five senses and has remained so to this day. When I hear a voice, this doesn't always mean the bearer of the voice is present. A gramophone or radio can produce a voice as well. My eyesight can't be trusted. A stuffed gull or a human being dressed in a bearskin are nothing more than facades designed for deception. But with smells, I'm not so easily fooled. I can smell whether a person smokes, likes to eat onions, has on new leather shoes, or is menstruating. The scent of perfume cannot cover up a sweaty armpit or the smell of garlic. On the contrary: It underscores these other smells, apparently unbeknownst to human beings.

A snowfield blanketed my field of vision. Far and wide, no other color but white. My stomach was empty, hunger stabbed at it from the inside, and soon I caught the scent of a snow mouse. I couldn't see the mouse, it was in the middle of digging an underground tunnel. The tunnel wasn't so deep, I pressed my nose against the snowy ground, following the mousy scent, which was in motion. I couldn't see a thing, but it was easy to pinpoint the mouse's location. Here it is—time to pounce! I woke up. The white surface before me wasn't a snowfield, it was a blank manuscript page.

My retinas have no difficulty recalling my first press conference. Every few seconds they were stabbed by flashbulbs. Ivan turned to stone in his suit, which was baggy at the shoulders and chest. Unlike at an ordinary circus performance, there were only ten people in the audience. "So listen, this is a press conference," Ivan said, inserting this disconcerting new word into my ear. We obediently took our places side by side on the podium. The flashbulbs assailed us once more like a sudden downpour. On the other side of Ivan sat his boss, whose hair odor and finger movements—they seemed at once cowardly and sadistic—made my hackles rise. One step closer, and I'd have bared my fangs at him. Apparently he noticed my antipathy and kept his distance.

"The circus is a top-notch form of entertainment for the working classes because ..." The boss had no doubt intended to enrich this skim-milk speech with a bit more semantic butterfat, but he was immediately interrupted by one of the journalists, who asked: "Have you ever been bitten by a wild animal?" The boss didn't have an answer ready. So then it was Ivan's turn to have questions thrown at him. They fluttered down from above like colorful confetti, confusing him.

"Is it true that you speak bear language?"

"Is it just a superstition to think a bear can rob a person of his soul, and then he'll die before his time?"

Ivan murmured incomprehensible words like: "Hmm, uh, I mean to say, well, beg your pardon, in a word, uh, but that doesn't mean …" Despite his poor answers, lengthy articles about us appeared over the following weeks, not just here, but in Poland and the GDR as well.

I have to admit: my life changed because I'd made myself an author. Or to be precise, it wasn't exactly me who did that, I was made an author by the sentences I'd written, and that wasn't even the end of the story: each result gave birth to the next, and I found myself being transported to a place I hadn't known existed. Writing was a more dangerous acrobatic stunt than dancing atop a rolling ball. To be sure, I'd worked myself to the bone learning to dance on that ball and actually broke some bones rehearsing, but in the end I attained my goal. In the end I knew with certainty that I could balance on a rolling object—but when it comes to writing, I can make no such claims. Where was the ball of authorship rolling? It couldn't just roll in a straight line, or I'd fall off the stage. My ball was supposed to spin on its axis and at the same time circle the midpoint of the stage, like the Earth revolving around the sun.

Writing demanded as much strength as hunting. When I caught the scent of prey, the first thing I felt was despair: would I succeed in catching my prey, or would I fail yet again? This uncertainty was the hunter's daily lot. When my hunger grew too strong, I was incapable of hunting. All I wanted to do was stop—before the hunt—at a first-class restaurant for a three-course meal. I also wanted to make sure my limbs were adequately rested before each big hunt. My ancestors had spent entire winters slumbering in their sheltered caves. How pleasant it would be to withdraw once a year until spring came to wake me. A true winter knows no light, nor sound, nor work. In the big city, winter shrank and shriveled, and the dimensions of life grew narrow too.

The memory of my first press conference remained sharp in my mind as if painted there, it hadn't faded at all, but I can scarcely remember the period that came afterward. One work after another. For ten years I labored without pause in a burning frenzy that was proof against winter. Everything that burdened or hurt me was instantly transformed into fodder for my career. That's why I couldn't remember anything.

My repertoire grew ever broader, my vocabulary ever larger, but I never experienced a greater or more illuminating surprise than the first time I grasped the true meaning of the performing arts. I kept having to learn new routines, which made me feel like a factory worker who, even after being given a new, more challenging task, still finds it monotonous, not a source of pride. "Performing in a circus can feel like assembly-line work," I once asserted at a conference on the topic Working Class Pride.

Sea Lion read my new manuscript and said: "It would be better if you skipped the political criticism—your philosophy is boring. What your readers want to know is how you mastered the high art of stagecraft without losing your wildness, and what that felt like. Your experiences are important, not your thoughts." I don't know exactly why, but his commentary made me furious, and on the way home I went into the government-run market hall, bought a jar of honey, and ate the entire thing right up, scooping it out with a shovel-hand. After that I stopped writing anything political, though I'm not entirely sure what's political and what isn't.

You might assume that I was born with acrobatic talent, that I trained hard to perfect my abilities and then proudly displayed the results to my audience. This interpretation is completely false. I never chose a profession, and there was never any question of my having talent. I rode the tricycle and was given sugar cubes as a reward. If I'd hurled my tricycle into the corner instead, I'd have gotten nothing to eat, just a whipping. Ivan had no choice either. Even the pianist, who was independent of the circus and played for us only occasionally, had probably never stopped to ask himself whether he happened to feel like playing the piano at a given moment. Day after day, all of us were stuck in a dead end, doing the minimum necessary for survival, which entailed maximal challenges. I was not a victim of Ivan's violence. None of my movements on the stage was superfluous or unnecessary: in other words, nothing I did was the result of external violence.

In life, we don't have a choice, because everything we are capable of is still not very much compared with life itself, not nearly as much as we imagine. And if we don't get this not-very-much exactly right, we will not survive. This fundamental principle can't be terribly different even for spoiled young people in a prosperous society.

If my physical abilities, or Ivan's prodding, or the audience's interest had subsided even a little, all our artistry and stagecraft would have been for naught.

My text, which had so quickly appeared in print thanks to my publisher's unorthodox approach to his métier, attracted the attention of readers in other countries who knew Russian. A Slavist named Eisberg who lived in Berlin translated the first installment of my autobiography into German and published it in a literary magazine. This translation was euphorically reviewed in a German newspaper of no small importance. The mailbox of the publishing house was soon filled with letters from readers asking when the next installment would come out. At the same time as the first part was published in Berlin, the second part appeared here in Moscow. The original and its translation began to play a fugue, though as far as I could see, it was more like a game of Cat and Mouse than a sublime musical form. As the mouse being pursued, I had to run faster and faster so the cat wouldn't catch me.

It couldn't have been Herr Eisberg who published my text illegally. Probably Sea Lion had sold Eisberg the translation rights without informing me. In this way, my text was transformed into West German currency that vanished in the depths of Sea Lion's pocket. After my superintendent painted a picture of this scenario for me, I visited Sea Lion and demanded an explanation. He said he knew nothing about it. His skin was so thick you could never see if he was lying or not. He turned his back on me, and even allowed himself an insolent bit of commentary: "If you have enough time to manage your translation rights, you ought to be able to write more installments!"

His words forced their way into my stomach and turned it— all I wanted was to retch them out again. A cruel idea occurred to me for taking my revenge; it was heinous, but I couldn't resist. From a phone both I called the superintendent of the building where North Star Publishing had made its nest and told him Sea Lion was hiding a large amount of foreign currency. Probably the super already knew about it, he might even have been in on the deal. But he had to consider the possibility that this anonymous phone call had come from the secret police, wanting to test his loyalty. For this reason, he couldn't afford to ignore the call. Otherwise he would be running a large risk of winding up in a penitentiary himself. And so he first informed Sea Lion and then denounced him to the police. All of this, by the way, being speculation on my part. When the police searched Sea Lion's office, they did not find so much as a smuggled chocolate bar, much less foreign banknotes.

Later I heard a rumor about a lady in Odessa who had purchased a snow-white Toyota from a Greek visitor to the spa. Her neighbors were surprised, wondering where she'd gotten all that Western currency. Shortly before this, Sea Lion had been spotted in Odessa. An eyewitness reported that Sea Lion had snuck into the lady's villa, carrying a large duffle bag. Already the scenario was taking shape in my head: Sea Lion had gotten his hands on a large amount of Western currency thanks to the sale of my translation rights, and then used them to buy his concubine in Odessa a car.

It was a great misfortune for me that Herr Eisberg was a talented translator. He turned my bearish sentences into artful literature that soon was praised in a celebrated West German newspaper. Admittedly there were no literary critics lauding my autobiography for its lyricism. All the praise was based on different criteria altogether, criteria I didn't understand.

At the time there was a protest movement in West Germany against the exploitation of circus animals. The movement's spokespersons argued that taming wild animals for the circus violated their human rights. According to the protesters, animals in the Eastern Bloc countries were even more oppressed than those in the West. Here in the East, a book appeared with the title *Tamed with Love*, written by one Dr. Aikowa. Her father was a zoologist. Perhaps this was one reason why she succeeded in teaching Siberian tigers and wolves to perform onstage without the use of whips or other threats. Most of the book was made up of interviews in which the author described her loving treatment of animals. Her book provoked a number of Western journalists. "Wild animals would never take an interest in the stage if human beings did not compel them by force. Aikowa is just trying to justify her circus, which is nothing but a pseudo-artistic endeavor by which Socialism intends to keep scooping up Western cash." This was more or less the opinion expressed by these aggrieved journalists. They discovered my autobiography as something that might be used as proof of the Socialist abuse of animals.

It wasn't long before the bureau responsible for such matters took note of my book's reputation in the West. One day Sea Lion informed me by telegram that my autobiography could not be continued. I was annoyed with Sea Lion, but as far as the future of my writing was concerned, I had no qualms. I would simply go on writing, even if Sea Lion didn't want to print what I had written. Perhaps I would even find a better publisher. Enough of those poisonous, barbed words Sea Lion was always using in his attempts to extract ever more lines of text from my paw-hands. No more taking anyone else into account—it was time for me to withdraw and enjoy some one-on-one time with my pen.

My life became as quiet as a fireplace long after the flames have gone out. It used to be I couldn't so much as go to the store for a few cans of food without being accosted by a fan. Now no one approached me. Even amid the bustle of the farmers' market, no one met my eyes. All the eyes flew away from me like mayflies, I couldn't catch a single one. I was delighted when the postman brought me a letter from my employer, but all it said was that I shouldn't return to the office until the situation improved. I was being relieved of my task of overseeing the project with the Cuban musicians; someone else had been assigned to it. I also stopped receiving invitations to conferences.

Sea Lion's journal couldn't possibly have held some sort of national literary monopoly, but for some reason no other magazine contacted me. The entire literary establishment had decided to give me the cold shoulder. My gall rose at this thought, and I slammed my fist down on the desk. It was a spontaneous reaction, but afterward I noticed I'd been holding a ballpoint pen. Too late.

The pen's neck was broken, its head lodged in the wooden flesh of my desk, while its body remained behind in my hand.

Formerly, symbolic acts had just seemed silly to me, for instance I couldn't have cared less about a two-legged author snapping his fountain pen in half to protest censorship. But now I myself had destroyed my pen. I would have expected a writing implement to lend me security in times of crisis, but in the end it proved just as fragile as a newborn's arm.

One day I received a letter from a domestic organization calling itself Alliance for the Promotion of International Communication. It was an odd-sounding request: "Wouldn't you like to participate in a project to plant orange trees in Siberia? It's very important for us to have a celebrity like you associated with this undertaking. This will help us draw a great deal of public attention to our work." Me? A celebrity? The words were like rose petals agreeably tickling the inside of my ear. Without hesitation I agreed to participate.

That same day, a few hours later, I wanted to take out the trash, and when I opened my apartment door, I saw the superintendent standing right in front of me. She asked how I was. It sounded like an excuse, but I had no idea what she might be hiding. "I'm planning to work in Siberia," I replied proudly and told her about the flattering invitation. The superintendent's eyebrows twisted with pity. "The point of this project is to grow orange trees in the cold," I added, wanting to eliminate any possible misunderstanding. My words brought her nearly to tears. She clutched her shopping bag firmly to her chest and excused herself, saying she unfortunately had to go now, since she had an urgent errand.

I was naïve and optimistic enough to believe that oranges could grow in Siberia. After all, they harvest kiwis and tomatoes in the Israeli desert. So why not oranges in Siberia? Besides, if anyone was a good fit for Siberia, it was me. Cold weather was my passion.

From then on, the super avoided me. Every time I came out of my apartment, she would quickly leave the stairwell and hide behind her apartment door. Glancing up from the side-

walk in front of our building, I observed her on several occasions watching me from between her curtains. Once, when I
needed something from her and knocked on her door, she
pretended not to be home.

Mold started to grow in my ears because no one ever spoke
to me. The tongue is not only for speaking; you can also use it
to eat with. Ears, on the other hand, exist only for the purpose
of hearing voices and sounds. All my ears ever heard was the
screech of the streetcar, so they began to rust like the wheels
of a neglected tram. I missed human voices. Then it occurred
to me to buy a radio, so I went to an electronics shop. But the
salesman told me that all the radios in the country were sold
out. I was almost happy to hear this, out of defiance. Even if I'd
been able to purchase a radio, it would probably have been of
such poor quality that I would scarcely have been able to distinguish its sounds from those of the screeching streetcar. On
the way home, I stopped at a stationery shop to pick up some
letter paper. I told the owner about the oranges-in-Siberia
project, and was treated to this reaction: "I'm so sorry to hear
that. But surely there's a way to get out of it." Perhaps I really
should have been concerned. When I was about to go back up-
stairs to my apartment, the super slid out of her apartment
and without a word handed me a slip of paper bearing the
name and address of a man I didn't know. At once I understood that this man was my salvation, but swift action is not
my forte. Another week passed without my doing anything
at all.

A new week began. A postman arrived panting, his cheeks
bright red, to deliver a registered letter. It was an invitation
to an international conference that was to take place in West
Berlin. The letter was written in a cold, acerbic style, which
made me all the more astonished to learn that the organizers
were offering an honorarium of ten thousand dollars for my
participation. I must have misunderstood, I thought, and read

the letter a second time, but the exact same thing was written there in black and white: "ten thousand dollars" and "West Berlin." Why were they paying so much? It was also strange that the money was to be sent not to me personally but to the Writers' Union in my country. Later it slowly began to make sense to me. Without the offer of money, I couldn't receive a permit to travel abroad. It took me less than two weeks to assemble all my documents, including an airplane ticket from Moscow to Berlin-Schönefeld.

I hardly had any luggage with me, as it was to be such a short trip. The airplane smelled of melting plastic, and sitting in it didn't make me feel any calmer, as the seat was built along narrow lines. The plane landed at Berlin-Schönefeld, and I was met by policemen who appeared to have been waiting for me the entire time. They got into a van with me and took me to a train station, where they deposited me in a dainty little train headed for West Berlin. When the border guard came through, I showed him all the paperwork I'd been given. The train was strangely empty, and landscapes empty of human beings flew by outside. They were deformed by the thick glass of the window. A fly bumped against my forehead, or wait, not a fly, a sentence: "I am going into exile." Suddenly I grasped my situation. Someone had devised this escape for me, to save me from a danger I hadn't known existed. Red plastic spectacles appeared before my eyes, it was a woman, still young, perhaps twenty or so. She asked me something, and I answered in Russian: "I don't understand." Then the spectacles asked in shaky Russian if I was Russian. Of course not, but how was I supposed to explain to her what I am. While I was hunting for the words, she said: "Oh, I see, you're a member of an ethnic minority, is that it? I wrote a term paper about the human rights of ethnic minorities, and it's the first time I got a good grade. It was a really wonderful experience. Long live minorities!" The plastic spectacles sat down next to me while I was still wrestling with the confusion in my head. Was my clan part of an ethnic minority? It's certainly possible that we are fewer in number than the Russians, at least in the cities, but high up in the North, many more of our sort exist in Nature than Russians. "Minorities are fabulous!" the spectacles exclaimed, apparently having skidded into some sort of manic state. She wouldn't leave me alone, kept bombarding me with questions, such as where I was going and whether I had any friends in West Berlin. I chose not to answer these questions so typical of a spy.

The plane trees that just a moment before had been jogging through the landscape with impressive speed now tottered like rickety old invalids with canes. The train crept into a gigantic cathedral, gave a screech, and stopped.

The station was a huge circus tent. A few doves were sitting on high perches, cooing. I knew these doves had emerged from a magician's bowler. An iron donkey loaded up with suitcases passed close beside me. A blinking magic slate kept announcing new circus numbers. Now a colorfully dressed woman appeared, her thighs exposed. The microphone announced the names of the stars to the audience. Someone whistled behind my back, and a proud dog dressed like a human being made his entrance. On the counter lay a pile of sugar cubes—the classic reward for stage artists.

My nose, which had been straying through the air, disoriented, suddenly had a bouquet of flowers pressed to it, there was a smell of nectar, and a word of greeting reached me through the flowers: "Welcome!" A number of hands were thrust in my direction: a swollen hand, a bony hand, a thin hand, hand, hand, hand, hand, hand. I shook hands like a politician, giving each of these unfamiliar hands a self-important squeeze.

I had never before seen such a lavish bouquet. What was it

for? It wasn't as if I'd just displayed any particular artistry. Was exile like a sort of tightrope walking, a feat worthy of reward? Admittedly it was a challenge to pull off such a stunt without rehearsal or support, but I wasn't finding it so terribly difficult. The woman with dyed red hair who'd handed me the bouquet probably wanted to say something to me, her mouth was moving as if in speech. But no words came out. In her place, a young man with appetizing baby fat said: "I apologize, but I'm the only one who speaks Russian. My name is Wolfgang. A pleasure to meet you." Beside him stood a sweaty man grasping a banner in his right hand and a plump valise in the left. The banner read: *Citizens Initiative KAOS —Keeping Authors Out of Siberia.* All of them were wearing neatly ironed jeans and well-polished leather shoes, no doubt a sort of uniform for this initiative.

I had no clue what they were discussing among themselves. One of them took his leave, then another departed as well, there were ever fewer of them, and in the end only Wolfgang and I remained. "Time to go."

To the left and right, buildings towered up in various heights, much smaller than the ones in Moscow. Some of the buildings reminded me of tastefully decorated cakes. The cars gleamed in the sunlight, I could even see my shape mirrored in their metal surfaces. Male and female legs in this city were clad in blue jeans. The wind offered me charred mammal flesh, coal, and sweet perfume.

Wolfgang stopped in front of a building and walked up the stairs. This freshly painted building, I thought at once, must contain my apartment. When I opened the refrigerator, a heavenly landscape of pink salmon appeared, cut into paper-thin slices and sealed in transparent plastic. I tried a slice right away, and it wasn't bad, though it had a smoky aftertaste. Perhaps the fisherman smoked too many cigarettes while he was working. It took a while before this smoky flavor started to taste good to me. Wolfgang looked around and said: "Beautiful apartment, no?"

The apartment didn't interest me particularly. All I wanted to do was crawl into the refrigerator and stay there. Wolfgang noticed that I couldn't take my eyes off the salmon, and laughed. "As you see, we did some serious shopping for you. That'll have to last you for the time being." As soon as he left, I quickly devoured the entire supply of salmon.

I stood at the open door of the empty refrigerator, enjoying the cold air. I pulled out a drawer in the bottom section. It was filled with attractive little ice cubes. I put them in my mouth and gnawed on them.

The kitchen soon began to bore me; I went into the next room, which had a television and a chair. I placed my rump carefully on the chair, gradually shifting my weight onto it, and right away there was a cracking sound. The chair lost a leg. Beyond this room was the bathroom, just as small as in the changing room of the traveling circus. I took an ice-cold shower and strolled out of the bathroom without drying myself off. At once, a large puddle appeared in the hall. I shook the water from my body, lay down in the bed, and suddenly had to laugh as a fairy tale popped into my head: Three bears cook some buckwheat porridge and go out for a walk. While they're gone, a little girl who's lost her way comes into the house, eats all the porridge, breaks a chair, lies down in bed, and falls asleep. The three bears come home, find the empty pot, the broken chair, and a sound-asleep girl. The girl wakes up, jumps out of bed in fright, and runs away. The three bears stand there, indignant and speechless. I was now in this girl's position. What was I to do when the three bears returned from their walk?

It wasn't the three bears who showed up the next day, though, it was Wolfgang, wanting to see how I was doing in the new apartment.

"How are we today?" he asked.

"I feel like the little girl in a bear book for children."

"Which bear? Winnie-the-Pooh? Or maybe Paddington?"

I didn't know either of these bears. "I mean Lev Tolstoy's *The Three Bears!*"

Wolfgang said: "I've never heard of that one."

There was a curtain of ice between Wolfgang and me. Ice appears to be a solid material, but it quickly melts on contact with body heat. I placed my arm on Wolfgang's shoulder jestingly but firmly. He broke free with remarkable deftness and speed, arranged his face in a rectangular configuration, and said: "I've brought you some paper and a fountain pen. We want you to continue your work. Please begin as soon as possible so that the work will be completed as soon as possible. We assure you that you will receive payment from us for your work." Wolfgang's mouth smelled of lies. There are different sorts of lies, and each one has its own smell. This particular lie smelled of suspicion: Wolfgang was probably reporting not his own thoughts but the words of his boss. Wolfgang was a liar, but fortunately he was still a young liar. His smell revealed that he was still a child, and a smell cannot lie. I gave him a playful shove, and when he didn't react, I gave him another one. He pursed his lips and shouted, "Stop that!" but then could no longer suppress his childish desire to wrestle with me. I threw him to the ground, being careful not to crush him. While we were playing, the smell of the lie disappeared from his body.

Soon my stomach was contracting with hunger. Paying no more attention to Wolfgang, I ran into the kitchen and opened the refrigerator. No more salmon, I knew it. Wolfgang came in behind me, glimpsed the refrigerator's empty shelves, and exclaimed: "Oh! I guess I shouldn't have been worried that you wouldn't like the salmon." He probably thought he could conceal his shock behind an ironic tone.

The next day, he visited me again, although I hadn't asked him to. Blinking frenetically, he stammered, "How are we today?"

"Not good." I hadn't mastered the smile technique and often gave the wrong impression.

Wolfgang looked at me, frightened, and asked: "You aren't well? What's the matter?"

"My hunger is making me sick."

"I don't think hunger is an illness."

I'd thought as much. I can't actually get sick. Someone told me once that illness was a traditional form of theater practiced by office workers, who were allowed to put on these performances only on Mondays when they didn't want to come to work. I'd never been sick in my life.

"What did you do last night?"

"I sat at my desk but couldn't write."

An ice-cold glint flashed in Wolfgang's eyes. "Take your time! No one is forcing you to work so fast that you lose your inner peace." Wolfgang was smelling of lies again, I shuddered involuntarily.

"Hunger isn't the best friend of poetry. Let's go shopping."

"I don't have any money."

"Then we'll open a bank account for you. Our boss already made the suggestion."

On the way to the bank, we passed two giant elephants standing at the side of the road. They were made of a gray substance, perhaps concrete.

"Is there a circus here?"

"No, that's the entrance to the zoo."

"Animals made of concrete live behind the gate?"

"No! Many real animals live in the zoo. They live on large properties surrounded by fences."

"Even the lions, leopards, and horses?"

"That's right. You'll find more than one hundred different species here."

I was flabbergasted.

What we did in the bank after this was surely not criminal, but afterward I had a bad conscience. We went into a building that bore a mysterious logo. Wolfgang whispered something to the man at the window, and they spoke for a little while in hushed voices. Then the man produced a paper with a magic spell on it. I stamped the shape of my paw-hand on the page instead of a signature and opened my first bank account. They said it would be one week before my ATM card was ready. Wolfgang showed me how to get money out of an ATM with a card. I noticed that he spread his thighs unnecessarily wide when he stood before the machine. Next he showed me a supermarket that had been built in the tunnel beneath a railway overpass. At the very back of the store, where the coldest goods were displayed in the brightest light, was the smoked salmon. "I won't be able to visit you for the next few days because I've been given a very important assignment. I'll be back in a week. Then we can go pick up your ATM card together. This ration of salmon will have to last until then. Don't eat too much!"

I ate the entire armful of salmon Wolfgang had bought me that same evening. During the days that followed I ate nothing at all but fortunately felt no hunger.

"You shouldn't eat so much Canadian salmon!" Wolfgang cautioned me in a measured tone of voice when he opened my refrigerator door the next week. I gasped because it was clear that on the inside he was berating me and would have liked to start screaming at the top of his lungs. But he kept his voice under control and spoke calmly, meticulously avoiding all discriminatory language. I felt like a circus performer who's made an acrobatic error in front of her audience. My thoughts kept circling senselessly around the question of why I shouldn't eat too much Canadian salmon. "What's wrong with Canada?"

Wolfgang appeared to be frantically looking for an image

that would explain the problem in simple terms. "Canada isn't to blame for the expensive salmon that find their way there. The problem is they're eating up your savings. It's important to save money." I didn't understand what exactly he meant by that, but I did note that the word "Canada" sounded beautiful and cool.

"Were you ever in Canada?" I asked him.

"No."

"Do you know what sort of country it is?"

"A very cold one."

When I heard that, I wanted to move to Canada right away.

The adjective "cold" has such an appealing sound. I'd give up anything to experience such cold, for Ice Queen beauty, for shivering jouissance. The ice-cold truth. Acrobatic marvels that give you cold feet. A talent that makes all your competitors blanch and tremble as if frozen. Rationality honed sharp as an icicle. Cold has a broad spectrum.

"Is it really that cold in Canada?"

"Yes, it's incredibly cold there."

I dreamed of a frozen city in which the walls of all the buildings were made of transparent ice. Instead of cars, salmon swam through the streets.

I lived with my windows open wide day and night. To me, Berlin was a tropical city. Some nights, the heat held me in its grip and wouldn't let me fall into sleep. Although it was February, the temperature rose to above freezing. I made up my mind once and for all to emigrate to Canada. Since I already had a successful experience with exile under my belt, surely it would be possible for me to go into exile a second time.

One week later I went to the bank, accompanied by Wolfgang, to pick up the new ATM card for my checking account. I pushed the hard, rectangular card into the slot in the machine, pressed the number 1 four times (that was my PIN), and watched the machine spit out banknotes. Then I pressed the number 2 four times. "What are you doing? You've already got your money," Wolfgang said in a low but razor-sharp voice. I wanted to know whether the machine might spit out something else, something more interesting, if I put in a different code.

The second time I visited the supermarket, my nose was immediately confounded by all the many smells. I couldn't remember where the salmon was. This supermarket was selling far too many absurd, unnecessary items instead of offering only what mattered—the salmon. I asked Wolfgang for an explanation of every product that interested me. "What's that? Can you eat that?" There were so many things I'd never seen before. The animal world is not without its culinary oddities, for example animals who prefer to eat leaves that have been stripped from their branches, roots dug up from the soil, or windfall apples. But this is nothing compared to the curiosities beloved by human beings: the grease they smear on their cheeks, the thick liquid they color their claws with, tiny little sticks they probably use to pick their noses, bags for temporarily storing things that will later be thrown away, the paper they use to wipe their bottoms, the round plates made of paper for throwing away, and the notebooks for children with a panda bear on the cover. All these products smelled strange. My paws started itching the moment I touched them.

I was sick of smelling the supermarket odor and just wanted to get back to my study, where my autobiography awaited me. When I said this to Wolfgang, he was relieved.

My desk wasn't to my liking anymore, it now seemed too low to me—too low for writing a proper autobiography. If the manuscript paper could lie right in front of my nose, close enough to soak up a nosebleed if necessary, I would be able to sit there calmly, letting the memories come as they would. Perhaps the solitude was weighing on me, though I'd been the one who'd asked Wolfgang to leave the room.

For days, I saw neither hide nor hair of him. Perhaps the bank account had been intended to take the place of a love affair. Money was wired to my account, I withdrew it, went shopping, and ate what I had bought. Then I'd come calling again, an impetuous lover ringing the doorbell, and my beloved would appear in the form of banknotes. I couldn't eat them, so I went to the supermarket and exchanged them for salmon. I ate and ate and ate, and it was never enough. I could clearly feel part of my brain regressing a little more each day. At night I tossed and turned, and then when morning arrived I couldn't heave myself out of bed. My limbs were as weak as noodles, my mood poorly lit. It was a degeneration. I wanted to do something to stop it. I dreamed of rehearsing a new number in bitter cold to reap the audience's thunderous applause.

I left the house. With an ear-splitting roar, a motorcycle flew by, right in front of my nose. I too had owned a motorcycle once, many years before, one made specially for me. The sound of its motor frightened me so badly that at first I kept my distance. I was quite good by then at riding my tricycle, but not a bicycle. So they made me a three-wheeled motorcycle that couldn't tip over. Ivan kept playing a tape of motor noise in front of my cage so I'd get used to it. Yes, I was in a cage. The word "cage" offended my sensibilities. I lost all desire to keep writing.

I tossed my pen aside and went downtown. The woman walking in front of me had on a fur coat. She looked as if she'd slipped into a pile of dead foxes. Through walls made of glass I could see not only the wares laid out for display in the shops but also what was on the plates of the guests in a restaurant. The boredom of the passersby was apparently considerable, since they scrutinized every product in the shop windows and every plate in the restaurant if the windows were big enough. If they were bored enough to take an interest in the meals being consumed by restaurant patrons they didn't know, surely they would find a story about a child in a cage exceptionally diverting.

Diagonally across from the bank was a bookstore. The bookseller's white sweater had recently caught my eye several times. On this day, I ventured to go into the shop because at first no one was visible inside. As I stood there dumbfounded amid the high shelves, it almost scared me out of my wits when a voice at my back asked whether I was looking for any book in particular. The white sweater was standing right behind me. Since it was blocking the exit, I couldn't beat a retreat.

"Do you have an autobiography?"

"By whom? If you don't mind my asking."

"It doesn't matter."

The white sweater indicated a shelf off to one side behind him, saying, "All of these are autobiographies!"

I was apparently now capable of improvising a brief conversation in German.

It was disappointing to know how many fat autobiographies already existed. They filled the ten stories of this bookshelf from top to bottom without leaving a gap. Apparently an autobiography was the sort of text that got written by anyone capable of holding a pen.

"All in German!?"

"What's so strange about that?"

"Must one write in German? I must learn German."

"Not necessary. The language you're speaking at the moment is what we call German."

"I can speak—that's in my nature. But reading and writing …"

"Then we should pay a visit to that shelf over there. We have a large selection of language textbooks. Would you like to have one with explanations in English?"

"No, Russian. Or Northpolish."

"I think I actually do have a textbook written in Russian."

My German textbook was more economically priced than a large package of salmon, but unfortunately harder to digest. The book's author explained in great detail—like the assembly instructions for a piece of machinery—each linguistic component, such as verbs, nouns, adjectives, etc. But it was unlikely that these explanations would enable the book's readers to build a machine themselves. At the back of the book, I found a section with the heading "Applied Grammar"; it contained a short story that one was supposed to read. I devoured it like the salmon, forgetting all about grammar.

The protagonist was a mouse. Her form of gainful employment: singing. Her audience: the people. On the vocabulary list I found the word *Volk*, which corresponded to the Russian *narod*.

There had been times when I was convinced that the word *narod* meant more or less the same as "circus audience." Later, at numerous conferences and assemblies, I came to realize that this supposition had not been correct, but I remained unable to define the term exactly, though my lack of knowledge was never conspicuous.

As long as the mouse went on singing, the *Volk* gave her its full attention. No one aped her, no one giggled, no one disrupted her concerts by making mouse noises. This is just how my own audience behaved, too, and my heart leaped as I remembered the circus. Every member of my audience was capable of walking on two legs or riding on three wheels. Nevertheless they gaped at me as if I were performing a miracle. And in the end they generously applauded. But why?

The second time I visited, the bookseller came up to me right away, gave a dry cough and asked whether the language textbook had been helpful. "I didn't understand the grammar, but the short story was interesting. The story of the mouse singer Josephine." My answer made him laugh.

"The grammar is superfluous if you understood the story." He plucked another book off the shelf. "This is a book by the same author. Among other things, he wrote several stories from the point of view of animals." When our eyes met, something seemed to occur to him that he found puzzling. Hurriedly he added: "What I mean is that this literature is valuable as literature, not because it was written from a minority perspective. In fact, the main character is never an animal. During the process by which an animal is transformed into a non-animal or a human into a non-human, memory gets lost, and it's this loss that is the main character." To me, his lecture was too much side salad without a main course. I couldn't follow, but I didn't want him to notice. So I lowered my eyes and pretended to be having profound thoughts about the book. After a while, a question finally occurred to me: "What's your name?" My question caught the man off guard. "Oh, sorry! I'm Friedrich." He didn't ask mine.

I opened the book the way you might break a loaf of peasant bread in two. My nails were too long to make it easy to flip through a book's pages. In earlier years, I'd attempted to trim them but wound up spilling a lot of blood. Now I just let them grow. From the open page of the book, a title containing the word "dog" leaped out at me. In all honesty, I couldn't stand dogs: cowardly, deceitful creatures who would innocently scamper up to me from behind, only to sink their teeth into my ankle at the first opportunity. I would have gone on avoiding all dogs if this animal hadn't been contained in the title rolling melodiously off Friedrich's tongue: "Investigations of a Dog." A dog, then, could possess an inquiring mind. This revelation took the edge off my bias against the species. Friedrich showed me another story from the book, the subject this time was an academy. "You might find this story even more interesting than the one about the dog." A happy schoolteacher would no doubt look exactly the way Friedrich looked at this moment.

I bought the volume of stories and right away read "A Report to an Academy." Unfortunately I must confess I found this ape story interesting. But my interest might be attributed to various causes, it might even have been prompted by rage. The more I read, the more unbridled my rage became, and I couldn't stop reading. The ape was of a tropical nature—cause enough for me to find this ape tale unpalatable. It struck me as the pinnacle of apishness to not only want to become human but to tell the story of one's own transformation. I imagined an ape aping a human being, and my back immediately started to itch unbearably, as though lice and fleas were dancing the twist in my fur. The ape narrator apparently believed he had written a success story. But if you asked me, I'd lose no time telling you I don't consider it progress to walk on two legs.

I felt sick to my stomach remembering how, as a child, I'd learned to walk on two legs. And I didn't just learn to do this, I even wrote and published a text about it. Probably my readers thought my apish report had been written in support of evolutionary theory. If I'd read the ape's report earlier, I'd have written my autobiography in a completely different way.

The next day, Wolfgang surprised me. Right away I told him about the ape, who was still on my mind. Wolfgang's reaction was a look of horror. "Write your own text if you've got the time to be reading other people's books! An author who does nothing but read is lazy. Reading books is robbing you of the time you could be using to write."

"But this way I can learn German. I'll write in German, and you can save time. No more translations."

"No, that's out of the question! You have to write in your own mother tongue. You're supposed to be pouring out your heart, and that needs to happen in a natural way."

"What's my mother tongue?"

"The language your mother speaks."

"I've never spoken with my mother."

"A mother is a mother, even if you never speak with her."

"I don't think my mother spoke Russian."

"Ivan was your mother. Have you forgotten? The age of female mothers is over."

I was confused because Wolfgang didn't smell of lies, in other words he was saying something he believed to be true, but I couldn't trust him. It was surely his boss's idea to impose Russian on me so his translator could twist my text to suit his political purposes. Bees can turn the nectar of flowers into honey. Nectar already tastes sweet in and of itself, but the deep, overpowering flavor of honey comes about through the process of fermentation set in motion by disgusting fluids disgorged from those insects' bodies. My knowledge, by the way, comes from handouts I received at a conference on The Future of Beekeeping. Wolfgang and his friends wanted to add their bodily fluids to my autobiography and turn it into a different product. To escape this danger, I would have to write directly in German. And this time I would supply the title.

Wolfgang said he didn't want to keep me any longer from my writing and left the apartment. I watched him from my window. Only when he had disappeared on a bus did I leave the house to pay a visit to my bookstore. This time, there was a customer in the store. He stood in a corner with his back to me. His hair was of a deep black hue that drew my gaze. Friedrich registered my presence and raised his eyelashes, making his eyes appear larger, while his lips assumed the shape of a friendly smile. "How are you? It's cold today," he said.

I always feel myself being thrust back into loneliness when someone tells me it's cold on a hot day. It isn't good to talk so much about the weather—weather is a highly personal matter, and communication on the subject inevitably fails.

"'A Report to an Academy' was entertaining, but I couldn't follow the ape's line of thought. It's ridiculous the way he imitates human beings."

"But did you ask yourself whether this was a voluntary choice on the ape's part?"

"He couldn't help it. That's what he writes. He had no other way out."

"Precisely. I think that's what the author was getting at. Even we human beings didn't become as we are voluntarily—we were forced to change in order to survive. There was never a choice."

At this moment the unknown customer, who until then had been immersed in a book, turned around and carefully used his fingertips to correct his eyeglasses.

"The brand name Darwin proves a bestseller yet again! Why do women paint their faces? Why do they lie? Why are they always jealous? Why do men go to war? The only answer to all these questions is: that's what evolution wanted. It justifies everything. But I can't think of a single reason why it should be good for the planet for noxious Homo sapiens to produce offspring. Can you, Friedrich?"

The voice of the one thus addressed cracked as he cried out: "My brother!" The black-haired man and Friedrich embraced warmly, but they immediately noticed when I tried to slip out of the store so as not to disturb them. Bookseller Friedrich ushered me back into the store and introduced me to his brother: "This is the author of 'Thunderous Applause for My Tears.'" I was astonished. All along, Friedrich had known who I was!

Friedrich was the main reason I visited his bookstore so often. The male members of the species Homo sapiens appealed to me a great deal. They were soft and small and had fragile but adorable teeth. Their fingers were delicately constructed, the fingernails all but nonexistent. Sometimes they reminded me of stuffed animals, lovely to hold in one's arms.

One day a woman lay in wait for me in the store. She was an acquaintance of Friedrich's, was called Annemarie, and belonged to an organization that worked in support of human rights. She wanted to interview me, to speak with me about the situation of artists and athletes in the Eastern Bloc. I replied that human rights weren't a primary concern of mine. She looked first disappointed and then, a second later, horrified.

I began to realize that my fate and the fate of human rights were inextricably entwined. Still, I didn't know the first thing about them. The concept of human rights had been invented by people who were thinking only of human beings. Dandelions don't have human rights, and neither do reindeer, raindrops, or hares. At most a whale. I remembered a text I had once read for a conference on the topic Whaling and Capitalism. It averred that larger mammals enjoyed more rights than smaller animals, like mice for example, and attributed the discrepancy to the tastes of a certain group of people, who valued larger things more than small ones. And among the mammals that are not vegetarians and don't live underwater, we polar bears are the largest. Apart from this theory, I couldn't think of any other reason why people kept chasing after me to give me human rights.

Annemarie had already left the shop. I stood empty-headed between the shelves, withstanding Friedrich's piercingly solemn gaze only with great difficulty. "Don't you have a new book for me?" Friedrich handed me a book. "Here, *Atta Troll*, that's one for you. A positively bearish text." The name Heinrich Heine was written on the cover. I opened the book at random to one of the few pages with illustrations and beheld a black bear lying with front and back legs outstretched. He was so attractive that I couldn't bring myself to put the book down. When I went to pay, Friedrich touched my paw-hand tenderly and said, "Your hand is cold. Are you cold?" My smile tasted bitter.

The next morning I had nothing but reproaches for him. "You sold me an indigestible book!"

"There are reasons for that. The author may have twisted things around to avoid being attacked by his enemies."

"What wolf do you suppose was after him?"

"The censor, for one thing."

"Zen sir? I don't understand."

"Censor. The sensor of power. Didn't you ever hear about censorship in the Soviet Union?"

I searched around in my brain for this concept but found only confusion. "Is that why writers write such complicated sentences?"

"Even when the author writes as simply as possible, it can still appear complicated to the reader." Friedrich picked up the book, leafed through it, and said: "You've got to read these lines! You won't regret having spent your money on this book."

The lines he was pointing to declared that Nature can't have bestowed any rights on human beings, since rights aren't natural.

Friedrich said: "If human beings want to possess human rights, they have to give animals animal rights. But how do I justify the fact that yesterday I ate meat? I lack the courage to think this thought through to the end. My brother, by the way, became a vegetarian some time ago." His gaze was prodding me for a response.

"I can't become a vegetarian," I said quickly, although I knew that my ancestors and distant relations got by without meat. They ate primarily vegetables and fruit, and only occasionally a brown crab or fish. I remembered a conference on capitalism and meat-eating at which I was asked why I killed other animals. I didn't know how to respond.

Sometimes I lashed out, which I feel ashamed of today. I can hear our teacher urging her charges on: "Now let's all dance together in a circle!" It was impossible for me to join this circle. The teacher took me by the paw and led me into the circle. Similar situations repeated themselves several times, and eventually the teacher stopped including me and left me alone. I stood in a corner of the room and observed the goings-on. One day a child asked the teacher why I wasn't participating. She replied that it was because I was egotistical, and in that same moment she received such a shove that she fell right on her bottom. It wasn't me—it was a muscular reflex that moved me to violence. Terrified by my own actions, I jumped out the fourth floor window, landing uninjured on the ground. Then I took off running in a random direction. No one could catch me. Since that day I was on the books as a problem child. I was seen as athletic but antisocial. I was to be shipped off to a special institute for talented children, since athletic ability was considered a valuable asset in our country. The so-called institute they brought me to was a cage. No ray of sunlight reached me there. A damp, dismal feeling returned to me as I remembered the cage. In front of the cage stood Ivan. My time in kindergarten seems to have preceded my first meeting with him.

Someone knocked at the door, my autobiography paused. It was Wolfgang, accompanied by a man I didn't know. As I then learned, he was the leader of the citizens' initiative KAOS. He had apparently been tipped off to the fact that my German sufficed for casual conversation.

"How are you?"

His question, which he posed with an artificial smile, sounded like a test. His last name was Jäger, which I knew meant "hunter." In my ears, the name sounded cruel and sly. He had a gentlemanly face. His white beard make him look like an officer. Men with this sort of visage sometimes sat in the front row at the circus.

"How is your autobiography coming along? Are you making good progress?"

Hearing this question made me defiant. I was afraid he was going to steal my opus.

"I am making slow, difficult progress," I said. "The language gets in my way."

"The language?"

"Well, to be specific: German."

Herr Jäger shot Wolfgang a reproachful look. I could sense that he was seething, but his voice remained calm and reserved as he said to me: "I thought we had communicated quite clearly that you are to write in your own language, since we have a fantastic translator."

"My own language? I don't know which language that is. Probably one of the North Pole languages."

"I see, a joke. Russian is the most magnificent literary language in the world."

"Somehow I don't seem to know Russian anymore."

"That's impossible! Write whatever you want, but in your own language, please. And you needn't be concerned about making a living. As long as you keep writing, we'll keep paying your bills." His face had a smile stretched across it, but the odor streaming from his armpits was one of cunning deceit. Human beings are constantly trying to sell me their generosity, the better to manipulate me. I wanted to ask Wolfgang for help, but all I saw of him was his back. He appeared more interested in the window than in me.

"I'm quite certain your autobiography will be a bestseller."

This visit by these two men made my pen go limp. Of course, the image of a pen standing up vertically or not strikes me as unduly masculine. As a female I am more inclined to say: The smaller the newborn text, the better, because then it has a better chance at survival. Besides, I require absolute silence. A mother bear gives birth to her children in a dark cave, all alone. She tells no one about the birth, uses her tongue to lick her offspring, which she can hardly see, and then feels the sensation in her breast when the newborns begin to suckle. No one may see her young: they are smelled and touched but never seen. Only after the children have reached a certain size does the mother leave the cave with them. It can happen that their father, half-starved, catches sight of these small animals and eats them up without knowing they are his own flesh and blood. A classic theme. The ancient Greeks wrote about similar cases. In my opinion, father polar bears ought to take a lesson from the penguins, with both parents incubating the eggs in shifts. For a penguin dad, eating the eggs would be unthinkable. He sits on the eggs, waiting day and night for weeks in raging snowstorms for the return of his wife, who's off looking for food.

"All penguin marriages are alike, while every polar bear marriage is different," I wrote in Russian and demonstratively placed the manuscript page on my desk so Herr Jäger would see it right away if he visited unannounced. As expected, Herr Jäger and Wolfgang showed up again several days later and immediately found the sentence I'd left for them. Wolfgang translated it into German and exclaimed euphorically: "*Weltliteratur!*"

Herr Jäger took my paw-hand and said: "Do keep writing. The faster, the better! Later there'll be time to cut and refine. The greatest possible error is to think too much and write too slowly." Apparently he meant to encourage me with these words.

"Before my exile, I had a lot to write about. The topics kept multiplying like maggots on a corpse. But now that I'm here, I've lost all connection to what I used to be. It's as if the thread of my memory has been cut. I can't find a way forward."

"Probably you aren't yet acclimated."

"It's unbearably hot here. I can't stand the heat."

"But it's winter, and your hands are cold."

"They're supposed to be. It's a waste of energy to always keep the tips of one's hands and feet warm. The main thing is that my heart stays warm."

"Maybe you've caught a cold."

"I've never been sick in my life. Just a bit exhausted sometimes."

"When you're exhausted, you can watch television, for example." Herr Jäger concluded his visit with this helpful suggestion and set off for home accompanied by Wolfgang. In their sagging shoulders, I discerned mild disappointment.

The moment the two of them had left my field of vision, I turned on the television. A woman who reminded me of a panda bear stood before a colorful patchwork map speaking in a high-pitched voice. Tomorrow, she said, it would be three degrees colder. Her voice sounded dramatic, as though this difference of three degrees would have an impact on world politics. I changed the channel and found myself looking at two panda bears. Two politicians stood outside their cage, shaking hands. I found these panda bears meddling in human politics improper. But then it occurred to me that I, too, was involved in politics, so in that sense I was no better than these pandas. Locked in my invisible cage, I am living proof of human rights violations, and I'm not even human.

I turned off the television, which wanted to go on torturing me with boring images. On the dark screen, the blurry figure of a corpulent woman appeared. This was me: a woman with narrow shoulders and a low forehead. Because of her pointy snout, she wasn't as cute as the pandas. I began to knead my inferiority complex like a yeasty dough. This activity was familiar to me from childhood. But then a pair of sparklers lit up in my eyeballs.

Yes, that's exactly how it used to be. There was someone to comfort me. When was that?

I was the only girl who was white and sturdily built; all the others were slender and brown. They had stubby noses and wide foreheads. I could see their pride in their shoulders. "I envy the other girls. They look beautiful," I said with coquettish sentimentality, "I want to be like them." Then the human being in question said: "They're all brown bears, and in case you don't know yet: not every bear is a brown bear. Stay just the way you are. Besides, given the wildness of your character, you could attract a large audience if you were to pursue a career on the stage." He stood there holding a broom in his hand. He was one of the many workers who cleaned the daycare centers and schools. They were always there, but I never learned their names. No one ever called them by name. During the day, they worked anonymously, and in the evenings they probably lived with their families, using only their first names. I thanked the man—one of the countless workers—for his words.

I was a strong girl and could toss my playmates around like nothing, and one day, when I was yet again flinging some kid into the air, the child called me an ugly name that surprised me. Suddenly I noticed that all the children except me wore the exact same kerchief tied around their necks. I did not belong. Unlike them, I didn't live with my parents. Perhaps that's why the stage became my home, and that's where my life unfolded. I was free, I received applause and experienced such ecstasy I nearly fainted.

Wolfgang visited me unaccompanied. Against my better judgment, I couldn't resist showing him my fresh-baked manuscript, so steaming fresh. Wolfgang read it through without taking off his jacket or sitting down. When he had read the last sentence, he plopped his body down into a chair like a heavy sack and said: "At times I felt so desperate I went back to biting my fingernails. It was a terrible task, trying to keep you motivated. Your creativity is back. I'm so relieved!"

"Do you think it's good?"

"Absolutely! Just keep writing. The neckerchief episode is sure to be a hit. All the other children belonged to the Young Pioneers—all except you. When I was growing up, we had an organization called the Scouts. My friends were all members, and they all had the same kerchief tied around their necks. I envied them; I wasn't allowed to participate."

"Why couldn't you participate?"

"My mother was against it. She said it was an ideology, and I didn't understand what she meant."

"What sort of ideology?"

"I'm not sure exactly. Maybe something like self-sacrifice. Sacrificing yourself for the fatherland, say. My mother said they shouldn't plant ideas like that in children's heads."

"That was her opinion?"

"Yes. What was your mother like?"

"The weather's so beautiful today. Let's go out."

"Where do you want to go?"

"I'd like to have a look at a department store."

The building that was called a department store was a somewhat sadder version of the supermarket. There were fewer goods for sale per square foot than in a supermarket, and hardly any visitors. A salmon grill. A flowered bedsheet. A large mirror. A ladies' handbag made of something like sealskin. We came to an area of the store with no customers at all. Loud music was trying to fill the empty space. A gramophone stood on a pedestal, and right beside it, a life-size, black-spotted white dog made of plastic. You could see his image on each of the phonograph records, which I found pathologically excessive. Wolfgang said, "a Dalmatian," adding with a proud expression on his face, as if he'd just made an extraordinary discovery: "You know what? Dogs can look so different, but they're all still dogs. Isn't that baffling?"

I wanted to respond that I had already read this very same idea in "Investigations of a Dog," but I didn't say anything, because I didn't want Wolfgang to think that I had gone and read a book yet again.

The department store didn't just absorb my attention, it consumed my strength, even though I wasn't looking for anything. I found no products I wanted to own. In the end, weariness overcame me, and all that remained was the feeling of being a loser. Next to the department store was an amusement park. I proposed that we pay it a visit. I realized right away that Wolfgang didn't want to, but, as if exacting my revenge, I didn't let up and kept sullenly and stubbornly insisting.

We sat side by side on a bench in the amusement park. Wolfgang asked me if I'd watched television.

"Yes, but it was boring. All you could see were panda bears."

"Why do panda bears bore you?"

"Since they're born wearing such impressive makeup, they don't make any effort to be interesting. They neither master any stageworthy tricks nor write autobiographies."

Wolfgang burst out laughing, which wasn't typical.

A bone-thin woman walked past, a leather leash rolled up in her hand. But it wasn't a dog walking in front of her, it was a tall man. Wolfgang got us ice cream in two ridiculously small paper cups. A single swipe of my tongue consumed all the vanilla ice cream. Then this same tongue gave voice to my deepest desire: "I want to emigrate to Canada!"

"What did you just say?"

"I want to emigrate. To CA-NA-DA!"

A bit of ice cream fell from Wolfgang's tongue-spoon. "Why pick such a cold place?"

"I know you find it comfortable here, but do you really still not understand that it's much too hot for me?"

Wolfgang's eyes filled with tears, making him look like a dog. In general, dogs tend to run around like mad in search of their lost pack-mates. They howl plaintively—not out of love, but in existential fear, believing they can survive only in groups. I'm not egotistical, but I prefer to remain alone because this is the more rational, practical choice for effective foraging.

I took my taciturn leave of Wolfgang, looking forward to continuing my work in peace. I urgently wanted to return to my childhood gramophone memories. But what came into my head in the end was the gramophone I'd just seen in the department store, and next to it, to add insult to injury, was that snotty Dalmatian, behaving as if his inclusion went without saying—and he wasn't even a real dog. The department store had replaced my recollection with a name-brand product.

Writing an autobiography means guessing or making up everything you've forgotten. I thought I'd already sufficiently described the character Ivan. In reality, I could no longer even remember him. Or rather: I was starting to remember him all too clearly, which could only mean this Ivan was now nothing more than my creation.

My memory lived in my arm's movement. It surprised me during that conference. Every time I tried to imagine Ivan's face before me, the painted face of Ivan the Foolish in a children's book appeared.

New misgivings about my work began to germinate in me. Instead of concentrating on my autobiography, I picked up a book that I didn't have to write myself, thank goodness, since someone else had already written it. I was reading to avoid writing, but perhaps it was more forgivable if I reread a book I'd read before instead of starting a new one. The dog in the story "Investigations of a Dog" was occupied with the present, he chose griping and brooding over cobbling together a plausible childhood. Why can't I write the present? Why do I have to invent an authentic-sounding past? The author of the dog story never wrote an autobiography. Instead he enjoyed being now a monkey, now a mouse. During the day he assumed human form and went about his professional business. At night he bent over his writing. Once I was in Prague for a conference. The name Kafka was never mentioned. This city, too, experienced a spring later on, but Kafka lived long before, even before it was winter. He didn't know life in our country, but he did know what I mean when I say that no one can ever act entirely according to his own free will.

One tropical day followed another. Within my roasting

brain cells, the scraps of thought refused to cohere. In a land of snow and ice, I could have cooled my head and felt fresh again. I want to emigrate to Canada! I'd already escaped from the East to the West. But how can one escape from the West to the West? One day, though, I was waylaid by the correct answer to this question.

While out for a walk, I discovered a landscape covered with snow and ice. It was locked up inside a poster. Other posters hung beside it on the wall, and I realized I was standing in front of a movie theater. Without hesitation I looked for the entrance and bought a ticket as casually as if I did this every day, even though it was my first time at the movies. A Canadian film showed me life at the North Pole. Arctic hares, silver foxes, white carnivores, gray whales, seals, sea otters, orcas, and polar bears. Life there struck me as unimaginable, but at the same time I knew that this was the daily life of my ancestors.

On my way home, I took the shortcut through a dimly lit alleyway behind the train station. Five teenagers were standing around, and one of them was using a spray can to scrawl mysterious symbols on the wall. I was curious, so I stopped and observed them without commentary. The smallest one noticed my presence and tried to shoo me away. "Get out of here!"

I just can't stand it when someone tries to exclude me from a group. Stubbornly, I refused to retreat even a single step. The other four youths one by one became aware of me. One of them asked where I was from. "Moscow." Suddenly all five boys jumped on me as if "Moscow" were a code word signifying "Attack!" I didn't want to injure these young, skinny humans with their soft, naked scalps, but I had to defend myself. So I distributed gentle blows with an open paw. The first boy fell on his bottom and, unable to get up again, gaped at me in surprise. The second one flew through the air, got up again, clenched his teeth and tried to ram me, but went sailing through the air once more, light as a feather. The third took a knife out of his jacket pocket and wanted to stab me. He approached, I bided my time, stepping to one side only at the very last moment, then turned around and pushed him— he slammed into a parked car, lost all self-control and hurled himself at me, his lip split open. I slipped aside again and gave him a gentle nudge from behind. He fell down, quickly got up—but this time, he took off. His friends were long since out of sight.

Homo sapiens is sluggish in its movements, as if it had too much superfluous flesh, but at the same time it is pathetically thin. It blinks too often, particularly at decisive moments when it needs to see everything. When nothing's happening, it finds some reason for frenetic movement, but when actual danger threatens, its responses are far too slow. Homo sapiens is not made for battle, so it ought to be like rabbits and deer and learn the wisdom and the art of flight. But it loves battle and war. Who made these foolish creatures? Some humans claim to be made in God's image—what an insult to God. There are, however, in the northern reaches of our Earth, small tribes who can still remember that God looked like a bear.

On the ground lay a leather jacket of good quality. I took it home with me as a present for Wolfgang.

As if on cue, Wolfgang showed up the next day.

"I found a leather jacket on the street, and it's too small for me. Do you want to try it on?"

At first Wolfgang glanced indifferently at the jacket, then his face froze. "Where did you get this jacket? Don't you see the swastika?"

There was in fact a sort of cross painted on the jacket. I was horrified. Had I beaten up a team of Red Cross workers? Quickly I hunted for an excuse: "They attacked me first. It was self-defense."

Fumes of rage were emanating from Wolfgang's face. Probably it was all a misunderstanding, I wanted to get it unknotted as quickly as possible. "Really, I hardly touched them. If necessary, I'll go see them and apologize. They misunderstood me. I said 'Moscow,' and the whole group attacked me. Is 'Moscow' a code word?"

Wolfgang sat down with a sigh and explained to me that according to recent statistics, most neo-Nazi attacks were carried out against Russian Germans as pale as me, as opposed to people with dark skin or black Ottoman hair. Those with radical right-wing leanings, he said, feared individuals who looked like them but were nonetheless different.

"I don't look like them," I protested.

"Maybe not. But a name like Moscow can stir up feelings, sometimes even rage."

Wolfgang called the head of KAOS and then informed the police. Later someone showed me a newspaper article about an author in exile being assaulted by right-wing extremists. Since I hadn't been injured at all, the article didn't say that the victim had been hospitalized with serious injuries, which would have made the story more newsworthy. I hadn't gotten so much as a scratch, but the fact is nonetheless that I—a female—had been attacked by five men, justification enough for Wolfgang and his friends to ask the Canadian embassy whether Canada would accept me as a political refugee since it was too dangerous for me to remain in the Federal Republic of Germany. I suspected KAOS of wanting to get rid of me because I was eating too much salmon and writing too little. "So now we sit back," Wolfgang said in a rosy voice with lots of thorns, "and wait to hear from the Canadian embassy."

My longing for this ice-cold land remained as powerful as ever, but an unexpected worry sprang up within me. At first it seemed insignificant, expressing itself only hesitantly in the question: Would I have to learn English? Had all the effort I'd put into learning German been in vain? I hoped it won't confuse me to be suddenly writing my life in several languages at the same time. Another worry that now surfaced seemed even more threatening than the first: Everything I've already committed to paper is safeguarded from loss, it's been saved. But what about the events awaiting me in the new world? I can't learn the new language as quickly as life moves forward. Something that can disappear is called "I." Dying means not being here any longer. I never was afraid of death before, but having begun my autobiography, I now felt frightened: I might die before I finish writing my life.

My ancestors were no doubt unacquainted with insomnia. Compared to them, I ate too much and slept too little. My evolution was clearly a regression. I pulled out the bottle of vodka that I kept in my hiding place behind the desk for sleepless nights. In Moscow, I'd needed my good connections to get hold of a bottle of Moskovskaya, but in West Berlin you can buy it at every train station kiosk. I held the bottle to my snout like a trumpet, and, as if blowing a fanfare, quenched my thirst. At some point I could no longer remove the bottle from my face. When I tried to pull it off, it hurt. It had grown into me. I was a unicorn and saw a polar bear approaching me, and my terror threw me into the ice-cold water. The polar bear stood there with no prey in his mouth, panting in irritation. I knew him, he was my uncle. Why did he want to eat me? "Dear uncle," I said in a friendly voice, but he bared his teeth at me and roared. Oh, that's right, he didn't understand my language. No wonder. In the water, I felt safe, the water was my element. Beside me, another unicorn was swimming. She whispered to me: "You can't afford to be drunk. Watch out! The orcas are coming."

"What nonsense. There aren't any orcas here," yet another unicorn replied.

"Yes there are. They're all emigrating because there's nothing left to eat in their native countries."

"Let's run away together!"

So the three of us swam north, shoulder to shoulder. We dove down into the ice-blue waves and popped back to the surface, we thrust our heads into the sea between bobbing ice floes, then jumped back out again. It was "beastly good fun"—as young people liked to say in those days—to cruise the ocean with friends. Knocking my head against drift ice didn't hurt a bit. I soon relinquished my vigilance. Then something breached the surface: at first it looked like a small, harmless ice floe, but it turned out to be a gigantic iceberg with only its tip visible. My horn struck the colossus with a cracking sound and broke right off. No matter, I thought aloud, the horn was merely decorative, but soon I was forced to realize that without the horn I had lost all equilibrium. My body spun around its spine and got sucked down into a whirlpool. Help! I need air! I saw many newborn seals struggling with their little hands. Apparently they were drowning just like me. I would have liked to make a snack of them if I hadn't been so caught up in my own drowning.

The images of the night vanished, I woke up and suddenly felt afraid of setting off for Canada. I forced myself to sit down at my desk, but was not yet in control of all my senses and let my gaze drift out the window. On the street, a boy was riding very slowly on a strange bicycle that resembled a dachshund. When he tugged hard on the handlebars, the front wheel rose up in the air, and the boy was riding on only the back wheel. He rode in a circle for a little while, then let the front wheel return to Earth. Then he turned around, still riding, so that in the end he was sitting backward. Clearly he was in training for the circus stage, even if he didn't know when or even if he would ever be allowed to perform. Then he fell over on his side as if a wicked, invisible hand suddenly had given him a shove. His bare knees turned red. But no pain could keep him from continuing. He got up and for his next number attempted a headstand on the moving bike. The words "steering wheel" occurred to me—that's it, a steering wheel is just what I need to steer my destiny. For this, I'll have to keep writing my autobiography. My bicycle is my language. I won't write about the past, I'll write about all the things that are still going to happen to me. My life will unfold in exactly the way I've set it down on the page.

At the airport in Toronto I was given a warm-hearted welcome by an icy wind. I knew how I could present a scene in which I was met at the airport by strangers, but that would have repeated the scene in Berlin which I had already written. How is an author to avoid repetition when one and the same scene keeps repeating itself in her life? How did others who emigrated to Canada write about their lives? When faced with such questions, the best recourse is to visit a good bookstore.

"The literature of migration is over there." Friedrich pointed me to a shelf that still bore its old label, Philosophy. There was such a large selection I couldn't decide which spine to touch first. Friedrich recommended three books to me, and I bought all three of them.

According to the first book, the Canadian state treated new immigrants well from the moment they arrived. For each newly naturalized citizen, a ceremony was organized at Town Hall at which the mayor himself appeared, shook the hand of each new citizen, and presented a bouquet. I copied out this passage.

In the next scene, the book's narrator was attending a language school. The thought of this new language was weighing heavily on my mind. German was still new enough to me, I didn't need an even newer language. A photo in the book showed a classroom in the language school, filled with flimsy, rickety chairs. I thought it might not be worth emigrating if it meant cramming my bottom into a narrow little chair to study more new grammar. And then the author wrote that the classroom was well heated, in fact almost so much so that you might worry about the waste of energy. But all such worries were ill-founded, the narrator explained, for Canada has an unlimited energy supply at its disposal. What a terrifying thought! I was fed up to my pointy snout with this book, so I threw it into a corner and picked up the second one. The author of this book had traveled by boat from the south of the New Continent to the north and secretly snuck into Canada. "I arrived at night, in the dark, in a small, deserted fishing village. I was freezing cold, so I took off my heavy, sea-water-soaked clothing and wrapped myself in a fishing net. The smell of seaweed filled my nose." The cold, soaked clothing and the smell of seaweed were so much to my liking that I greedily copied out this passage. But this author didn't stay on the beach for long either, the next day he went straight to the authorities, and later he too wound up in a language school. I shut the book and opened the third one approximately in the middle, I wanted to land right in the middle of life. Awaiting me there, I found a first encounter, longing, a first kiss: I was immediately drawn in.

I enrolled in a vocational training school. At first the only goal I had in mind was learning English. In those days I enjoyed speaking with anyone and everyone, and wasted no time worrying about what others might think of me. In the course of the weeks I spent there, I was increasingly struck by the fact that I was the only one in my class with a snow-white appearance. A feeling of inferiority blossomed like a poisonous flower. No one was insulting me, and probably no one paid any attention to my coloration, but the mirror showed me a pallid face and whispered that I looked unhealthy and sad. I began spending time after class beside a lake at the edge of town, lying in the sun and awaiting the brown miracle, but my nature would not allow any color to stick to me. In my class there was a boy named Christian who made a pleasant impression on me. He asked whether there was something troubling me. Instead of answering his question, I suggested we go swimming together on Sunday. He immediately agreed without making me aware of the slightest barrier.

We lay beside the lake, our bodies wet, showering in the tiny, gentle particles of light cast by the evening sun. Christian was also pale like me, and it was inexplicable to me that I had never before noticed this. I told him of my distress, and he told me the story of the Ugly Duckling. Christian was proud of the town of his birth, Odense, which was also home to the author of this fairy tale. A strange gaiety came over me, our eyes met, and I laid my paw-hand on his head. He slowly bent down and pressed his snout-nose against my breast. While we were flirting, the sun descended the last few steps and disappeared into the basement. The three of us lay there together: Christian, me, and the night.

Christian said he didn't want to marry me in a church because as drugs go religion was outdated. We celebrated our marriage within our own four walls. Just like that I got pregnant and gave birth to twins: a girl and a boy. The boy died before he had been given a name. I named the girl Tosca.

While I was copying out these passages from the book, I entered the story being told as its protagonist. I wanted to adopt what was being told as my own life story and live it myself, down to the last punctuation mark. I read every sentence aloud and copied it down, but at some point I stopped looking at the pages—a voice from inside the book was whispering the story to me. I listened and wrote. This activity cost me a great deal of my life force.

My husband and I graduated from the vocational school, adding the crowning achievement of finding work with a watchmaker (him) and as a nurse in a doctor's office (me). My husband soon joined the Tradesmen's Union, engaged himself politically, and never got home in time for dinner. On weekends, instead of resting, he would fight even harder for the workers' cause. Our daughter Tosca grew up raised by me alone. She was a cheerful creature, a source of joy, but she sometimes also brought me embarrassment. She would dance and sing on the street, and when passersby would enthusiastically applaud, she would refuse to stop. One day my husband surprised me with a suggestion: "Let's flee to the Soviet Union." An incurable disquiet crept into me. It had cost me so much effort, so much suffering, to leave my native land behind me. What would happen if I were to be recognized there as a traitor? When my husband learned of my worries, he stopped talking about emigrating. I was relieved and thought that the topic of exile had been settled once and for all. My love for Canada was great, though I don't want to overemphasize this love, since I also loved the United States, or at least the pancakes that were produced there. One week later, I realized I had underestimated my husband's tenacity. He approached me with a different proposal: "Let's flee to East Germany! They don't know anything about your past there. We'll submit our applications as Canadians and say we want to contribute to the creation of an ideal state. I love Canada as much as you do, but the entire first world is at an impasse. I already told you that my mother in Denmark lost her job because she participated in a leftist demonstration. She came with me to Canada and was soon murdered here by her neurotic lover. If we stay here, we'll have to keep slaving away and will never earn any more than we do now. We won't be able to give Tosca a first-class education. She's extraordinarily talented. In the East, she would receive specialized training for free. She can become a figure skater or a ballet dancer." When I heard that, my decision to go to East Germany with my family was virtually assured.

•

Out of relief, I sighed, threw myself into bed and let my ear sink into the soft pillow. I lay there like a croissant, embracing Tosca, who had not yet been born. She was still a part of my dream as I gently slept. One thing was certain: one day my daughter would stand on a theater stage, dancing the lead in Tchaikovsky's *Polar Bear Lake*. Later she would give birth to a son who would look so adorable that everyone would immediately want to cuddle him. I would call him, my first grandchild, Knut.

I gaze out at the wide field: not a house, not a tree, everything is covered in ice all the way to the horizon. With the first step I take, I realize that the ground is made of ice floes. My feet sink along with the floe I've just stepped on, already I'm up to my knees in ice-cold water, then my belly is wet, then my shoulders. I have no fear of swimming, and the cool sensation of the icy water is rather pleasant, but I'm not a fish and can't stay in the water forever. There's a surface I took to be an edge of the mainland, but the moment I touch it, the entire thing tilts to one side and disappears into the sea. I stop looking for the mainland—just a substantial chunk of ice will do. After several disappointments I finally find an ice floe sturdy enough to bear my weight. I balance on top of it, staring straight ahead, feeling the ice melt away from second to second beneath the warm soles of my feet. This ice island is still as large as my desk, but eventually it will no longer be there. How much longer do I have?

II

THE KISS OF DEATH

Y SPINE STRETCHES TALL, MY CHEST BROADENS, I TUCK my chin slightly and stand before the living wall of ice, unafraid. It isn't a struggle. And in truth this ice wall is really just warm snowy fur. I gaze up and discover two black pearl eyes and a moist nose. Quickly I place a sugar cube on my tongue and stick it out as far and as high as I can. The polar bear bends down toward me slowly. She bends first at the hip, then at the neck, balancing on her hind legs. She exhales forcefully, and the smell of snow streams powerfully from her throat. Then her tongue swiftly and skillfully snatches the sugar from my mouth. Has one mouth touched the private interior of the other or not?

The audience holds its breath, forgetting to clap, frozen at that moment—one thousand eyes are fixed in terror on the polar bear Tosca—for no one in the audience knows that she's not a source of real danger. To be sure, my life would instantly end if Tosca, standing nearly ten feet tall, were to deal me a blow with her powerful paw. But she won't. Danger will arise only if the ensemble of nine polar bears ranged behind her in the background were to cease to be harmonious. It would take just a single one of them getting twitchy, and that minuscule flame could ignite the others' latent agitation and quickly flare into a major blaze, engulfing the entire stage and burning us all up. For this reason, I keep a close watch on everything, the bears standing behind me included. My entire body is a feeler—each pore is an eye, my back covered with eyes—and each hair on the back of my head is an antenna, monitoring the shifts in power among the bears. Not for an instant does my attentiveness flag, except when Tosca and I kiss. At that moment, our mouths claim all my attention, and I can't keep track of the ensemble. My left hand, which holds a whip, gives a brief flick at the moment of the kiss.

The audience believes my whip ensures my dominance over these beasts of prey. In reality, this leather snake is as innocuous as the little baton a conductor uses to beat time. No musician in the orchestra is afraid of being struck and injured by the baton. But that thin little stick is the embodiment of Power, perhaps because it's always one step ahead. That's just how it is with my whip and my animals.

I am the smallest, weakest, and slowest of all the creatures onstage. My sole advantage is that I can precisely anticipate and gauge the fluctuations of mood among the bears. If the balance of power among these nine bears were to shift, if two of them were to suddenly attack each other, I would be unable to stop the fracas using my own strength. For this reason, I send my whip whistling through the air and shout to distract the bears whenever I sense even the faintest enmity stirring. Such a conflict might quickly escalate to the point of no return.

Nine polar bears stood upon the Drum Bridge, resembling mythology's Naga, the nine-headed snake. One head swayed like a grandfather clock's pendulum; from the depths of the second's throat, a deep voice rose. All these heads were waiting for it finally to be their turn to receive a sweet reward.

My skirt was short, my boots tall, and my long curly hair was tied back in a ponytail. I was 5'2", and no one could tell I was already over forty. Because of my appearance, it occurred to the circus director, Pankov, to develop this number. "One little girl has ten enormous bears in her power—ravishing! I have goose bumps already. We've really needed something more sensual in our program. Polar bears are much larger than brown bears, and because they're white, they look even bigger. If you line them up in a row, it'll look like a gigantic icy cliff. Magnificent!" Pankov's hoarse voice resounds in my ears to this day. His cigarette consumption knew no planned economy. "So what do you say? Are you up to the challenge? Why not give it a try? Don't be afraid of failure. Even if it bombs, I won't fire you. You can go on working here as a janitor." A malicious laugh. For years I mucked out the circus's stables until I got my hands on the keys to my present career. Pankov knew this perfectly well. He was testing me. Maybe he wanted to see if I'd lose my temper and blow up at him.

I'd had no experience with polar bears beyond a single failed experiment—one, however, that represents a brief but unforgettable phase in my life. At the time I was training a troupe of big cats, and one day I was forced against my will to accept a polar bear into the ensemble. I love all mammals, but I hated the popular circus numbers that put various beasts of prey onstage together. More specifically, I abhor the human stupidity and vanity that takes pride in forcing tigers, lions, and leopards to sit nicely side by side. It reminds me of the government choreography that displays brightly garbed minorities in a parade, minorities granted a crumb of political autonomy in exchange for providing an optical simulation of cultural diversity in their country of residence. But wild animals (as opposed to humans) form groups according to species to enjoy specific benefits. Wild beasts of prey maintain a mutual distance to avoid having to pointlessly fight and kill. Human beings lock these creatures up together in tight spaces so it looks like a page in an encyclopedia of animals. I often felt ashamed to be standing onstage as a representative of Homo sapiens, that idiotic species.

My boss and his boss decided that my wild-animal number would lack interest without a polar bear. In retrospect it's clear to me that they themselves were living like beasts of prey in their own political ensemble, each constantly afraid of being devoured by some other functionary. After the death of Stalin in 1953 it became difficult to predict who would be the next to get gobbled up, or by whom. Increasingly we had the sense that it was impossible for a privately run circus to survive. We felt a new sort of uncertainty. No one knew if we could go on working like this or whether a storm would suddenly tear our circus tent from its foundations.

By merging to become the national circus of the German Democratic Republic, in 1961, the three circus companies Busch, Aeros, and Olympia were successfully reborn. I hoped that this national circus would decide to drop the mixed wild-animal act, since its primitive brutality was not in keeping with a modern state's notions. But my request to establish a peaceful lion family number was soundly rejected in the circus world. The audiences were clamoring for dangerous assortments of predators.

At the time I wasn't yet certain whether or not polar bears were creatures as peace-loving as lions. Besides, I had the suspicion that Pankov had made his suggestion only because he wanted to make trouble for me. In the end, though, I decided to accept his proposal. I didn't want to close a gateway to my own advancement.

By the time I met my husband, Markus, his glory days as a bear trainer were already behind him. I'd been one of his bear act's many admirers for several years. Under his guidance, the bodies of the bears flowed across the stage like particles of light—bright, weightless, resplendent. At the time when I fell in love with Markus, he was in crisis. I happened to be in the room during one of his rehearsals. He was surrounded by interns who worshipped him. His hair was always carefully combed, and although this was only a rehearsal, not a performance, he wore English riding trousers and elegant boots. He stood there like a master with years of experience, but in his face I saw signs of bewilderment and the beginnings of fear. A brown bear refused to obey one of Markus's commands, and I even thought I glimpsed contempt in the bear's eyes. Brown bears have the ability to ignore the presence of human beings when it suits them. Even when the bear finds himself in closest proximity to a human, he can continue to behave as if he were alone. Animals compelled to share their cramped living spaces with others grow wise in this way. It lets them avoid unnecessary conflict. I've heard that Japanese office workers—who must ride to work each morning in overstuffed subway cars—possess this same wisdom.

But no brown bear can ignore a person who is goading him. Markus had unintentionally provoked the bear, and this was a serious error of the sort no bear trainer can allow himself. Was I the only one among those present who noticed? Markus was experiencing an existential crisis: he could no longer understand the bears. At the same time, though, he opened his heart to human beings, something he'd never done before. After the rehearsal I sat down beside him on a bench. Both of us were breathing in the same rhythm, which rapidly decreased the distance between us, and it wasn't long before our marriage was inscribed in the state registry. It was my second marriage. Markus made no reply when I told him that my daughter from my first marriage lived with my mother. He didn't flinch when I told him my first husband had also been a bear trainer.

Markus was planning to present a new number featuring a Kodiak bear in the coming season. The new bear was not yet acclimated and kept looking at us petulantly, as if to say that he wouldn't so much as waggle an ear for a whole bucketful of sugar. When Pankov put in an appearance at rehearsal, Markus would crack his whip several times in quick succession to make it look like he was working. With every passing day, he became more disheveled. He showed up for rehearsal barefoot, in a faded old dark-blue tracksuit; his thin, sweat-moistened hair was no longer combed.

There was still plenty of time before the premiere, no need to rush things, but it was worrisome that he didn't notice the bear's anger until it bared its teeth at him. He was like someone trying to bluff his way through a conversation in a language he doesn't speak. I broke out in a cold sweat and wanted to shut my eyes.

Markus was relieved when Pankov suggested handing off the Kodiak bear to an animal psychologist for a while, since the creature's behavior was problematic. "Instead," Pankov said with a grin that none of us understood, "we'll get some polar bears." Horrified at first, Markus calmed down when Pankov said he wanted to see me onstage with a polar bear act.

My husband was in a very different place in his life than I was: he neither wanted a large audience nor was he hungry for a new career. Deep in his heart, the desire to leave behind the role of wild-animal trainer forever was taking root. Unfortunately you can't just jump off a speeding train unless you want to end your life. But if someone had commanded him to transfer from the commuter train to the polar bear express, he'd probably have preferred to jump out the train's window instead. Polar bears were considered particularly aggressive and unpredictable.

In those days he would suddenly start screaming in the middle of the night, still caught in his nightmare—screaming like a little boy who's been bitten by a large dog. I knew this scream well. As a child, I was once forced to witness a friend of mine being attacked by a dog.

Apparently Pankow already had a fairly clear picture of this new number in his head. He wanted me to wear a headband to expose my forehead, put on a short skirt, and then breezily order the polar bears about with the effortlessness of a fairy. Markus was to stand in the wings keeping an eye on the bears to shield me from any danger. The audience would probably just think he was my assistant. In truth, though, he would be the locus of power controlling everything from the shadows. Pankov chose his words carefully, not wanting to offend my husband, while Markus himself enjoyed a deep sense of relief with no qualms. Finally Markus asked in a cheerful voice: "So how many polar bears are we getting?"

"Nine of them," Pankov replied.

Markus remained silent for the rest of the day.

Later I learned the backstory: The reason Pankov was so desperate for a new idea was that he'd just received nine polar bears as a gift from the Soviet Union. Never before had our circus received so generous a present. Everyone was secretly wondering what had prompted this superpower to give such a gift to its insignificant German neighbor. Perhaps the gift's giver was afraid of being abandoned by its recipient in favor of her former partner, West Germany. Or else the Soviet Union was trying to compete with an Asiatic neighbor who kept expanding his circle of friends by handing out panda bears left and right. In any case, the commodity in question (the polar bears) was immediately forced on our circus.

If someone gives you a cake, you should eat it as soon as possible. If the gift is a painting, you should hang it on the wall. This is how the recipient of a gift displays good manners. The nine polar bears weren't knickknacks to be placed on a shelf, they were professionally trained dancers. According to the

letter that accompanied them, these polar bears had graduated from Leningrad's Academy of Arts with excellent marks
and thus were qualified to appear onstage starting immediately. The government bureau responsible for overseeing the
gift was applying pressure: before the next state visit from the
Kremlin, Pankov was to put together an unforgettable show,
with the nine polar bears as the highlight of the evening. As
with earthquakes or storms, it was impossible to predict exactly when the next Kremlin visit would come. Pankov was in
a panic, he had to get the new show up and running as soon
as possible.

When I heard the words "polar bear," I thought not only
of the problem bear I'd tried to integrate into that old wild-
animal ensemble, but also of a bear I'd seen in a theater production for children. She was an actress, and if I wasn't mistaken, her name was Tosca. Probably I'd been given a ticket
by a professional connection and went to the show to pass
the time. I'd never heard of Tosca, but when I took my seat in
the theater I heard the couple next to me talking about her.

Though she'd graduated from ballet school with top hon-
ors, Tosca hadn't been able to land a role in a single production, not even in *Swan Lake,* as everyone had expected. And so
she was regularly performing for children. Her mother was a
celebrity who'd emigrated from Canada to Socialist East Germany and had written an autobiography. The book was long
out of print, and no one had ever read it, so it was really more
of a legend.

I was sitting in the first row and caught my breath when
the gigantic white soft body appeared onstage. I'd never seen
anything like it: a soft, feather-light living mass that made me
feel its weightiness, its warm flesh.

In this play for children, Tosca had no spoken lines, but
sometimes her jaws moved. I stared at her mouth and soon
found it difficult to breathe as it became clear to me that she

was trying to speak. I couldn't understand her. The stage lighting was no doubt avant-garde for that period: the curtains, simulating the Northern Lights, constantly dispatched mysterious waves of light in our direction. The color of Tosca's fur changed along with the light, shifting from ivory to hues of marble and hoarfrost. During the performance, our eyes met a total of four times …

To our surprise, the nine polar bears formed a union only a week after their arrival. The demands they presented to Pankov were anything but demure, and when he ignored them, they began a tumultuous strike.

These polar bears could deliver political speeches in fluent German. From their mouths I learned new terminology that no doubt had its origins in the labor movement. None of their demands seemed exactly typical for bears. The overtime pay; the monthly paid leave for women; a cafeteria serving fresh meat and seaweed from the Baltic; shower facilities with ice-cold water; air-conditioning; and a library for the use of all circus employees. Even though we humans could have used showers and a cafeteria, we'd never have had the courage to confront Pankov with such demands. Our days and nights were filled with such frantic labor that we had long since forgotten the very terms of our contracts.

Pankov was red-faced with fury when the union representative read out the list of demands. "Shower facilities? A cafeteria? Are you nuts? You can go wash outside somewhere, and eat as much of your weird seaweed as you like, I don't care. But none of that has anything to do with me. How dare you even think of organizing a strike here! Our country is the Land of the Workers. That's why we don't have strikes here! Get it?"

Deep inside, Pankov was a man of the Middle Ages; he didn't think bears possessed human rights any more than slaves. But remnants of a weakness for the life of the mind could still be discerned in him: he rejected all the bears' demands, with the exception of promising to build a small library. These bears had come from a great nation and weren't accustomed to making compromises with small countries like ours. The most familiar form of approach to them were military invasions. They had no intention whatever of ending the strike or of thanking Pankov for the library.

When I knocked on Pankov's door to give him a bottle of illegal vodka, he'd already been living under siege for ten days. He looked like a wilted houseplant. When he saw the vodka in my hand, he gave a feeble smile. Then he pulled out two glasses that looked like they were meant for holding toothbrushes, and poured the vodka. We raised our glasses, I pretended to drink, and Pankov really did toss back the spirits. He temporarily recovered his strength, and I took advantage of this interlude to tell him about Tosca. Hearing the words "polar bear" immediately sobered him up again, so he poured himself another big glassful and swallowed it. I waited a few seconds and then suggested that we invite Tosca to join us and put together a show with her. "If I can conjure up a beautiful number with Tosca, the skepticism of our visitors from the Kremlin will instantly melt away, even if the strike proves as eternal as Siberian frost. Don't worry, the Russian politicians will never notice that Tosca is not from the Soviet Union but from Canada."

For polar bears, national identity has always been a foreign concept. It's common for them to get pregnant in Greenland, give birth in Canada, then raise the children in the Soviet Union. They possess no nationality, no passport. They never go into exile and cross national borders without a visa.

Like a drunkard clutching at a straw as he drowns in a vodka sea, Pankov clung to my words. He instructed his secretary to call the children's theater, then fell snoringly asleep on the sofa before hearing the results. The secretary made all the necessary arrangements by telephone to invite Tosca to be an artist-in-residence. She didn't have a role at the moment and was bored. The artistic director of the children's theater immediately authorized her to work in our circus.

Later I learned that all this information had been altered if not falsified outright. It wasn't true that there hadn't been any suitable roles for Tosca. She could have had a role, but she hadn't liked it. She'd protested, and a dispute with the theater had ensued. An East German playwright had crowbarred Heinrich Heine's epic poem *Atta Troll* into a children's play in which Tosca was to play the role of Atta Troll's wife, the black bear Mumma. Tosca said she had nothing against playing Mumma. She'd even consider it an honor to paint her body black, allow a bear tamer to place her in chains, and perform an obscene dance in the marketplace. But she was unwilling to accept the plot in its current form. Her husband (and dancing partner) had longed for freedom and liberated himself from the bear tamer's chains. Tosca was offended by the assumption that Mumma was less noble-minded because she didn't also strive for freedom. Was it subservience to present one's art on the street—art created using one's own body—and to demand payment for this? Was a Hanseatic merchant more respectable than a street artist, even though he too worked for money? And what about the prima donna of the Soviet ballet in Leningrad who exposed large portions of naked skin for her audience?

There was something else too that troubled Tosca: Mumma was raising her child on her own, as had always been the norm among bears. But a mother bear biting off and eating one of her youngest son's ears out of love was something that could never happen in nature. Tosca felt that the playwright should revise this passage. She was also put off by the mocking tone in which the narrator spoke of the success Mumma enjoyed in the capitalist city Paris and the white bear she took as a lover. *What do you have against Paris? What do you have against polar bears?*

The director and dramaturge both found it inappropriate, if not unforgivably impertinent, for an actor to criticize the content of a classic work. The dramaturge felt this to be an affront to his dignity, and the director burst into tears and complained to the theater's administration. The artistic director was equally outraged when he heard about Tosca's audacity, but worker protection laws prevented him from firing her. Just as he was stamping in rage, the query arrived from the circus, asking about Tosca's availability for a residency.

Tosca accepted the invitation at once, overflowing with joy. But when she arrived at the circus, transported in a splendidly ornate cage with large wheels, her first disappointment awaited. When her vehicle passed the quarters of the nine polar bears, they immediately began to heckle her: "Strikebreaker! Scab!"

When Tosca set eyes on me, a flash of recognition lit up her face. She tried to rise to her feet, but the ceiling of the cage was too low. I walked over to her, she gazed at me and sniffed my breath. I thought I saw a sort of affection in her eyes.

That night I couldn't fall asleep for a long time, just like when I'd gotten my first puppy as a child. At five in the morning I woke for the last time from a shallow sleep and couldn't stay in bed any longer. I pushed the wagon cage into the rehearsal space and sat down on the floor in front of Tosca. She regarded me with curiosity and pressed her paws against the bars as if she wanted to join me. Time stood still, I didn't move. When I was certain that Tosca was completely calm, I opened the cage. She slowly stepped outside, sniffing at my body here and there, licked the palm of my hand when I showed it to her, and finally rose up effortlessly on her hind legs. She was at least twice my height. At that moment I realized how small the brown bears were. I placed a sugar cube on my hand, and

Tosca returned her front legs to the earth to sweep the sweetness from my palm with one swipe of her tongue.

"She has no difficulty at all standing on two legs. This ability is probably rooted in her genes." I heard the voice of my husband, apparently he'd been watching us the whole time through the crack of the door.

"What are you doing up so early, Markus?"

"Tosca inherited her abilities from her mother. Her mother was a circus star."

"I don't think you can inherit things like that," I replied absentmindedly.

With a gesture that swept my opinion to one side, my husband went on: "Why not? It took so-and-so many thousands of years before humankind could walk on two legs. But it only takes us a year to learn this. In other words, the results of the training have been inscribed in the genetic code and passed on."

In the course of the afternoon, an arch-shaped bridge was delivered, constructed of massive iron rods. We had it assembled and placed in the rehearsal room. Tosca put one paw on the bridge and carefully, one step at a time, climbed up it, stopping when she reached its peak. Then she sniffed the air all around her, extending her neck as far as she could and swaying her snout slowly back and forth. It might have been a scene in a theatrical performance. "This scene here is already a work of art fit for the stage!" my husband said, nodding in satisfaction, and suddenly Pankov was standing beside him with a proud expression on his face. "Sooner or later the nine polar bears will give up their ridiculous strike and come back to work as nicely as you please. Then we'll have all of them stand in a row on this bridge. It'll look fantastic! I had this fake bridge built to bear at least ten thousand pounds. I even have a name for it: the Bridge to the Future. Pretty swell, right? When it's a hit, please don't forget that the name was my idea."

In the afternoon, Markus brought a blue rubber ball he used for training the seals. Tosca sniffed at the ball, then gave it a shove with her snout, and when it started rolling, she ran after it light-footedly. As a reward for this, she received a couple of sugar cubes from me and then repeated the game.

It was too easy—and for this reason almost frustrating—to rehearse a new scene with Tosca. I didn't have to teach her anything. I only had to get her to repeat the things she'd done out of curiosity, and then combine them into sequences. All I had to do was figure out how to make certain that Tosca really would repeat certain things during the performance. This would guarantee enough of a show to make our audience happy.

Relieved, Markus and Pankov went and got a crate of beer to celebrate, but I wasn't satisfied yet. Pushing a ball around with her snout wasn't really in keeping with the divine aura of Polar Bear Tosca. Any second-rate actor could ascend the Bridge to the Future and gaze longingly into the distance. No, there would be no embarrassing overacting with Tosca. Wasn't there a refreshing idea that would shake the audience awake? I smiled self-ironically, because my ambition had suddenly returned.

At that time, the first tentative signs of a depression had been making their appearance, much as they had shortly after my first wedding. Back then, no one in our country spoke about depression. I secretly called it "my tristesse." My first tristesse arrived when I had given birth to my daughter and was spending most of my time, like any other mammal, nursing my baby and changing her diaper. On the side, I had to help my first husband with his paperwork, do his laundry, and iron his costumes. I had given up my career as a wild-animal trainer and for a while was just the housewife of the circus. The vacuum I felt inside me was not without weight. On the contrary. Every time I briefly stopped moving my hands, pausing in my work for a few seconds, the vacuum in my chest swelled up, stifling me. During the night I would turn over in bed every five minutes because the vacuum had settled in my chest and I couldn't breathe. I wanted to stand onstage again beneath a shower of spotlights, my eardrums split in two by the crowd's applause. Above all, I wanted to work with animals again. It seemed to me that if I kept playing housewife, the world would soon forget all about me. Moved by this worry, I'd immediately said yes to the risky offer to try an act with predators and had entrusted my little daughter to my mother's care.

And then, after I married my second husband, Markus, that old tristesse returned. Only performing onstage could punch a hole in the dismal sky, surprising the audience with a bright, sunny blue.

Markus, concerned, asked what was wrong—it had been quite a while since I'd last uttered a word. "The sky is so triste," I said.

"Your Anna has been with your mother all this time, you never see her. Is that really all right for you?"

I was surprised to learn my husband had been thinking about my daughter.

"Why don't you go visit her?"

"I don't have the time. You know the bus is on a ridiculous schedule. I can't let myself think about her. That won't help anything."

After German reunification, people might be criticizing my parenting style, but at the time there were many mothers who had no choice but to leave their children in the hands of official caregivers and visit them only on weekends. Some professions even forced women to go for months on end without seeing their children. No one held this against them. We were unfamiliar with maternal love—it wasn't even a myth. The churches in which the Virgin Mary held her child in her arms as a model to us all had been shuttered. When the suppression of religion came to an end, the myth of maternal love rose like a fata morgana from the horizon of the border. It pained me that after 1989 Tosca was so harshly criticized for having rejected her son Knut. Some said that Tosca had relinquished her son to strangers because she was from the GDR. Others wrote in their newspapers that Tosca had lost her maternal instincts while working in a circus known for its animal abuses, under typical Socialist stress levels. Invoking "stress" in this context struck me as misguided. There was no stress before 1989, only suffering. Equally misplaced was the notion "maternal instinct." With animals, childrearing is a matter not of instinct but of art. It can't be very much different for humans or they wouldn't keep adopting children of different species.

Maybe it was my fear of the next tristesse installment that so inflamed my ambition. "I'm not satisfied with just presenting some ordinary act with Tosca on the bridge or with the ball. We have to offer the audience something completely new, something that has never before existed in the circus world!" I slammed these intentions down on the table without concealing my ambition. Pankov stopped pouring the beer down his gullet and remarked that perhaps we could find some new ideas in books about ethnology or collections of myths. People in the circus generally tried to avoid giving much of an intellectual impression, risking as they did attention from the secret police. Besides, they were afraid of spoiling their audience's appetite with intellectual displays. With his ill-tempered vulgarity, Pankov was trying to make everyone forget he held a PhD in anthropology.

My husband and I got the day off for research. Pankov wrote us a letter of introduction and sent us off to a public library since our own new library didn't yet exist. We immediately found several reference books about the North Pole and immersed ourselves in them, forgetting both our objective and ourselves.

For a long time, polar bears had no contact with human beings and had no way of knowing how dangerous these small two-legged creatures were. It was reported that one polar bear's curiosity had driven him to approach a small airplane that had landed in his territory. The amateur hunter got out of the airplane, took his time aiming his rifle, and shot the bear dead. It would have taken a miracle for the bullet to miss its mark. Polar bear hunting became a popular sport, as it required neither technical skills nor the willingness to take risks. To be sure, a person who wished to derive actual profit from bears was obliged to capture them alive, and this did require some skill. Despite all efforts to the contrary, some bears died of the anesthesia, and others during transport. In 1956, the Soviet Union outlawed polar bear hunting, but the U.S., Canada, and Norway refused to stop. In 1960 alone, more than 300 polar bears were killed by amateur hunters.

I gasped with animalistic fury. My husband was probably hoping to calm and relax me when he said: "What if you dress up as a cowboy and pretend to shoot at Tosca? A sound effect, Tosca falls to the ground and plays dead."

"I'm afraid it might just look silly. But then what?"

"Suddenly Tosca gets up again and devours you. In other words, the victim of human violence rises from the grave and in the end conquers the evildoer."

"That won't work. A circus audience isn't looking for Socialist moral realism. Let's try to find a mythological plot instead."

"So let's read some books about Eskimos!"

We read that the Eskimos—which is what we called the Inuit people in those days—possessed a great deal of knowledge about polar bears, but that scientists generally refused to accept it. The most frequent justification for this refusal was the absence of scientific proof.

"We aren't scientists—it's OK for us to believe the Eskimos."

"Agreed. When I was a kid, I wanted to be a zoologist. Now I've finally found a good reason to be glad that didn't happen."

This same book said that Eskimos believed that polar bears plugged up their anuses when it was time to hibernate.

"How about having Tosca put a cork in her butthole onstage and then shoot it into the air with a fart?"

"Hmm, tasteful. Why don't you perform that one yourself?"

A few Eskimos report having seen polar bears pushing ice floes around with their snouts while swimming in the sea. This was presumably a clever hunting strategy, allowing them to approach their quarry undetected. I thought of Tosca and the way she immediately started pushing the ball around when I placed it in front of her.

"What if you get into a baby carriage and let Tosca push you around with her snout?"

This idea struck me as not half bad. "But are these the roles the audience expects of us? With me as the baby and Tosca as the mother? Should I really let her mother me?"

"The founders of the Roman Empire were suckled by a she-wolf. All heroes capable of earth-shattering deeds were adopted and nursed by animals."

"How about a musical? At the beginning we'll show my childhood, with me drinking bear's milk, and in the end I'll be the Empress."

"Excellent idea. But maybe you've forgotten: we've come to the library to look for an idea that can be staged quickly. I don't think that in a matter of days we can write and compose a musical."

We went on reading. Several Eskimos report that polar bears press snow into their wounds to stop the bleeding: a beautiful image, but not really suitable for the stage.

Many Eskimos believe—the book claimed—that polar bears are left-handed. It could be interesting if Tosca were to go into a classroom set up onstage and write words on the blackboard with her left hand. From Pankov's point of view, the most important audience members were the Russians, so Tosca would have to write using the Cyrillic alphabet. I had a feeling that Cyrillic script might be too much for the left hand of a polar bear. My husband replied: "But Chinese ideograms are much more complicated than Cyrillic script, and in China the panda bears are capable of writing ideograms—or at least the simplified characters mandated by Communist reformers."

When I told Pankov about the literate panda bears, he gnashed his teeth in envy and claimed that was just propaganda: pro-panda propaganda disseminated by the Chinese government in an effort to justify their writing reforms. I asked him what made it propaganda. Was it the message that even bears can write if there are fewer brushstrokes in the characters?

"What was his answer?"

"He just kept insisting that pandas can't write. Regardless how simplified the ideograms, written characters are written characters, and panda bears are panda bears. But I asked myself what we would do if the pandas did in fact turn out to be naturally more intelligent than we were. Probably the best we could do would be to conceal this fact from our Kremlin guests."

"You can't compare the intelligence of different sorts of animals. Besides, the circus stage isn't the place to demonstrate one's intelligence. And in any case feeling envious of the pandas and their brains won't do us any good. Every bear species has its own strengths. It isn't the point of a circus to demonstrate the national IQ. By the way, do you remember the children's story *The Three Bears*?"

As always, I was surprised by Markus's sudden change of topic. "It could look sweet and interesting if the bear were to do banal things onstage such as humans perform every day:

sit down at the table, place a napkin on her lap, open a jar of jam and spread the strawberry jelly on a slice of bread, drink cocoa from a mug, and so on."

My husband remained in a good mood for quite some time, and even the insolent tone adopted by the librarian who shooed us out of the building before closing time didn't bother him.

"Who'd have thought it? I actually like spending time at the library. Doing research and collecting ideas for choreography are activities far better suited to me than ordering dangerous animals about onstage."

His cheeks looked sunken, his eyes were encircled by shadow. His hair had already taken on the whiteness of hoarfrost, while his eyebrows had grown too bushy. He no longer had to grapple with live bears: this thought filled him with relief, opening the floodgates within him, and the years that had been dammed up inside him all this time now flowed back out, causing him to age drastically in the space of a few days.

The next morning we got an early start practicing scenarios with Tosca that were borrowed from everyday life. She could effortlessly open a jar of jam, but smearing the jam on the bread proved impossible for her. It wasn't that she lacked dexterity, it's just that she preferred to take all the jam out of the jar at once, using her tongue. I couldn't think of any trick that might get her to do what I wanted, and she couldn't be talked into it either, since we lacked a common language.

"I'm out of ideas. Back in a minute, I'm going for a smoke," my husband said, and left me alone with Tosca. He'd been smoking more and more, and taking ever more frequent sips of vodka. I looked wistfully at Tosca. She lay on her back like a baby, like my daughter Anna when she was small. My thoughts drifted to Anna, I wondered how she was, whether she'd made any friends at school.

The next day Markus returned to the library, this time alone.

Even though we didn't know yet what our show was going to look like, I could still get started rehearsing Tosca's entrance and exit with her, elements whose importance is underestimated by laypersons. I strode into a corner of the rehearsal room, taking care never to turn my back to her. On the ground were balls, a bucket, and stuffed animals. Tosca hurried over to me and sniffed at various of my body parts, paying particular attention to my rear end, but also to my mouth and hands. I thought I'd have to suppress a laugh, but found it was far more than laughter I needed to suppress.

My husband hadn't yet returned for lunch, and my stomach was growling. I asked Tosca to go into her cage and wait for me there. At that very moment, Pankov's secretary came into the room, bringing a piece of equipment, apparently some sort of weird tricycle.

"I thought you might be interested in this tricycle for small bears. We just got it as a gift from a Russian circus. It's a hand-me-down and not in perfect condition, but it still works," she said. The tricycle was solidly built, and I sat down on it, but couldn't make the pedals move. Tosca was watching me enviously from her cage. The tricycle was obviously too small for Tosca. I'd have to ask Pankov to have a tricycle specially built for her and then listen to a lecture about being over budget.

With my knees up near my ears, I sat on the tricycle, thinking back on the days when I used to deliver telegrams by bicycle. My current wages were certainly not high, but my memory of that period bore the heading "Poverty." Later on, all the financial reports in the GDR were black and gleaming. Being in the red, someone told me, was an attribute of capitalism and not relevant to our way of life.

Every day, riding between the Telegraph Office and my clients' doors, I'd practice bicycle tricks. When I increased my speed to cut a sharp curve without stepping on the brakes, my ankles just grazed the earth racing past beneath me. Centrifugal force held an erotic attraction for me. Sometimes, wanting to rise into the air, I would pull the handlebars up to my chest until the front wheel left the ground. There I would be, cruising along on just my back wheel, filled with euphoria, even pride. Or I would lift my butt off the seat, slowly shifting my weight onto my wrists and raising my hips up high until eventually I felt that I could take both feet off the pedals simultaneously to execute a headstand on the moving bike. I was spontaneous, courageous, fearless. Acrobatics was my dream—I wanted to jump over a rainbow and ride a cloud.

I saw the black flame in Tosca's pupils flicker. Everything around me was filled with light, so bright it blinded me and made the line dividing the wall from the ceiling disappear. I still felt no fear of Tosca, but there was something frightening in the atmosphere surrounding her. I'd entered a realm where it was forbidden to set foot. And there, in darkness, the grammars of many languages lost their color, they melted and combined, then froze solid again, they drifted in the ocean and joined the drifting floes of ice. I sat on the same iceberg as Tosca and understood every word she said to me. Beside us floated a second iceberg with an Inuk and a snow hare sitting on it, immersed in conversation.

"I want to know everything about you." It was Tosca who said this to me, and I could understand every word. "What were you afraid of when you were little?" Her question surprised me—no one had ever asked me about my fears. I was a famous trainer of wild animals, afraid of nothing. But in fact there was something that frightened me.

As a child, I sometimes felt behind my back the presence of insects. One late-summer dusk, I was playing alone in the front hall of my apartment building when I sensed that someone was standing behind me. I turned around and saw an old beetle, its feelers rolled halfway up. Its legs were so thin as to be almost invisible, it was all they could do to drag the unwieldy carapace along with them. I was no longer sure whether the legs were the main part of the insect and its back only a sort of luggage, or whether the hard shield also had blood flowing through it, assuming insects had blood at all. I just wasn't sure. The knapsack with school books on my back was a carapace shielding me from attackers. I'd kept it on so long it was growing into my flesh. Like plants sending out their roots beneath the earth, my veins without my noticing grew out of my back and into my knapsack. If I were to take it off now, my skin would come off too and bleed.

"Are you there?" my mother asked. "I have to go take care of something. You can have dinner alone."

"Where are you going?"

"To the doctor."

"To the dentist?"

"No, the gynecologist."

I ran outside when I heard the word "gynecologist." I still hadn't had a chance to take off my schoolbag. I ran in the direction of green surface, the familiar landscape around our house was no longer visible, there was a smell of dark green. The color green smelled green. Everything red smelled red, it smelled of blood and red roses. The color white smelled of snow, but winter still loitered at a distance, the snow would remain out of my reach for a long time yet. I stopped, unable to go on running, breathing like a bellows, both my hands propped on my knees. On the crown of my head, a tiny aviator with silk-thin wings alighted. I brushed it away, and it flew off but then at once came back again, returning to land on exactly the same spot. I reached out my hand, blindly grasping for my prey. Before my eyes, I slowly opened my fist, in which the powdery-dry remnants of wings glimmered in the cold light. The insect's belly was no longer there. Had it been flying without its torso when I caught it? Or had its belly disappeared into thin air when I squeezed too tightly? Who knows, perhaps even the hairs on my head were nothing more than insects. Each hair was a terribly thin, long animal that had clamped its teeth into my scalp to suck the blood from my head. I began to hate my hair and plucked out strand after strand of it.

On the back of my left heel, I discovered a birthmark I'd never seen before. I touched it cautiously—and it turned into an ant. I was all eyes, trying to read the face of the ant. Beneath my focused gaze, the tar-black mask expanded: it had neither eyes nor mouth. My bladder was suddenly full, I stood up and opened my legs wide. The exit path for the urine grew warm, but nothing came. I stared at the ground with its ant-body punctuation. Ants everywhere! Nothing but ants! When I finally understood this, something hot passed through my urethra, bubbling and running down the inside of my thigh. The ants were getting a shower, but this only seemed to strengthen their life force, and they began to climb up my legs, following the path of the urine. Help! Help!

I laid my head in Tosca's lap and sobbed. Finally, at my age, I'd found a friend in whose lap I could weep over a terrifying memory. The tears tasted like sugarcane, it would have been a shame to stop crying too quickly, so I raised my voice and recommenced bawling at the top of my lungs. "What's wrong with you?" asked a voice on a completely different wavelength from Tosca's. The night-table lamp came on, and I saw my husband's plaid pajamas. Presumably I'd just been dreaming.

"Did you have a nightmare?"

The situation to me was more embarrassing than anything else, I quickly wiped my tears away with my fingers. "As a child, I was afraid of insects. I just dreamed about that."

"Insects? You mean like ants?"

"Yes."

My husband laughed using his entire upper body, even his pajamas crinkled with laughter.

"You aren't afraid of lions and bears, but you're scared of ants?"

"Yup."

"Do worms scare you too?"

"They really do. But spiders are the worst." I was alert now and knew I wouldn't be able to get back to sleep quickly, so I told him about horrific spiders.

At the time, I knew a boy in my neighborhood named Horst. Unlike other boys, he smelled refined—though I couldn't say exactly what he smelled of. "There's an orchard behind the train station. Let's go steal some fruit."

I didn't care whether he was lying or not, I found the idea exciting and followed him. There really was a hidden orchard in which numerous apples were ripening blood-red. Their branches formed a ceiling that was low enough for our robber hands to reach. When I stood on tiptoe and tried to pluck a large, gleaming-red apple, a spider suddenly descended on its thread elevator right in front of me. A grimace—or, no, it was the pattern on its back, but it looked like a face, and it was screaming so loudly it hurt my eardrums, I thought, but no, that's my own voice! The owner of the orchard heard my screams, hurried over and found a girl lying unconscious on the ground. He tended to me. When I recovered my senses, he brought me home without a scolding. A few days later, Horst suggested another prank. This time he wanted us to steal sweets from an emporium's warehouse. The main impediment was a watchdog kept chained to the warehouse door. The dog pulled back his upper lip and gave a warning growl. His language was unambiguous. I said to Horst, "He'll bite if we try to pass. Let's go home!"

"Are you saying you're afraid of this little dog?" Horst spat in disgust and began to advance.

"He'll bite!" By the time I got the words out, the dog had already sunk his teeth into the boy's calf and was shaking his head without letting go. Horst's screams are engraved on my eardrums forever.

Later Horst and I happened once to walk past the warehouse. On that day, the dog was in a good mood and wagged his tail at us. His eyes invited me to stroke his head. Without hesitation, I walked up to him and patted him between the ears. Horst stared at me, aghast.

The thoughts of animals were written clearly on their faces as if spelled out with an alphabet. I found it difficult to understand that this language was not just illegible to other people but in fact completely invisible. Some people even claimed that animals didn't have faces at all, just snouts. I didn't put much store in what's known as courage. I would just run away when an animal hated me, that's all, and conversely, I could easily tell when an animal loved me. Mammals were easy to understand. They neither put on makeup nor engaged in play-acting. An insect, on the other hand, frightened me because I couldn't get a sense of its heart.

My husband listened to me attentively this entire time. When I'd finished speaking and fell silent, he said melancholically: "I no longer understand the feelings of animals. It used to be I could sense them precisely, like an object I was holding in the palm of my hand. Do you think I'll ever regain that?"

"Of course you will! Right now you're just spinning your wheels, but sooner or later you'll be back in peak form." I turned off my bedside lamp, as if to extinguish my bad conscience.

The next day, Tosca and I once more practiced coming onstage, bowing, and exiting. From time to time Tosca looked deep into my eyes and seemed to be alluding to something. Apparently it wasn't just in my imagination that we'd spoken: we really were entering a sphere situated halfway between the animal and human worlds.

Around ten in the morning, Pankov showed up. His beard

was still smeared with yolk from the soft-boiled egg he'd eaten at breakfast. He asked how our rehearsals were going.

"The jam didn't work," I said, "so now we're trying it with honey."

"Aha. And what's this honey number supposed to look like?"

"We're going to attach wings to Tosca's back so she'll look like a bee. She transports the nectar from the flowers to the bees' hive and produces honey. In the next scene she'll turn into a bear and gobble the honey up."

A dark cloud covered Pankov's face. "Can't you just put together a straight acrobatic number? Dance on a ball! Jump rope—play badminton! Don't you know that with difficult-to-interpret productions, people can accuse us of secretly engaging in social criticism?"

To calm Pankov down, I asked him to order a ball for Tosca. A tricycle would have been too expensive, but maybe a ball wasn't too much for him. Besides, for badminton we would have needed not just the shuttlecock but two racquets as well. It could have proved difficult to get a racquet custom made for a bear. And jump ropes? I found a rope, but fortunately Tosca was incapable of jumping over it. I was against the idea from the start, anyhow: Tosca's hind legs were too delicate in relation to her weight. Jumping rope might injure her knees. I knew that the Russian circus employed several poodles who could jump rope, but my voice involuntarily rose: "If we start imitating the Russians, we'll never have a future of our own!" My husband pressed his index finger to his lips, whispering: "The ears of the secret police are in every wall." We knew for a fact that bugging devices had been installed somewhere in the circus.

My husband and I slept and ate in our circus trailer, and our office was in a trailer, too. For rehearsals, we used a large room in an auxiliary building. There were colleagues who liked to rent a small room in town and didn't sleep at the circus. My husband and I were true circus people: we lived entirely on the grounds of our circus as if unwilling to be parted from it even for a second. In all honesty, I was afraid—a fear I concealed—that this husband I knew so well might suddenly seem like a stranger to me if I saw him outside the circus. More than the physical intimacy we shared, it was the bears who brought us together so intensely.

Yet another day passed without our making any progress. Secretly all day I was just waiting for sundown. I quickly ate a piece of stone-hard dark bread with cheese, gulped down a mug of black tea and brushed my teeth at breakneck speed. "Are you going to bed already?" My husband was staring at me with astonishment. In his right hand, he held the box with the Go set in it, and between the fingers of his left, he'd skillfully wedged both a bottle of vodka and a pack of cigarettes.

"My brain is full of knots today, probably it's a rope we can't jump." I didn't want to spend the evening with him, since I neither drank vodka nor played Go. For these things, he had Pankov's secretary.

A snowfield extended between me and the jagged horizon. I spread a piece of hide on the hard, snowy ground and sat down. Tosca followed, placing her chin in my lap and closing her eyes. She had no voice. The ice goddess had lost her voice after going several thousand years without speaking. I could read her thoughts, they were as clear as if they'd been written in soft pencil on drawing paper.

"It was pitch black. I was an infant, I was freezing cold and pressed against my mother. She was tired, and ate nothing. Until we came out of the hole one day, I saw nothing, heard nothing. Later I asked my mother if I'd been born premature. She answered that it was perfectly normal for a baby bear to be born early. What sort of woman was your mother?"

Her question surprised me and brought me back to the present; I'd been feeling like a bear child. Now it was my turn to talk—the human being's turn.

For as far back as I can remember, I lived alone with my mother. She told me my father was living by himself in Berlin. I didn't know Berlin, but still couldn't get the city out of my mind. I can remember the pattern of the wallpaper in our apartment quite well, but not the face of my father.

Once I saw my parents' wedding photo. Or at least it seems to me I can remember the white gloves and the hem that melancholically drooped from the bottom of my mother's gown. From my father's breast pocket, a rose hung its head. It's possible my father lived with us at the beginning of my life. This is only a vague inkling, not a solid memory. I don't know when or why my father quarreled with my mother and left us.

My mother worked in a Dresden textile factory. One day she was transferred to another factory in the Neustadt district and wanted to move with me to a new apartment on the edge of town that was just as far away from her new workplace as the old apartment had been. From the new place, she would have a direct bus connection to work, she explained, but I instantly sensed she had another reason. Perhaps the move had something to do with the neighbor my mother sometimes conversed with in whispered tones. In any case, I was against the move and protested. I didn't want to be separated from a mouse that lived in the basement. My mother said: "Moving often brings good luck. New places, new animals!" She only said that to placate me, but by chance it turned out that she was right. The famous Circus Sarrasani had set up camp half a mile from our new apartment.

I awoke from my dream and saw my husband's back. Soon the sun would rise. He turned around and asked me what I'd think about dancing with Tosca onstage.

"Did you go on thinking about the act all night long?"

"No, it just came to me as I was waking up."

"Dancing isn't my forte, but maybe it's worth a try."

During the day I couldn't speak with Tosca about our dreams because we lacked a common language. But now and then something in her eyes or gestures showed she'd just remembered our conversation from the night before.

When I stood facing her and took her paws, I thought how odd we must look as a dancing couple, considering that she was twice my height. The record player Pankov had provided for the rehearsal was of even worse quality than I'd feared. I stumbled while attempting to fish the melody of "La Cumparsita" from its crackling background and stepped right on Tosca's foot. Fortunately I was light as a feather to her, so it didn't hurt. She bent down and licked my cheek, which possibly tasted of breakfast jam. The music abruptly stopped, and I heard my husband messing around with the record player, muttering: "That's odd. Could it be any *more* kaput?" Cautiously I touched Tosca's belly. There was a firm layer of thick fur, and beneath it, a soft layer of short, fine hair. Touching her brought back the memory of my first tango lesson. A female voice hummed a tango melody inside me while giving instructions: "Back step, back step, come to the cross, side step!" What was the owner of the voice called? "Turn to the left and back step." I obeyed the voice and danced. Tosca looked at me, faintly puzzled, but when I tugged at her arms, she took a step forward without hesitating. When I pushed against her, she took a step back. "Come to the cross, side step, forward step." It was an aerial acrobat who had taught me the tango. Her mother was from Cuba. As we danced, I fell down, and our lips met.

Pankov sat in a corner of the rehearsal room, watching us. I hadn't noticed him come in. "The two of you are no good at dancing, but the way you stand face to face is artistic, like a painting. Hahaha. If the tango is too hard, maybe you should play cards instead."

My husband gave a whistle. "What about having them play Go?"

"Is that the Japanese checkers you're always playing to pass the time?"

"Exactly. We use white and black stones to play, exactly the right colors for our cast of characters. Ten polar bears—the white stones—locked in battle against ten black stones. We can borrow ten sea lions to represent them."

"Then the white stones will eat the black stones, leaving us in the red. Besides, why Go and not chess? The Russians will think we have something against chess because so many world-famous chess players are Russian. Avoid ambiguous references! By the way, we're going to have a visit today from a young director who has something important to tell us. Can you join us for the conversation? Apparently he used to work with Tosca. Maybe he'll have some good ideas for us."

The young director was named Honigberg and had been part of the casting commission for the *Swan Lake* production. Despite his support of Tosca, the commission voted not to give her a role. To this day he felt guilty about not having been able to get her accepted. At the time, he was working in the provinces as the choreographer of a ballet company. Exasperated with the conservative members of the commission, he kept trying to get them to understand Tosca's magical talent. He'd even gone so far as to blurt that he could no longer stand by and watch a genius being forced into the shadows where she would quickly be forgotten, while Tosca's untalented former classmates like Ms. Magpie and Mr. Fox were being catapulted into successful stage careers.

The oldest member of the jury had informed him—it was meant as a warning—that sturdily built female bodies were not in keeping with contemporary tastes. "For male dancers, a compact body is de rigueur, but where the ladies are concerned, the audience still expects to see delicate fairies floating through the air." Honigberg, appalled at his colleague's festering spirit, paid Tosca a personal visit at her home, surprising her with a somewhat overhasty proposal: "There's no point staying in this country for you. Let's escape to West Germany together! We can go to Hamburg and work with John Neumeier. It's surely a splendid place to work." Tosca was taken with his suggestion, but her elderly mother, who'd had an unusual past, was against the idea. West Germany, she said, was like heaven: nice to dream about, but you don't want to end up there too early. Tosca's mother had been born in the Soviet Union, had emigrated to West Germany, and then continued on to Canada, where she married her husband and gave birth to Tosca. Then at the request of her Danish husband, she'd moved to the GDR. She was all exiled out. "If you really want to go to Hamburg, I won't stand in your way. But we'll probably never see each other again. Take a copy of my will with you!" Tosca opted out of exile, found a position at the children's theater, and awaited her come-what-may. Then the query from our circus arrived. When Honigberg heard that Tosca had shifted her allegiances to the circus, he decided to bid farewell to the hopelessly outdated Literary Theater art form and seek the future of the stage arts beneath the big top. He wanted to become Tosca's personal artistic director. "I'm like a teenager who's run away from home. I have nothing left, no place to sleep, no bread to eat. Could I sleep here in the circus and share your meals? I'll help out with the production and won't ask for a fee." Honigberg was confident, self-assured, as though it were his right to be accepted by us.

Pankov and Markus glanced skeptically at Honigberg's too-tight jeans; I, on the other hand, felt no need to subject his legs to interpretation. Just the chance of finding out more about Tosca made him interesting to me. "What plays has

Tosca appeared in?" I asked, trying to make my voice sound friendly. He replied with a significant smile but said nothing.

The next day, we gathered in front of Tosca's cage for a small consultation, three chairs arranged in a circle.

At first, my husband was skeptical of the young man, this homeless Honigberg, but in the course of the conversation, both men gradually relaxed their muscles. Markus claimed that the development of children's theater was responsible for the destruction of the modern stage, since so much of what made theater interesting was diverted to the children's theaters, leaving nothing behind for the adults. Honigberg agreed, saying that the circus was the true seat of art, since it did not exclude children. The result of this exchange between the two men was the beer that the two began to drink even though the sun still stood high in the heavens. I asked them not to smoke in front of Tosca. "Then we'll continue our conference outside. Beer without a cigarette is like a meat dish without salt."

Change of scene. We sat down beside the laundry area where the circus employees' linens fluttered in the breeze as though butting into our conversation. Honigberg answered my questions listlessly, but still in reasonable detail, recounting how Tosca was discriminated against because of her figure and language.

I imagined Tosca's sufferings and suffered along with her, thinking: "How wretched is the life of the stage artist!" No matter what torments she may have suffered in the course of her career, she will be judged by her audience solely on the basis of her latest performance. Everything else remains unseen, unless of course the artiste becomes famous enough that an author writes her biography. If Tosca were human, of course, she could write an autobiography and have it printed at her own expense. But as an animal, she is doomed to have the pain-filled, female life journey she has embarked on as a bear forgotten after her death. Unfortunate creature, thy name is bear! I was alone with my thoughts. The two men formed a unit and fell away. The more they drank, the more solid their manly bond.

"Tosca on a bulldozer—how about that?"

"She can wear a helmet and carry a pickax."

"Let's drink to the lady workers of the world!"

Even the darkness that had placed a gentle cap upon each of our heads couldn't deter the two men from continuing to sit there drinking. I went in and took a shower to wash their words from my body. It was only nine when I went to bed.

"My mother wrote her autobiography."

"That's fantastic."

"Many stones lay in her path. She stumbled often and fell down seven times, but she got up again eight times. She never gave up writing." Tosca's voice was as clear as a thin, transparent sheet of ice. "I, on the other hand, can't write anything at all."

"Why not?" I asked.

"My mother already described me as a character in her book."

"Then I'll write for you. I'll write your life story so you can escape from your mother's autobiography."

When I made her this promise, I didn't realize it would be too difficult for me to keep. I woke at four and right away asked myself how I could possibly write Tosca's biography when I'd never written anything at all besides a few simple letters. Next to me, my husband was snoring, and I thought of a locomotive. I slipped stealthily out of bed, went to the empty dining hall and sat down at a table. Propping up my chin, I let my thoughts drift, and my eyes drifted too. Soon they landed—on a pencil stub lying on the ground. What was this if not fate? I had been born as a human being so I could write Tosca's biography! All I lacked was decent paper. In our country there was a permanent paper shortage, even in the circus. Sometimes an odyssey through the entire town was required to find a roll of toilet paper. In the dining hall I looked behind each of the shelves and eventually found an old list the cleaning crew had left behind. The back of the sheet was blank.

I should have been grateful to have found any paper at all for my debut as a writer, but still I felt ashamed. In other places, even a tomcat could find the paper he needed to write his autobiography. Admittedly, the backs of his manuscript pages were just as written-upon as mine, but the text they held was far more interesting than the cleaning staff's notes. Man needs paper. The pages don't have to be all that big, and preferably not as huge as the snowfields on which polar bears write their lives. For me, one sheet of paper a day would suffice—that was as much as I could fill in a day without writing myself into the ground. I ironed smooth the cleaning list with my hand, then picked up the dwarf pencil, and began writing Tosca's biography in the first person.

When I was born, it was dark all around me, and I heard nothing. I pressed myself against the warm body beside me, sucked sweet liquid from a teat, and fell back asleep. I'll give this warm body the name Mama-lia.

There was something that made me feel afraid: the giant. He came to us from someplace and tried to force his way into our cave. Mama-lia bellowed at him—her voice was a strong arm expelling the giant, but eventually her voice grew hoarse, and already a giant leg was planted right in front of me. Mama-lia shrieked, a piercing sound, and the giant, excited, started barking. "What's the matter? What are you doing up?" my husband's voice asked. He was standing behind me. Quickly I covered the freshly written sentences with my left hand.

"What are you writing?" He sounded astonished.

"Nothing."

"I'm thirsty, let's have tea."

An intern arrived with a large thermos filled with black tea. I tried to unscrew its old-fashioned top, but I couldn't get it open—the air inside had cooled, exerting suction. I held the thermos tightly in my left hand, bending over as I labored to uncap it, as if I were trying to twist a gigantic screw into my own chest. My right hand had been transformed into an eagle's talons.

"Is everything all right? Should I open the stupid thermos for you? Or maybe we should have Tosca open it onstage!"

"That's not a bad idea. Let me ask in the office if they can get us a new thermos to use in the show."

"I'll come with you. Is Honigberg up yet?"

We visited the trailer that served as the main office and asked if we could have a new thermos bottle to use in rehearsals. The man whose face was the embodiment of circus administration replied at once: "Out of the question. There's a severe shortage of thermos bottles in this country at the moment. In recent years, thermos production hasn't been able to keep up with demand. We can't even replace the ones that get broken. So of course you can't have one to use onstage."

Pankov walked into the room holding a big stack of paper in both arms. "You still don't have an idea for the polar bear show? What a hopeless pair of long-distance runners." He disappeared again right away—apparently he really did have a lot to do.

For once I sensed a certain human warmth in Pankov's commentary: my husband, however, detected ice-cold criticism. He jumped out of the office trailer, sat down on a wooden crate, and wrapped his arms around his lowered head. Even though of the same species, it seemed he'd lost his ability to interpret the emotions of his fellow humans. It wasn't only the bears' thoughts that had slipped beyond his reach. Or had my skin become too thick to feel Pankov's coldness?

Markus looked as if he never wanted to get up again. To shift his train of thought, I began to tell an old story: "I must have told you at some point that my debut was a donkey routine. What if I try the same thing with Tosca?"

As if he'd been waiting for me to speak these very words, Honigberg turned up just then in his pajamas, and said: "A donkey routine? How delicious! Please do tell us your story." Honigberg sat down right beside Markus, who seemed pleased and remarked oddly: "Were you asleep all this time? I was worried. I thought: Perhaps the fellow's run off." Markus placed his hand on Honigberg's shoulder.

I owe my breakthrough as a circus performer to censorship. I was only twenty-six and not particularly hardworking, in fact I was as lazy as a donkey. What I mean is that it was lucky that our circus poster was subjected to rigorous scrutiny by the culture police (as we called them) and rejected. There was a young clown named Jan. Everyone used to say that the circus director relied on this young man for any decision requiring a precise understanding of numbers and letters. At the time, I was responsible for keeping the equipment and premises clean as well as caring for the animals and children. One full moon night, I was out searching for a moonstruck child who'd sleepwalked out of bed, and spotted a flashlight beam in the office trailer. I thought the child must have picked the trailer as a hiding place, so I tiptoed to the windowsill—and heard Jan's voice, sounding different, more self-possessed than usual. I also heard the voice of the director agreeing with Jan or asking for further clarification. In any case, the two spoke as if they were on an equal footing. Although I didn't mean to eavesdrop, I couldn't tear myself away. Jan was explaining like a teacher to his charge: "When they ask you about the intention behind the poster, make sure to emphasize that we intentionally placed this important sentence right in the center: 'The circus is art that comes from the lives of the people.' A quote from Lunacharsky." Jan's voice sounded almost overbearing, while the circus director seemed almost timid, asking: "Will we even manage to attract an audience with such a stuffy-sounding slogan?"

"Certainly. The sentence is printed in big letters in the middle of the poster, but you don't really notice it—the color blends in with the background. The gaze of the typical viewer will first be drawn to the name in smaller letters: Circus Busch. It's more a logo than a word. As images, logos call forth an immediate emotional response. Like the Coca-Cola logo. Then the viewer's gaze will continue on to the golden lion and the erotic woman in the swimsuit. It's all a matter of design. We can manipulate vision. In our country, there's still been almost no research done on consumer psychology. I'm positive the official inspectors won't be able to see through our strategy. Seeing our poster, a person will succumb to its sensory appeal and come to the performance, but no one will accuse us of using decadent methods to make money."

"But to be honest, the woman looks like a striptease dancer."

"If the officials say the woman looks too decadent, just tell them she's wearing one of the official Olympic swimsuits. Training wild animals is a sport, and the trainer's arms and legs must have complete freedom of motion, otherwise the body of the working class is in danger."

"Who counts as working class?"

"Everyone who works in the circus is working class. That's only logical."

The circus director, a man who usually never missed a chance to display his power, was quite deferential toward Jan. Only later did I learn the reason for this.

Several days later, gentlemen with severe expressions paid us a visit. They restlessly wiped perspiration from their foreheads. I went on grooming the horses, assuming this visit had nothing to do with me. But the circus director led the men over and addressed me in a supercilious, deep register as if he were lifting a rabbit up by the scruff to display it to a would-be buyer. The men circled me, surveying my body from chest to thighs. The director said with a self-satisfied air: "This is the woman I mentioned. At the moment she's dressed simply because she's tending to the animals, but as you see, she's obviously a great beauty as well as athletic. Now we'll put on her stage costume and present her to you. Might I ask you for a bit of patience? Why don't you enjoy a beverage over there while we wait?" Jan repeated the expression "a beverage," his skilled clown hands miming the knocking back of a glass of vodka. For the first time, the men laughed, while Jan's eyes remained cold.

Somewhat later, I finally learned what had led up to this farce: the censors had deemed our poster suspicious after all and were torturing the director with unexpected questions. One of these questions was: "Who is this fictional decadent woman pictured on the poster? The wild-animal trainer is a scrawny man with gray hair, isn't he?" The director was stumped, but Jan stuck out his rescuing tongue quickly: "Now we're going to have to reveal something to you—and of course we're glad to—but please treat this information confidentially: in our troupe we have a talented young woman who is going to crown our next season with her surprise debut as a wild-animal trainer. At the moment she's still officially employed as an animal keeper, becoming better acquainted with our animals' particular characteristics—but if all goes well, next season will find her onstage. And so, to account for this eventuality, we have included her likeness in one corner of the poster. Of course, it's impossible to tell in advance how things will go in rehearsal. One never has beasts like this under control one hundred percent." Jan saved the day with such a high-caliber lie that reality could only submit to it. I can't believe he thought of it just like that, on the spot. The officials visited the circus with the assignment of verifying with their own eyes the existence of this talented young woman.

Jan led me into the changing-room trailer, undressed me, clothed me in a pink costume belonging to the director's former mistress, and piled up my hair so that it rose like an onion dome atop my head. Then he added fake eyelashes that fluttered like butterflies, smeared my lips pink and greasy with a salmon-tinted hue, and led me into the room where the officials, their mood much improved by the vodka, were waiting. They immediately accepted me as the promising egg about to hatch into stardom and showered me with generous applause.

At some point the officials left the circus grounds. I wanted to return to the trailer and take off my costume, but my colleagues stopped me. "Not so fast. It's exciting to see you like this—it's as if we'd hired a new girl!"

"In all honesty, I've often wondered what you would look like in costume."

I was floored. A compliment from woman to woman!

"You're the ugly duckling who turns out to be a beautiful swan."

"What a rotten thing to say. It's not true at all that she was ugly before."

"But somehow you never noticed her, right?"

Some of them nodded to me, and others sighed and energetically spewed words I struggled to interpret, unsure whether they meant to praise me or insult me out of envy. Jan suggested to the director that they give me a five-minute act, since a lie is the best mother of truth. In the presence of his colleagues, Jan addressed the director with polite reserve. Now the director had to ask the master animal trainer whether he could imagine taking me under his wing. (The director was no match for this master trainer, his respect for him was too great.) The master's stern face showed no expression as he replied: "She's a beginner, so I recommend that we start with a donkey." It sounded like a grandfather ordaining his grandchild's choice of profession: with authority, but also with love. His astonished colleagues gaped first at him and then at me. The master had never before allowed anyone to appear onstage with his animals.

Thanks to Jan, the poster was approved and quickly sent off to the printer. One week later, plainclothes policemen arrived to observe our rehearsals. I took up my position beside the master and pretended to be diligently rehearsing. The policemen didn't even look at me. Instead they asked to speak with Jan, and when he appeared, they grabbed his arms and took him away.

I slept restlessly, not just that night but also the ones that followed. Once, finding myself unable to remain lying there in the muggy, stale air of the trailer, I went out in the dark and heard a woman sobbing. I followed the sound and found a red-haired woman crouching in tears beneath an illuminated window. She'd once been rumored to be Jan's secret lover.

"Are you worried because Jan hasn't come back yet?" My question was cautiously tentative, but she furrowed the skin above her nose and answered:

"Why don't you just say clearly that he was arrested. I know everything. I even know who betrayed him."

"The circus director?"

"Never. Who would send his own son to prison?"

"What? Jan is the director's son?"

"Of course. You didn't know?"

My husband interrupted me and said: "What sort of act was the donkey number? Your story is interesting, but it's much too long."

"Let me tell it the way I want to. It's good practice for when I write a book someday. You have to present concrete details."

"You're planning to write a book? Not an autobiography, by any chance?"

"No, I want to tell a certain person's life story. I'm practicing on my own life story. Listen, now comes the chapter about the rehearsal with the donkey. You'll have to pay attention."

"We have to start rehearsing. There isn't much time left before the premiere. You and this donkey are going to have to fill the gap left behind by Jan's disappearance." My master's full-bodied voice came back to me. My donkey apprenticeship began, but my lessons weren't given by the master himself, but by Professor Beserl, who would come to the circus with his donkey. His academic title was by no means a nickname. He had once taught in Leipzig, at the university, and was well respected in the field of behavioral science. After his retirement, he debuted a donkey act in a circus and became famous overnight. A few years later, though, he developed knee problems and was forced to stop several times in the course of any performance to sit down and speak gently to his knees, caressing them. The doctor, who'd no doubt been bribed by the circus manager, gave the old donkey professor false hopes, praising his endurance, and the donkey act kept being performed. But one day, after a last loud creak, the professor's knees definitively gave up the ghost. Everyone in the audience heard it. Ever since, the professor had lived the life of a recluse in a small, dilapidated cottage, living modestly but happily with his donkey. When he received the circus director's query, he was overjoyed, gladly taking upon himself the long trip to the circus so as to pass on the secrets of donkey artistry to the next generation.

On our first rehearsal day, he said to me: "You must love only vegetarian animals. If you have an affair with a carnivore, your fate will run amok. Take a good look at him! Isn't he sweet? A donkey is no daredevil, nor is he a coward. In other words, he is perfectly suited to acrobatics." The professor's donkey was named Platero.

Putting great faith in their eyes, human beings, when they first meet a new individual, quickly take in the person's figure, clothing, and face. Donkeys, on the other hand, place a great deal of importance on the tastes a person has to offer. The professor said that I should start by impressing the donkey with carrots. The next time he saw me, he would immediately think of carrots. I held a carrot before Platero's muzzle. He nibbled on it, making an appetizing sound that sounded like "carro, carro." Then he pulled back his upper lip, displaying his proud teeth. He looked as though he were soundlessly laughing. It was impossible to tell by that laugh whether he was happy or making fun of someone. "Doesn't he have a splendid laugh? He laughs to remove the traces of food from his teeth. You can give him something sticky to eat and then talk to him just before he's finished chewing. For example, like this." The professor gave Platero a carrot smeared with a sticky substance and asked him: "You wouldn't be making fun of me, would you?" Platero moved his mouth as though he were grinning, at precisely the right moment. "You can combine little scenes like this to create an act."

"I didn't know you used tricks like that!"

"To manipulate the people, politicians use their own carrots and sticks. We're just using our brains to animate animals." The professor pulled back his upper lip just like his donkey and laughed.

"You can't make art just by working hard. You have to achieve something effortlessly and naturally. When your art looks like magic to your audience—not like back-breaking work—then it's exactly right." It seemed to me that at just that moment, I saw Platero nodding in approval, but it was just the sunlight playing a trick on me.

Beneath his long lashes, Platero's eyes had such a gentle

gleam that I found them almost uncanny. Do vegetarians never fly into a rage? Do they never tear at each other in fury? Does the character of a human being change if he becomes a vegetarian?

The premiere was just around the corner, so we took advantage of every possible shortcut. We worked constantly, our eyes fixed on the future, laboring without respite. Platero had already mastered his skills; I was the one who still had many new things to learn. I tried to slip into the professor's role. A long road lay before me.

Large cards with numbers written on them were arranged in a row. I asked Platero what two times two was. He went over to the card with the number four written on it. This card had been smeared with carrot juice, and the others not. The trick was perfectly simple, but it still wasn't easy to get the donkey to walk up to the same card every single time. "It can happen that the donkey chooses a different card, even though he knows perfectly well which one smells of carrots. Human beings sometimes behave like this too: doing something on purpose, even though it means giving up a reward. So it's possible even when you've rehearsed enough for things to go wrong. Let's say the trick fails to work one time out of ten. So the question is: How can you prevent this ill-fated occurrence while you and the donkey are onstage? Do you know how?" I shook my head until my hair stroked my cheeks.

"You have to achieve a certain mental state in which failure is no longer possible. You are as relaxed as if napping beside a lake in the springtime, but your head is clear as glass. You are free of worries, but still attentive. Your entire body functions as a sensor, registering everything that takes place around you, but this places no burden on you at all. You respond automatically to everything because you are part of everything that occurs. You act without intention, but always correctly. Onstage, you must find a way to enter this state. Then you will never fail."

The donkey went over to Card Four every time I gave him the multiplication task "two times two." When I saw the circus director walking over, I thought this would be a good opportunity to show off my skill. Lovingly I stroked Platero's ear and asked him what two times two was. Platero did not move from the spot. The professor sat, his face expressionless, on a wooden crate in a corner of the rehearsal room, unwilling to help. I repeated the question, stroking the donkey's ear once again, but Platero refused to budge. The director sighed in disappointment and left us. I wanted to burst into tears. Somewhat later, the professor casually remarked: "You stroked Platero's ear that time. You'd never done that before. He wanted you to keep stroking him, that's why he didn't move. He picked you over the carrot."

"Why didn't you tell me right away?"

"Is that my duty? I'm here for my own entertainment. I enjoy watching young people suffer."

"That's so mean!"

"Onstage, you can't just stroke the animals when you feel like it. In the circus, even the tiniest gesture counts as a signal—you can't just sneeze onstage, or blow your nose."

I didn't have time to go on feeling distraught—or to celebrate every little insight either. First of all, I had to teach the donkey to answer the audience's math problems by going over to the appropriate card and stopping in front of it. It was this donkey's habit to stop short whenever he saw someone standing right in front of him. And when I stood behind him to the left, he would take a step diagonally to the left. When I stood behind him to the right, he would go to the right. It was my task to use these rules to bring the act to its finale.

The donkey would shake his head when I touched his ear. He nodded when I touched his chest. We practiced answering a question with Yes or No. We rehearsed from morning till night, and when I was desperate for a break and went out for a breath of air, all the people I saw had donkey faces. I saw a man scratching behind one ear and immediately wanted to lend a hand, but then remembered that you can't just touch other people like that.

The professor usually went home as soon as rehearsal was over, but one evening he stayed late to talk with me. "Platero is old, and so am I. We have to take into account that we may not exist much longer." His voice sounded cheerful even though he apparently intended to talk to me about the time after his death. "What if you have to start over with a new donkey after we're both dead? I am going to initiate you into the final secret. Until now I have never shared it with anyone. This is like making you an heiress to a large fortune. You were at a great disadvantage when you came to the circus, because your parents were not circus people. You must have noticed that, didn't you?" I remained obstinate, refusing to nod. "Fine. You don't want to admit you're disadvantaged. You have a strong will. You'll succeed."

My debut with the donkey took place shortly after my twenty-sixth birthday. It was an incandescent success, even though it was just a brief, unremarkable number featuring an unprepossessing animal.

"Arithmetic! Should we try it with Tosca? Maybe she has a talent for math." Inspired by my donkey tale, Markus decided to paint numbers on large cards. Since we didn't have any cardboard, he used veneer panels that he'd taken from the basement of an abandoned building without permission. There were cards with the numbers one through seven, and only one of them had been smeared with honey. Tosca immediately went over to the sweetened number and started licking it. "Tosca keeps sniffing at the card and licking it. I'd be surprised if no one in the audience saw through our trick. Besides, there's something not terribly convincing about the idea that a bear can add and subtract. Why are we so quick to believe that a donkey can?"

"Probably because there are donkeys in children's books who can read and write. Do you remember the donkey in *The Merry Pranks of Till Eulenspiegel*? Wasn't there that trick with the donkey reading aloud?"

"That's right. On the other hand, everyone thinks donkeys aren't particularly clever. So the contrast is humorous. We ought to be staging the opposite of some cliché."

"What's a polar bear cliché?"

"Polar bears are always sitting on ice floes."

"What's the opposite of ice?"

"Fire."

Making big cats jump through flaming rings was an obligatory offering of every circus. My husband and I knew we wouldn't be able to avoid it forever but it would be too banal to just send Tosca through the flames. We needed at least some sort of backstory, we could for example turn the fairy tale "Snow White" into a musical and have Tosca leap over the flames in the heroine's role. In my opinion, though, we didn't need any additional infernos at the circus—we were so deep in the red that the ledger-books' numbers were fiery enough. But Pankov instructed his secretary to retrieve the large fire ring from the warehouse without consulting us. The next morning, all the equipment was gleaming, freshly polished, in the rehearsal space. I pretended not to see it and practiced with Tosca how to walk side by side and stand facing each other.

The sun set, and when sleep made its entrance, I was allowed to visit the world of ice. Every time, I could recognize an evolution that progressed with each passing day. Nothing there was in the red or in the black—there was only progress. There was no industry, no hospital, no school. There were only words exchanged between living beings. "I've started writing your biography," I said to Tosca, who sneezed in surprise.

"Are you cold?"

"Very funny. I have a pollen allergy. Here at the North Pole, no flowers bloom, but there's still pollen in the air, and I can't stop sneezing. It's uncanny, having pollen without flowers."

"I've written up to the period just after your birth. Your eyes weren't open yet. Your mother and you weren't alone, there was a third shadow."

"My father wanted to live with us, but my mother couldn't stand him. She used to snarl whenever he came within sight of us."

"Isn't that normal for a mother bear?"

"Maybe it was normal once, but even Nature changes over the course of history."

Mama-lia's voice was terrifying, and I found myself feeling afraid of her, even though I knew perfectly well I was in no danger.

Humans can roar too, to intimidate others. At first they use words that mean something; after a while, however, all you hear is a bellowing that has grown out of speech, and a person being roared at has no other choice but to roar back. This thought made me suddenly remember how my father left us and went to Berlin. With the sixth sense of a small child, I felt the tiny thorn in my mother's voice just before she started shouting. I began to cry at the top of my lungs to distract her. She tried to calm me and forgot my father. But then he said something else that grated on her nerves. My mother gave him a sharp look and, with an edge to her voice, said something, and my father answered explosively as if he wanted to flip the dining table upside down.

This memory suddenly assailing me might well have been an invention on my part. My mother and I never talked about my father. She left the house early every morning. By the time I got back from school, she would be home already. She was a beautiful woman, but her eyes would be shriveled up in the morning, and in the afternoon her cheeks sagged. I often felt the urge to study her face more intently, but she would turn away from me quickly and busy herself with housework. On the back of her shirt, the garish printed pattern on the smooth, cold polyester resembled a tarantula, twitching along with the movements of my mother's hands. But why am I writing about myself? "What was your father proud of?" I asked Tosca.

"He sometimes liked to tell people he came from the same country as Kierkegaard. That made him very proud. My mother would laugh and say: How nice to come from a small country—if I were to start counting off all the cultural luminaries born in mine, I'd never finish."

"That was a bit mean."

"My mother was highly intelligent and infinitely inquisitive. That's why she went into exile and wrote an autobiography. But I can't write at all—I always have to ask humans for help."

"Accepting help from others is also a skill. Let me write about your life!"

In the interior of my head, a thick fog had gathered. Which way should I go?

"What's the matter?" someone asked. It was neither Tosca nor my mother. "Have you fallen in love?"

Finally I pried my eyes open and saw before me the face of my husband, at first grinning but then showing signs of worry when I didn't respond. "Who are you running around with? You're always so busy! It's not like you have time for an affair. Is it someone from the circus?"

"Now you're talking garbage—let's go rehearse."

"This whole time I've been telling you my ideas for the performance, but you weren't listening."

"My thoughts wandered ... all the way back to my childhood."

"Again? Maybe we should take a walk instead."

"Not the worst idea. Let's clear our heads."

Pankov came toward us, from the direction of the front gate. We probably looked exhausted—that was the only explanation I could think of for the benevolent tone in which he addressed us. "Tosca is a consummate actress, she always shines onstage. I am confident that your number will be a success."

The moment Pankov left, my husband whispered: "He's being ironic, right? How could we possibly be successful? I'm going back to the library. Here at the circus, no ideas come to me—the feeling of being penned in is unbearable. I don't understand how I've been able to spend my entire life here."

Markus exited my field of vision, and I sat down cross-legged in front of Tosca's cage. The feeling of being penned in at the circus was hard for me to understand, since everything you could think of was here, and everything was always returning to the circus: one's childhood, the dead, friends. What good would it do me to look for anything elsewhere?

I went on sitting cross-legged there, silent and immobile in front of Tosca. She got bored, lay down on her back and played with her own hind claws. I felt warm breath at the nape of my neck, turned around, and found Honigberg standing behind me. "Are you alone?" he asked with a grin.

"Can't you see there's two of us? If I count you, that makes three."

"Has Markus taken off again? You're always all by yourself. Aren't you lonely?"

"Don't come too close. Your shoes are filthy. How'd you get them so dirty?"

"I've been to the place where no one's allowed to go." His relentless grinning gave me the creeps.

I remember that there'd been a swampy field surrounding the circus. Coming home from a secret visit, I often found a map made of dirt on my shoes. Once, a stain horrified me because it looked like a stepped-on moth. On the other shoe, I could make out its shadow. With a handful of weeds, I tried in vain to wipe my shoes free of insects. The mud was viscous and foul-smelling; perhaps it contained carnivore droppings. This thought made the mud on my shoes suddenly appear holy to me, and I no longer wanted to scrape it off. The lions—which I had never seen before except in picture books—lived right in my neighborhood here in the circus, and as proof of this I was wearing their scat!

I concealed my soiled shoes behind a bucket on the veranda. My mother, who couldn't risk missing the five-o'clock bus to work, had to get up before four a.m., and at nine p.m. she would close her eyes beneath the covers. I listened, wanting to be sure she was breathing slowly and deeply. Then I snuck out on the veranda to investigate the condition of my shoes. The gooey earth had turned the leather stony and yellow. I put them on and tried walking a little way. With every step, the stiff leather scoured my heels like sandpaper. I had no choice but to adopt a bow-legged gait to minimize the pain. In this way, I became an iguana. Cold-blooded animals like reptiles and insects had always aroused my hatred. I took off the shoes and my undergarments as well. My thighs and belly were covered with snow-white fur. The moon glanced out from sooty clouds, illuminating my bare loins.

I woke from my slumber to see Tosca—curled up, asleep, her left arm was her pillow—and, her mirror image, I lay in the same position. My skirt was obscenely rumpled, no longer even covering my thighs completely. I tugged it straight and gave my hair a quick combing with the finger-comb. At this moment my husband strode up to me imposingly, having apparently just returned from the library.

"Were you sleeping?"

"So it seems."

"Was someone with you?"

"Who?"

Beside the hem of my skirt I saw a footprint. Someone with dirty shoes must have stood there.

The following weeks brought several surprising bits of news. First, Honigberg announced that he was joining the union. There was a labor law that prohibited the union from barring entrance to anyone based on ethnic differences, so the polar bears were forced to accept Honigberg, the dodgiest Homo sapiens of all, into their union.

One day after joining, he proposed to the union leadership that the circus be incorporated. But he wanted the change to be a secret, necessitating double-entry bookkeeping, since the circus had an obligation to open its books to the government. But, under his plan, members of the circus community could develop their own free-market economy. When stock prices went up, expensive stage sets could be purchased: an attractive new stage would drive up ticket sales and profits. The next season, he insisted, was sure to be a hit; what a shame it would be to give these profits away to government officials. The officials would just squander the profits like water, shoveling caviar down their gullets in Western-currency-only restaurants and bathing in vodka. The money shouldn't just be dumped out like water, instead we should freeze it for the sake of investing sensibly in the future of our stage. Of course, the *entire* profit wouldn't be invested. Every stockholder would be able to buy a transistor radio with his dividends, or honey, or other products. The nine polar bears, who at first did not understand Honigberg's explanations, were eventually delighted with his plan and wanted to buy stocks at once. Pankov, too, accepted the proposal ... but my imagination was not powerful enough to divine the young man's actual intentions.

"What's he up to?" When we were alone, Honigberg was all my husband ever wanted to talk about these days. If I failed to look interested enough, he would dig in his heels. "Come on, tell me what you think." I felt like a mouse trapped in a corner, and tried counterattacking with a question of my own: "Why can't you get this infantile young man out of your mind? Don't you have any vitality of your own left?"

"Just as I thought." His bloodshot eyes gleamed as if I'd just confirmed his insinuations. "How do you know so much about his vitality? I've known it for a while now. You're having an affair with him."

"When could I possibly have had time for an affair? And you've been right next to me this whole time."

"But I can feel when a period of time has a hole in it, even on days we spend fully occupied. You use this hole to meet secretly with someone." Perhaps my husband was already halfway to madness by then.

I myself was dimly conscious of being in love—but not with Honigberg. That was unthinkable. I wasn't trying to hide anything from anyone; I myself didn't know whom I was in love with. When I was a child and kept going to the circus every day, I never suspected I was in love with the circus. I kept my visits to the circus a secret from my mother, but not because I wanted to conceal my infatuation. I just didn't want my mother to keep me away from the lions because of my dirty shoes. There were other things I hid from her too: for example, that I never managed to make any friends, or that my teacher had said I was very talented, especially in the natural sciences. "Why did you keep all these things a secret from your mother?" Tosca asked me.

"I don't know. A child's instincts. For a woman to find the friend with whom she'll willingly share her stories, she might have to grow to adulthood."

One day, my secret visits to the circus came to light. I'd been afraid my mother would scold me for my dirty shoes, but that didn't happen. Instead, she calmly instructed me to buy a ticket and go in through the main gate. Those who used the circus's rear entrance, she said, would wind up backstage among the artistes.

I'd never heard the word "artiste" before. The word inflamed my imagination. Any fire my mother was trying to keep me away from always inspired my burning interest.

Even after my mother had learned of my visits to the circus, I didn't want to give them up. I would take off my shoes en route and hide them in a bush. It was strangely disconcerting, and at the same time exhilarating, to cross the swampy field barefoot. It tickled a little, maybe the ghosts of the underworld were licking the soles of my feet. Amid the smell of unknown animals, I crept into the labyrinth of circus trailers, and let my nose guide me. Suddenly I saw in front of me a horse's face. The horse stared at me without blinking. His long eyelashes gave him a gentle look. The odors rising from the earth were suffocatingly sweet, my chest was tightly constricted, and I could hear my heart pounding. Was this a sexual stirring? The horse's ears flicked, and I heard footsteps.

Someone gave me a little shove from behind: a clown with a painted white face. It appeared to have been a while since his face paint was applied: The white coat had cracks in it, accentuating deep laugh lines that weren't currently laughing. The star-shaped tears, no longer crying, were smudged. It was unclear whether the clown was a woman or a man, and for this reason, I couldn't think what to say. And so I quickly made a bow by way of apology and ran off. Since then I have seen many clowns, but that first clown remains forever preserved in my memory.

The next day I visited the horse again to admire the size of his nostrils. This time the clown approached me slowly and cautiously, holding up an index finger vertically before his lips. Today the clown wore makeup only around the eyes; his lips were thin, and around his mouth I saw freshly shaved skin with a bluish tinge. He was apparently making an effort not to frighten me. I felt paralyzed with insecurity, but nonetheless waited as he approached. "Do you like horses?" he asked, standing so close that I could feel his body heat. I nodded, and he went over to a trailer and beckoned me to follow.

The scent of hay tickled the little hairs in my nose, and then it filled the barn of my lungs. "The hay has to be chopped up and fed to the horses," the clown said. He took an armful of hay, placed it on the huge chopping block and hacked away at it rhythmically with his rusty knife. He tossed the chopped hay in a bucket and we returned to the horse with this freshly cut fodder. "What do you think? Wouldn't you like to play Take Care of a Horse? If you come back at the same time tomorrow, you can chop the hay and feed the horse yourself."

And so it came to pass that every day after school I would hurry to the circus to perform my duties. Soon I was even allowed to use the curry comb, and to cart dung to the compost heap. I was motivated and unpaid.

While I was attending to the horse with my delicate child arms, the clown would practice doing headstands on the back of a chair or wiggling his hips while balancing on a ball. Now and then the thought floated into my vicinity that perhaps he was exploiting me, but even if that was true, it didn't bother me. I developed my own economic theory: all losses immediately turn into gains when you touch a horse.

Soon other people began to say hello to me. To be sure, I was an illegal worker who'd been secretly smuggled in through the back door. But I felt accepted at the circus, which certainly wasn't the case at school. It was a long time before the clown asked me: "So what's your name, anyhow?" Till then, he'd just used "Hey, you"—either civilian names meant nothing to him or he'd thought he would be responsible for me if he knew my name.

"My mother sometimes calls me Bar as a joke, since my name is Barbara."

"That's good. Bar as in Bear."

Back home, I told my mother there was a bear hidden in the name Barbara. She raised her eyebrows. "How ridiculous. Do you think I'd name you after an animal? Who's been telling you such rubbish?" I was forced to confess my daily visits to the circus. My mother was not surprised—she seemed to have suspected as much all along. She told me to always be home by sundown and gave me permission to go on playing circus employee.

When I curried the horse, my spirits rose with every stroke of the comb. The horse had a funny sort of hair that tended to remain pleasantly dry even though its body would sweat. The flesh beneath the hair was trustworthy and firm, emanating a reassuring warmth. The desire that arose in my hand while I was combing crept up my wrist to enter my body and swim in my womb like a carp. "When you were a child, the horse was much bigger than you. You gazed up at it, and now standing like that is coming back to you again," Tosca said. Her eyes and nose were three black dots in the snowy landscape. If you connected the three points, it made a triangle. Tosca's white body was perfectly camouflaged in the snow, I couldn't see it, I spoke blindly to the triangle's invisible midpoint: "Sometimes I think it doesn't get me anywhere to think back on my childhood."

"My mother believed that we have to find our way to the time before childhood," Tosca replied.

"I'd love to read your mother's autobiography."

"Unfortunately it's out of print. At the North Pole, all the books are out of print, and all the printing presses have melted, so it's no longer possible to print a new edition." Tosca rose melancholically to her feet. Her chest was thin, making her elegant neck appear even longer and her front legs even shorter than they were. Tosca was about to depart, leaving me behind. "Wait!" I shouted.

"What's wrong? Did you have a nightmare?" It was Markus, acting as if he had no idea what to do because he couldn't understand my condition. Meanwhile I knew he'd started spreading rumors about me, saying I was crazy and constantly under attack by hallucinations and nightmares. Maybe he was hoping in this way to conceal his own weak nerves and pathological jealousy. Pankov stood there too and said: "I hear you're refusing to attempt the fire act. Has your passion for the stage been extinguished?"

"Extinguished?" I replied. "I'm not the one on the point of a burn-out, it's my husband, and the fire singeing him is Jealousy. Can't you save him? I can't take his heat, that's why I keep running out into the snow. In a snowy landscape, I can recognize Tosca right away by the three black dots."

Pankov burst out laughing. "If you see three lights in the form of a triangle coming closer, it's a locomotive. Are you planning to throw yourself in front of a train? You mustn't do that. Please, get some rest."

My husband's jealousy intensified by the day, without any cause. While Tosca and I were practicing our bow, Honigberg walked into the rehearsal room, followed by my husband, who, accusing me of having made eyes at Honigberg, quickly gave my shoulder an irritated shove. Tosca growled threateningly, and Honigberg turned pale when my husband pushed me again. "Stop it!" Honigberg said, grabbing my husband's arm. He dragged him into the corner of the rehearsal room and kept him there.

"Let go of me! What are you trying to do?"

"Don't you see that the bear is getting angry? You're in serious danger."

Pankov ordered me, my husband, and Honigberg to report to his office. I was prepared for trouble, but there was none. "There are rumors that we're going to have a visit from the

Kremlin next month. I'd like to start the new season early so that by the time our important visitors arrive, everything will be running smoothly. We're not looking to present a ritual sacrifice, so let's not have Barbara get eaten by a bear in front of the Russian officials." Pankov's expression was grave, but Honigberg replied with self-confident levity: "Not to worry! We're almost done rehearsing. Barbara and Tosca have developed a true friendship. They'll go onstage together, eat cookies from a bag, pour milk into their cups from a jug, and drink. Then Barbara will place a fashionable lady's hat on Tosca's head and put a vest on her as well. The two will stand side by side before a mirror, and everyone will see what good friends they are. That's enough—the sight of true friendship will move every heart in the audience, even if there's nothing spectacular about it."

"The friendships of women are wonderful, but not an appropriate subject for a circus routine."

"Not to worry! The nine polar bears standing on the bridge behind them will provide all the masculine dynamism we need. Each of these animals weighs well over a thousand pounds, and the nine of them together come to nearly five tons. Little Barbara will swing her whip, and these white giants will obey. These creatures weigh more than twenty sumo wrestlers. Impressive, no?" Honigberg seemed to be looking down on Markus and me, as if he were Pankov's deputy, but really he was just a vagabond whose presence in the circus was merely tolerated. Markus, trying to extend his neck so as to look taller than Honigberg, hastily asked: "Wait a minute— what's happening with the strike?" Honigberg calmly replied: "The strike is over. Starting tomorrow, all the polar bears will be back at work." We looked at Pankov, he looked at the floor. Honigberg continued in a self-assured tone: "There's no longer any reason for a strike. The polar bears all bought stocks and withdrew their demands. I told them they weren't allowed to hold strikes any longer because now they were stockholders, not workers."

Markus cast a hate-filled glance at Honigberg's thin, denim-covered legs and said with visible annoyance: "So you used monkey tricks to betray their innocent animal hearts. You're a disgrace to humankind!" My husband was looking like a frill-necked lizard. I wanted to brush the bloodthirstiness from his ruffled collar, so I rested a hand on his shoulder, but he shrugged away my touch, saying churlishly: "So now you're on his side."

It seemed to me important to clarify the situation to keep things from escalating. "You're jealous because you suspect us of having an affair. That's absurd. You're really imagining things." My words took him by surprise, as if the possibility of something going on between Honigberg and me was only just now occurring to him. He started screaming, and Honigberg—who appeared equally shocked—was soon screaming too. Pankov heaved a sigh, and on his way out, he said: "Barbara, you're not well. You've got to see a doctor."

It wouldn't be the first time I'd been compelled to pay a visit to a psychiatrist. As soon as I was old enough to leave school, it was decided that instead of pursuing a university degree, I would work as a domestic. I soon suffered from hallucinations: everywhere I went, I saw the buttocks of a well-to-do man. I didn't mind shoveling horse dung, but it filled me with revulsion to imagine cleaning the toilet seat on which my wealthy employer had placed his fat, sweating butt cheeks. These buttocks followed me all through the streets, leaving me gasping for breath. I tried to hide by diving into a crowd, but the phantasm gave me no peace. I told my mother about it, and she replied that I shouldn't think so much. "Think only of things that actually exist." But what about the things that didn't exist but nonetheless showed themselves to me?

It hadn't originally been my mother's intention for me to

become a domestic servant. If I'd gone on to be a scholar, I'd have allowed myself to think about nonexistent things. My teacher had told me I should continue my studies, but I'd rejected her suggestion with defiant resolve. My mother learned of my refusal, which must have come as a shock to her. I saw her sitting at the kitchen table as if turned to stone. She'd at least managed to make tea, but drinking it was beyond her. Her hands propped up her heavy head, and her eyes lay in deep hollows in her grayish skin. In those days, it didn't go without saying that a mother would send her daughter off to college. I no longer remember what objections I had to university studies. At times I even dreamed of researching the lives of mammals and receiving an academic degree for this work. But just as I hid my favorite books about horses behind the armoire and only read them when I was alone, my dream refused to come out of its hiding place. Ernest Thompson Seton's animal stories gave me the idea of becoming not just a zoologist but an author as well.

"Why do you have regrets now for not having studied? The circus is your university." Tosca's words comforted me; perhaps, I thought, I'd made the right decision after all. But back then I was filled with despair, and the rich man's buttocks continued to haunt me. The doctor who examined me didn't take me seriously. He said dismissively that I was suffering from weak nerves and prescribed some drugs.

Either the doctor had gotten his medications mixed up, or it was my fault. In any case, when I swallowed the pills, I was immediately filled with the irresistible desire to work in the circus. I quarreled with my mother and ran out of the house, speeding as fast as I could all the way to the circus like a motorcycle burning fury as its fuel. My circus friends were sitting in a circle, drinking beer in the twilight. They let me join their circle at once, but as soon as I asked them to accept me into the circus troupe as an official member, they looked embarrassed. I was about to start crying when the oldest man got up and rested on my shoulder the fingers he'd just been using to twirl his beard. "Many customs and modes of conduct seem perfectly natural to people who were born in the circus and grew up here. But these same things can appear incomprehensible or unacceptable to the children of workers. Of course a lot of this can be learned retroactively. But there are too many things that are nowhere written down. This is why a normal citizen can't really survive in the circus. A lion can't become a tiger. It would be better for you to look for a job in the city." I burst into tears. The tightrope walker Cornelia got up and said: "I'll take her to Mr. Anders. Maybe he can find a job for her." A longstanding fan of the circus, this gentleman worked as a department head at the Telegraph Office. Cornelia set off with me trotting behind her, walking at such a clip that it was all I could do not to lose sight of her back.

A man with broad shoulders opened the door, and immediately I noticed an odor I'd never smelled before. He looked at us, and at once his eyes narrowed with pleasure. I had never before set foot in the apartment of a well-to-do, well-educated man. Intimidated, I sat on the leather-covered sofa with its hand-carved side panels. Upon a silver plate lay roast beef, bread, and fruit, just like in an Old Master painting. Cornelia kept her stiff smile on her face while she elastically juggled the first words. Every now and then she signaled to me conspiratorially with her eyes. Apparently hypnotized by Cornelia, Mr. Anders promised to give me—a girl of unknown origins—a job.

I wasn't accepted into the circus, but my paranoid delusions ceased. My mother was thrilled to learn I'd found a job in the Telegraph Office. Working for a government agency, she said— any agency at all—made me a public servant, and this, unlike circus work, meant security. But later the circus was nationalized, and all of us, even the clown and an animal trainer like me, became government employees.

•

"I promised to write down your life story. But so far I've only been talking about my own. I'm terribly sorry."

"That's all right. First you should translate your own story into written characters. Then your soul will be tidy enough to make room for a bear."

"Are you planning to come inside me?"

"Yes."

"I'm scared."

We laughed with one voice.

I became a government employee and rode around on my bicycle all day long. After the first month, you could see the muscles on my thighs and calves. I could ride faster and thus saved time and no longer felt I had to rush, so now and then I would practice bicycle acrobatics in a park or even right on the street.

Once I tried to do a headstand on the bicycle. "You need a special bicycle for that, a custom-built model," a passerby said. I wanted to engage him in conversation, but he was already gone. I began to sense on my skin the presence of spectators. When I had an audience of even a single person, it was no longer a paranoid delusion, it was a proper rehearsal. And if a rehearsal was possible, there might also—someday—be a premiere.

I trained ever more diligently. One day I was observed by a relative of my boss as I clattered down some stone steps on my bicycle and I received a stern reprimand. Worried about the bicycle, the boss exclaimed: "You aren't working in a circus, do you understand?" It had been such a long time since I'd heard the word "circus." It was true enough, just as the boss said: the Telegraph Office was not a circus. The circus was where I wanted to work.

The war broke out before I could start my new life in the circus.

"I envy the inhabitants of the North Pole. There aren't any wars there."

"There aren't any wars. But people with weapons keep arriving all the same. They shoot at us."

"Why?"

"I don't know. I've heard that humans hunt instinctually. But instincts are a mystery to me."

"I think hunting used to be important for human survival. That's no longer the case, but they can't stop. A human being, perhaps, is made up of many nonsensical movements. But they've forgotten the movements necessary for life. These humans are manipulated by what remains of their memories."

My father returned home once during the war. I saw a man walking back and forth in front of our house. I don't know what gave me the idea that it could be my father. He looked at me in such a way as to signal that I should follow him. We walked for a while until we reached the bank of our small river, where we sat down on a bench. I looked at his yellowed fingers holding a cigarette stub. "I started torturing animals as a child, just the way many adults torture their children. I killed animals—a cat, for example. I plunged my knife into its heart and was able to watch calmly as it died. It was important to me not to lose my self-control. I required ever new victims, in the end, I even killed an army horse. The military thought it was an act of antiwar resistance."

I told my mother about my encounter with this man. She was furious because she thought I'd made up the story. "It isn't possible that your father is still alive. You can't go around telling people nonsense like that."

The Telegraph Office soon closed, I lost my job, and began working in the armaments factory along with my mother. On Sundays I washed our clothes in a tub and cooked for us. I would walk into town carrying a large cloth bag to buy the week's food. The people I would see on the way had coarsely whittled faces. When two people who didn't know each other crossed paths on a desolate street, they would exchange distrustful glances. Fate might at any moment turn anyone at all into a murderer or a victim. The sight of a soldier standing at an intersection was enough to make me start shaking, even though the soldiers were ours. But what did that mean: ours? Every soldier was prepared to kill. My wish was always that he would shoot somebody else instead of me. I was forced not only to suffer hunger but to be distrustful too. When winter came, it brought not greater hunger but a hunger more intense. My eyes were constantly mistaken, and I rarely raised them from the ground. In the mirror I saw cracks in my skin. It wasn't just me—others I saw in the street had ruined skin too. Their eyes were inflamed, and they couldn't stop coughing. My mother was afraid I might accidentally tell someone about my father. "If anyone asks, say that you were separated from him as a baby and can't remember anything."

The neighbors' eyes sometimes spoke a language I couldn't understand. I often turned around while walking, as if someone had pasted an invisible label on my back. I imagined being arrested and forced to stand against a wall to be shot. "Why do you keep bringing up these fantasies? There's no reason for anyone to arrest you," my mother's voice said. My nose was strangely reprogrammed, and I smelled the dead bodies, a vague but persistent odor, and I didn't know if I was imagining it or not. It was practically a miracle I was still alive. My mother once asked me if I was a member of a resistance movement. But for this I was too apolitical, alas—I didn't know anything at all about the resistance.

After the big air raid, the city's walls and roofs collapsed to form heaps of rubble. When I could think again, I'd been evacuated to a factory building, and the woman lying next to me was my mother. When the moonlight shone gently on the windowsills, the smell of sweat from all the people packed in together intensified, lethally cloying.

I found a scorched lump of iron and thought it had to be the corpse of a bicycle. I began to collect useful items and fragments of broken objects and machines and sold them to a workshop. But even when I managed to come by a little cash in this way, it wasn't easy to exchange for decent bread. For this reason, I was glad to have the opportunity to visit relatives who had a farm outside of town to help in the fields. I still remember the turnips and cabbage, and especially the rutabagas.

The Telegraph Office was reopened. Among the new management, there were only fresh faces to be seen, and none of them wanted to offer me a job. I helped acquaintances of my mother's and was given food in return. I cleaned everything that was dirty, and tried to procure everything that was lacking. I also took part in the city's rubble-clearing operations.

"Why do I feel so lonely?" I asked Tosca.

"You aren't alone. I'm here."

"But no one except me believes I can speak with you. Sometimes I wonder if it's even true. Lots of people want to talk with me—but not about the war, they only want to talk about the circus. They always start their conversations with the same question: How did I end up joining the circus? I tell them that as a child I helped out at Circus Sarrasani, and when I was twenty-four, I was accepted at Circus Busch as a cleaning woman. No one wants to hear about what happened in between. They say: We all know about the war. It's not that I want to talk about the war, it's just that it makes me nervous to have a hole in my circus biography. A hole that big might one day become my grave."

"I'll listen to you."

"How can I be sure it's you? How do I know I'm not dreaming?"

Somewhere a dog barked. "Rich people were resurrected after the war as rich people, even though their money had burned to ash. Don't you find that strange?" This wasn't Tosca's voice, it was the voice of a vital young man. His dog was named Friedrich. Friedrich would always jump up on me when I came to the apartment and try to lick my face with his large, moist tongue. "Class society doesn't vanish in a war. On the contrary: the difference between rich and poor is increased by a war and during the postwar period. For this reason, we need a revolution as soon as possible." The young man, Karl, had chatted me up on the street. I was quickly drawn into a conversation, it felt as if I'd known him a long time, so I followed him to his apartment, which was filled with vintage furniture. His sofa and bed didn't look as if they'd been subjected to an air raid, in fact there was nothing in his apartment that appeared in urgent need of repair or replacement. The books on his shelves, unlike the furniture, were all recent. I pulled out a book with a red spine. Before I'd finished reading a paragraph I'd chosen at random, I found myself being embraced and engulfed from behind. I was all bones, and my breasts were only just starting to show signs of future roundness. His hands boldly crushed them. With all my strength I twisted my head around, he placed his hands a bit lower down, applying pressure to my abdomen while using his chin to hold my shoulder in place the way a paperclip holds a sheet of paper.

"It was like a lightning bolt from a clear sky. I didn't have time to long for love, to fall in love, or even to notice the taste of my first kiss."

"And if you had gotten pregnant, Nature would have quickly attained her goal."

"Nature, for all her greatness, is small: all that interests her is dividing tiny cells into even smaller ones. I can certainly understand that my heart is of no particular concern to Nature. Cell division and more cell division, that's all she cares about."

"Did you go to see Karl every day?"

"We immediately started fighting."

"Why?"

"I talked with his dog Friedrich too much. Karl didn't like that. Maybe that was the bone of contention."

One day I contracted a high fever, it went to my head and swept away my thoughts. I was sent to bed, my mother filled a bag with ice cubes, I heard the glassy clicking sound of the ice, and then coldness surprised my burning forehead. I heard my mother speaking with a doctor, their voices withdrew. My consciousness wanted to travel to far-off lands. I stood in a flat landscape, a snowscape, the snow blinding me. Staring into it, I saw a snow hare leaping across the snowfield, and a moment later he vanished from sight. With every step I took, the shaft of light changed its angle, negating what it had shown me just before.

A snowy wind boxed my ears but it didn't feel cold. The frozen ground was as milky as a pane of frosted glass. Through it, I saw the water and two seals swimming by, probably mother and child.

After a long journey I woke up and felt something wild, unripe, unpredictable inside me. I kicked off the wool blanket, quickly got dressed and slipped into my shoes. My mother tried to stop me—she wanted at least to know where I was going. I myself didn't know. Walking made me dizzy and I lurched but didn't fall because the wind was propping me up on both sides. Before me I saw an advertising pillar on which a poster bloomed like a bright tropical flower: Circus Busch! I studied the dates and saw that the final performance had taken place the day before. In front of the pillar stood a bicycle that wasn't locked. I sat on the metal horse, pressing the pedals with all my strength. The city fell away, a field of rapeseed received me in its yellow arms, and far off in the distance, a circus caravan was crossing the horizon.

Left, right, left, right, I pushed down on the pedals as if possessed, terrified that the rickety old bicycle would collapse beneath this pressure. I panted, spinning the wheels of my dreams, trying to catch the images flashing past in my brain. Eventually I caught up with the procession of circus wagons and from atop my rolling bicycle asked a man sitting in the last trailer where they were going.

"To Berlin!" he replied.

"Do you have performances in Berlin?"

"Yes. Berlin is the greatest city in the world. Have you ever been?" At this moment it became clear to me in a flash that I wanted to go there too. Could I manage it with this bicycle? The sky suddenly grew black.

"You'd better ride home as quick as you can. It's going to start pouring in a minute."

I looked up, and a fat raindrop fell right into my eye. "Please take me with you to Berlin!"

"Not possible. Maybe the next time we're in town. We'll pick you up."

"When?"

"Just be patient and wait for us."

I woke up and saw that I was lying in my familiar bed. My mother said I'd been asleep for two days. I still had a high fever.

"You'd better go to the doctor. Your illness is coming back. You seem off somehow." It wasn't my mother saying this to me, it was my husband.

"Huh? What do you mean by *off*?"

"You don't answer when I ask you a question, and your eyes have a strange gleam."

There was something off about my husband. That's probably why he was telling me I was off.

Was my fever dream the place where I caught up to the circus troupe on that old bicycle? One week later I happened to see a poster for Circus Busch plastered on an advertising pillar in town. Their engagement had ended just one day before I'd had the dream. I kept this discovery from my mother. You can't reproach a child for never telling her parents what occupies and troubles her heart. It's just a childish attempt to become an adult. Parents, on the other hand, would much rather lie to their children than reveal their weaknesses. If my mother had suddenly lost her nose, she would have covered her face with a handkerchief and told me she had a cold. What was great Nature thinking when she gave us these characteristics?

"You say I shouldn't have conversations with your dog. It's not an insect I'm talking to. A dog is as much a member of the class of mammals as we are. Why shouldn't I exchange words with my fellow mammal?" This was the argument I used to defy Karl's prohibition. When he started shouting, I could feel his body temperature rise: "A human being is fundamentally different from a dog. But what's a dog, really? Just a metaphor." Karl loved the word "metaphor" and used it to intimidate me. After I told him about my lifelong dream of working in a circus, he replied: "The circus is nothing more than a metaphor. Since you never read actual books, you believe that everything you see is real." Lovelessly, he threw a volume of Isaac Babel in front of me. I haven't seen Karl since then. For a long time, the book stood in a corner of my bookshelf, observing me resentfully. I didn't expect Karl to ever come back to me, but I wanted the circus to come back.

"You can wait for him as long as you like, he's never coming back." I returned to my senses. Before me stood my husband. He grinned and went on: "I locked him in the bathroom." Since I thought my husband perfectly capable of imprisoning

Honigberg, I turned my attention to the bathroom door. But it was Pankov, not Honigberg, who now emerged with a self-satisfied expression and asked: "Something wrong? What's the matter?"

"Where's Honigberg?"

"Right over there!" Pankov's finger indicated two people standing behind me immersed in conversation. The one with his back to me was unmistakably Honigberg.

I knew that my husband's nerves were worn thin and vulnerable. If one more shred of nerve ripped, he might attack Honigberg, fatally even. This thought left me no peace. As a child, I repeatedly dreamed of a dog and cat trying to kill each other and would try to the best of my abilities to prevent this mutual murder. But the desire to kill danced about wildly in the air, provoking both of them and seducing them into this struggle to the death. It was my task to end their battle as quickly as possible. I was still an infant, and already my head was filled with worries. The one thing I don't know is what my worries looked like without language.

I didn't want my child to witness my husband causing harm to a human life. Perhaps it would be me he attacked, not Honigberg. Perhaps in the end he would be his own victim. Best for my daughter to go on living with my mother.

If I'd ever given serious thought to how my husband would die, it would have been clear to me what his end would look like. But from where I stood in the middle of life, I was incapable of seeing anything in sharp focus. Otherwise I'd have been able to predict the fall of the Berlin Wall and its effect on my life. The GDR perished, and so did my husband.

When I raised my head, Pankov placed a notebook with white paper on the table and said: "This is a gift for you. I don't want you using our important documents for your manuscripts." Ever since the Soviet Union had given us the polar bears, Pan-

kov had avoided the word "gift." So it was all the more remarkable that he used this word now, giving me permission
to write. I thanked him but went on writing on gray recycled
paper.

For me, a girl who dreamed of circus life, the wait proved
worthwhile. In 1951, Circus Busch posters went up all over
town. In those days, our daily life was low on color: tabloids
with full-color photographs didn't yet exist. The bright circus
posters looked flowery against our drab backdrop. Every time
I caught a glimpse of them, the curtain rose in my mental theater. Drums and trumpets announced the prologue, the cylin-
drical light embodied a promise, and creatures from distant
planets with luminous dragon scales made their entrance.
Some could fly without wings, others spoke with animals. All
the excitement, applause, and cries of delight were too much
even for the circus tent—the air began to split it open.

Three days still remained before the first performance, then
it was only two days, then only one, now it's today, in two
hours, in an hour—now the curtain opens. A clown with an
apple nose stumbles onto the stage, tripping and turning a
somersault. The circus has developed its own natural laws: A
person who looks clumsy just walking is an athlete. A person
who can make the audience laugh is someone to take seriously. I thought that maybe there was something I too could
contribute, maybe I could fly. A woman dressed in a shimmering silver costume climbed ever higher up a rope until she
almost disappeared from sight. A muscle-bound man strode
into the middle of the stage. My eyes slid from his close-fit-
ting white costume to the black chest hair that the costume
didn't quite manage to cover. I began to feel strange as the flying trapeze performance commenced. As if hypnotized, I rose
swaying to my feet. The man behind me hissed: "I can't see. Sit
down!" With effort I forced my bottom to return to the seat.

After the trapeze act, the band playing the music switched from the tango to an oozy melody. Iron railings slid into place like a long folding screen, separating the audience from the stage. I saw a lion and at once felt dizzy again. I got up, walked down to the stage, gripped the bars of the railing and pressed my face to them. Lion eyes stared at me. Behind my back, unrest was stirring, but that did not concern me. A circus employee who was responsible for audience security that evening hurried over. But the lion was faster. He leapt toward me and lovingly pressed his cold snout against my nose.

My mother, picking me up at the police station, asked what in the world had made me get up to such a stunt. My answer was almost too simple to be understood: "Because I want to work in the circus." She stared at me, horrified, and then went the rest of the day without saying another word to me. I thought her anger would last a long time. But the next day she surprised me, saying that she had finally understood that I really wanted to work in the circus.

I owe it to my mother that I was soon accepted into the circus. "Thank you."

"What for?" My mother's hands were terrifyingly large.

"Why are your hands so big?"

"Because I'm Tosca."

At the time, a huge number of people wanted to work for the circus. Even a highly skilled acrobat had to fight for a position. My mother thought up a strategy. She asked Circus Busch to take me on as an unpaid worker responsible for cleaning and taking care of the animals. Her parting gift to me was this bit of advice: "It doesn't matter how you got in. Everyone who gets inside has the chance to rise all the way to the top."

I had to go for an official interview even though I'd already been informally accepted. Into the cigar fumes separating the boss from his future employee, I explained how as a small child I'd volunteered at the circus, performing menial tasks.

And hoping to spruce up my paltry circus résumé, I confessed that during my employment at the Telegraph Office I'd taught myself acrobatic bicycle tricks. The director of the circus asked my age, and I gave the honest answer: "Twenty-four." With the instruction "Wait here," he left the office trailer.

A man soon appeared who looked like a clown even without makeup. He showed me the stables and the barn. That was Jan. "If you want to spend the night here, you'll have to sleep in the children's trailer and look after them. Is that all right?" I nodded. In the so-called children's trailer, blankets and clothing lay scattered everywhere. Supposedly seven children lived there.

I got up at six in the morning, tended to the animals, tended to the humans, cleaned, mopped, and scrubbed. I washed clothes, brought each child to perform its task, ran errands, put the children to bed, and another day would be over. During the night I was often woken by small, crying children.

Children are born in the circus just like anywhere else. Many members of the circus community love children, but none of them are able to parent their children full-time. At the moment when I arrived, three of the seven children were going to school, but there were also times when school was impossible because of the touring schedule.

After school they had to participate in training sessions, and after that they did their homework. I would help them. Some had trouble with math, others were learning Schiller's ballads by heart and wanted me to listen patiently to their attempted recitations. Once, I asked the children in jest: "You kids are seriously diligent even though no grown-up is forcing you—do you like studying?"

"Of course! We want to show the workers' children that we're better than them."

These children used textbooks especially prepared for the children of itinerant performers. With this clever system of study, it didn't matter in which order you studied the material. The subjects were not kept separate from one another. In every workbook, you could learn reading, writing, arithmetic, geography, and history. In one of them, I found an afterword written by the editor, a circus historian who lived in Dresden. He believed that in the future, all professions would take on the highly mobile nature of traveling circuses. And then, if not before, the true value of his textbooks would be recognized.

The circus children couldn't carry around many thick books. They also didn't have time to pursue several different subjects at the same time. For them there was only a single subject, which they called "studying." It would also have seemed strange to them to separate studying from working. There were no physical education classes at the circus, but as soon as children could walk, they were introduced to acrobatics as part of everyday life. There were no music classes, but every member of the circus had to be able to play at least one instrument. Virtually all the useful skills I possess today are things I learned along with the children. The children were still children all the same. When I sprayed them with cold water, they were as happy as little bears. I washed their clothes in an old tin washtub and hung them out to dry on a clothesline I'd stretched between two trees. When the wind was rough, the wash on the line would flap self-destructively. Some of the laundry flew away on gusts of wind, never to return.

I was just hanging out the wash when the circus director happened to pass through the laundry area. "You are wise. Young people today always want to become a star right away. But I need someone to take care of the animals, run errands, and look after the children. You're not just seeing your own needs, you see the circus as a whole. You understand what we need. Bravo! You should probably be running the place." With this last sentence, he burst into unrestrained laughter. Yes, he was praising me, but in truth he was just happy to have found a worker he didn't have to pay, one who'd arrived out of the blue and volunteered. Knowing this didn't prevent me from continuing to put all I had into my labors.

When I felt like sitting down with someone for a cup of tea and a chat, I would instead go and tidy the children's rooms. If I had a craving for something sweet, I ate nothing and did the laundry. I was disciplined. The thing I'd most looked forward to was taking care of the animals. At first I was only in charge of a horse, but later on, the big cat trainer—the one all the others called "the Master"—entrusted me with his lions.

There were various sorts of dung. Horse dung looked dignified. I could have brought it to church as an offering like the sheaves of wheat placed on an altar during the harvest festival. Horse dung took on the form of an artwork when it fell to the ground—I wanted to learn to fall as skillfully as it did. The lions' poop was like the poop of housecats but monstrous in size. I practically suffocated when I inhaled its odor. I tried to breathe only through my mouth, but this made me sick to my stomach.

It wasn't easy to get by on the amount of food allocated to us. We secretly stockpiled the flesh of mice we'd caught with mousetraps in a special hut. Often I had to mix groats into a lion's food to make it go further. The lion would become impatient and aggressive when he was dissatisfied with his food. Chills ran down my spine when the Master said: "It's your fault if the lion is forced to eat you. That's not his preference."

Occasionally I had to resort to visiting a meat-processing facility to ask for the half-rotten scraps. While I was chopping hay, the question came to me: How can horses run like the wind if all they ever eat is dry grass? If hay provided sufficient nourishment, why were there animals who went to such extreme lengths to eat meat? Once, I was caught pondering this question as I worked. "What are you thinking?" It was Jan who asked.

"Why are there carnivores? To me it seems normal to be a vegetarian."

"In Nature, it's hard to find enough edible grass. Then you have to eat all day long until the meadow is bare and right away move on to the next one," Jan replied.

"Were the carnivores once vegetarians?"

"Bears, for example, used to be vegetarians, but some of them had to change their diets. Think of polar bears! There's no grass at the North Pole. You won't find nuts there, or berries. Polar bears have to withstand extreme cold, their females even give birth during hibernation and nurse their young without eating anything themselves. They have to store fat in their bodies, and this is only possible if they eat fatty meat: I think that's why they developed from vegetarians into carnivores. Seals aren't easy to catch, and they probably taste disgusting. But that doesn't matter. Every living creature has to try to find out how to maximize its chances for survival. Generally it's possible to just squeak by. I find it lamentable that we have to keep eating all the time so as not to just die on the spot. I detest 'gourmets.' They act as if food were an ornament that increases the aesthetic value of their lives. Which only works if they suppress all thought of how miserable it is that they have to eat at all."

Sometimes I had the feeling we circus folk existed outside society, that we were even independent of civilization itself. Sometimes when I couldn't manage to dispose of the animal dung during the day, I would secretly dig a hole at night on the circus grounds to make the overproduction disappear. Dead mice had to be dried in secret before they could go into storage as backup provisions for the big cats. I went hunting for medicinal herbs to help the sick children recover. There were many things we improvised instead of buying.

The postwar period passed so quickly I barely saw it. When I was running an errand in town and happened to look up, I'd be surprised by the new facades of an era that had apparently started without me. There was even a rumor that soon television sets would be available for purchase. We remained isolated from all such developments—the circus was an island.

"You had a lot of success with your donkey once. Wasn't his name Rocinante? You went to Spain with him too, right?"

Markus brought this up several times when we were freshly married. He was envious, and wanted a piece of my past to call his own. "It's true, I went to Spain, but we weren't tourists, there wasn't any time at all for sightseeing. During the day we had rehearsals, and at night were the performances."

"But surely you went to restaurants and ate paella."

"Not even that. We'd brought plenty of bread and pickles with us, and tons of Hungarian salami."

During our performances in Spain, I could feel success tingling on my skin. But I didn't know what enormous praise my modest donkey act had garnered in the Spanish press. The circus director knew, but he kept it from me. Perhaps he was afraid I'd become stuck up instead of continuing to work for him with such gratitude and industry.

I woke up in the middle of the night, the air sultry. Thirst pulled me from my bed, I crossed the laundry area and saw the trapeze artist sitting on a shabby plastic chair. Perhaps she'd come outside to cool down. When she caught sight of me, she quickly looked around and then beckoned me over to her. "The newspaper said: 'Her proud, feminine contours and an innocent, solemn face framed in blond enchanted the audience.' Do you know whom they were talking about?" I thought for a moment, then my cheeks burst into flame. "Yes, that's right," she said, "they were talking about you. A Spanish newspaper wrote about your act in great detail. That's fantastic. Your donkey act has won the heart of the country that knows the donkey best. I understand Spanish, my mother was from Cuba. Have you heard about the passionate nature of Latin Americans?" I was confused, didn't know what to make of her question. "I can teach you how to dance the tango. Then you can fly to Argentina and enjoy enormous applause thanks to your new tango number." She placed her hands on my hips, hummed a tango melody, and taught me the first steps. It wasn't just two legs I had, there were an indefinite number of them. I tripped and fell to the ground, my legs twisted, imagining myself lying helpless on the beach, a skinned rabbit with naked pink skin. A rescuer found me and stroked my head, even my hip and belly were given a cautious massage. Life returned to me. But I mustn't continue, a voice within me said. "The night air is beginning to grow cool. Shall we go in?" I was hoping to use these words to escape from my rescuer, but she replied: "At the North Pole, a tongue can be hot." On this day I learned for the first time how thick a human tongue can be.

After learning from her how to stop time with a kiss, I never again had the opportunity to enjoy a similar encounter with another member of my sex. The Latin American night was interrupted, though it would be reprised again much later on.

The director of the circus was searching in vain for a good stage idea that would satisfy the public's expectations. People wanted to see me back onstage again next season. Thinking I should take the offensive, I proposed working with the big cats and bears.

You have to be prepared to surrender your own intentions the moment you catch a whiff of danger: this is the most important thing to remember when working with beasts of prey. You have to understand that courage alone is of no use. Even when my condition and motivation were at their peak, I often had to break off a rehearsal if the leopard was in a bad mood. I had to stay relaxed, fill my empty day with other tasks, and not impatiently count the days until the premiere. It was like mountain climbing in the snow. The climber who lets his ambitions drive him is the most likely to suffer a fatal accident. Fear isn't something to be overcome, it's there to protect us from an untimely death. I never went anywhere near these animals if I sensed even the faintest trace of fear inside me. But after several days without a rehearsal, the pressure was almost unendurable. The director didn't always understand my situation. He would snarl at me: "Why aren't you working? You didn't work yesterday, and today you want to laze around again?" The Master, who always understood, had to gesture to the director to leave us in peace.

One day a couple of policemen appeared from nowhere and took the Master away. The director told us several days later that the Master had secretly been arranging his own exile. Back then, the word "exile" sounded to me like the name of a ghost. The director now had quite different worries than we did. He gazed despairingly at the little circle gathered around him, as if hoping to find an answer in one of our faces. "What can I do? The police brought me in for interrogation too. I told them there won't be a next season for us—without the animal trainer, there's no circus! Then one of them said to me ironically: 'What's the problem? Don't you have that new girl who trains the big cats? You don't need your old Master anymore.'"

"It doesn't matter if he meant it ironically or not. Let's make the most of it—don't worry, I'll manage something."

"But you don't know how to do anything yet."

"The Master trained me to be ready to go onstage all by myself next season." The director gaped at me in surprise, then this expression was replaced by a calm look that was perhaps nothing more than despair run aground.

My number began and ended successfully. Knowing the limits of my artistry, I reduced my performance to the simplest possible elements. To distract from the simplicity, I put on a striking, glittery costume and asked the lighting engineer and musicians to transform the stage into a fantastical realm. A leopard, a brown bear, a lion, and a tiger sat together in a pretend living room. One beast sat nicely on a chair, another on a bed. They were harmoniously distributed across the stage. Through the painted windowpane, you could see a projection of the full moon trembling in the nocturnal mist. The animals kept changing places, slowly and calmly. At the end, the lion gave me his paw as if to wish me good night. I knew that somewhere in the middle the tiger would roar. The audience shrank in horror, I cracked my whip, and the tiger fell silent. He never meant to threaten me. He knew he'd get a meatball as a reward for roaring loudly at this point. But the spectators thought that by using my whip I'd brought the difficult relationship between these animals back under control, and there was thunderous applause.

After the show, a journalist with flushed cheeks burst into the dressing room and said: "It was wonderful to see a delicate young woman with several dangerous beasts of prey in her power!" I was surprised and for the first time realized that in the eyes of these others I appeared delicate and young. In a newspaper the next day I read that a beautiful young woman had by force of will freely governed the movements of these beasts of prey. The expression "beasts of prey" troubled me.

Since the act had gone well, I ventured to suggest to the director that he let me work with an all-lion group. My wish was fulfilled, but unfortunately I couldn't lead this group for long. If I hadn't kept a photograph, I might not remember this peaceful island in time that I spent among the lionesses. You can keep a photograph, but not the sense of satisfaction. Who took this photo? Five lionesses and me in a room: one lay stretched out on a sofa, while another, out of personal preference or solidarity, had selected a hard wooden chair. No housecat could display so peaceful an expression as any of my lionesses. It was as if they meant to say: No drudgery for us, we wish to rest, and only after resting shall we undertake something ... provided it accords with our whims and desires.

I'll stop rhapsodizing about the lions. As long as bears exist, there's no reason to speak about the past. It may be that the lion is King of the Beasts, but the bear is President of the Animals. The age of the lion monarchy has ended. When you see ten polar bears standing in a row, you forget all the other mammals.

Just five minutes till curtain. I sat on a stool, shifting my buttocks uneasily back and forth. The clown adjusted his collar for the nth time, the director drank his clear liquid from a bottle, his free hand trembling. The music started in, the seven-hued light licked the stage with its colorful tongues. Markus stood in the wings behind the curtain on the left, grinning. He was the husband of the animal trainer the public so revered. Today he would play the role of an assistant whose name wouldn't even be mentioned. He seemed satisfied with this status. I surveyed the colleagues around me: some of them accepted the fact of their own stage fright, while others struggled to relax. I had never before consciously observed my colleagues' art. For a Homo sapiens, it was certainly quite a feat to be able to leap from one branch to the next like a squirrel, or to clamber up a rope like a monkey, but I'd never been attracted to acrobatics of this normal sort.

After dreaming up and then abandoning the most motley and outlandish stage ideas, my team decided to show the audience simple, quotidian scenes. Sitting on a chair; lying on the bed; opening a box on the dining table, removing some sweets, and then snacking on them. Pankov was capable of uttering mortifyingly official sentences with a straight face: "The function of the circus is to demonstrate the superiority of Socialism." We'd come to the conclusion that it was already

glorious enough if we—humans and bears, such different creatures—could join together to meet the challenges of day-to-day
life without slaughtering each other. That's what gave us the
idea of showing a peaceful, uneventful, ordinary day. When
Pankov dropped in to observe our rehearsals, he remarked
that our performance bored him to tears. He wanted to see
us dancing the tango on top of a large ball. He insisted, and I
thought: I can put on an ordinary acrobatics show anytime—
that's what would be boring.

Barbara and I decided on a certain finale for our act without
informing Pankov and Markus. We rehearsed in our shared
dream. I was scared because I wasn't sure if I'd only dreamed
this on my own or if Barbara had really had the same dream
too. What would I do if I realized in the middle of the number
that I was the only one who'd had the dream? This thought
made the sweet taste of the sugar turn sour on my tongue, and
I felt my back stiffen unpleasantly.

Finally it was time for our grand entrance. Barbara and I
walked onstage hand in hand. The audience clapped enthusiastically even though we hadn't yet done anything. I sat down
on the stage relatively close to the audience, and stretched
my legs out like a human child. When Markus gave the command, the nine polar bears marched onto the stage. Three of
the most athletic bears balanced on large blue balls, rolling
backward. The other six waited on the bench to the side. Barbara struck the floor with her whip. The three balancing bears
skillfully spun their balls around, displaying their white back-
sides to the audience. For some reason the entire audience
burst out laughing, and Barbara made a deep bow. I didn't

have time to find out why the audience found white polar bear bottoms so funny.

Markus brought out a sled and hitched two of the polar bears to it like sled dogs. Barbara got into the sled and took the reins. When her whip whistled, the sled glided off, circling the iron bridge. Next, all nine polar bears climbed onto the bridge, and at a new signal from the whip, they all rose to stand on two legs. At precisely this point, the band started playing a tango melody. I slowly got to my feet, took up my position in front of Barbara, and began with the first steps. My dancing, I believe, was magnificent. When the tango music came to an end, I was given a sugar cube, stood facing the audience, holding hands with Barbara, and took a bow. That was the end of the official program.

I was nervous until I saw Barbara's fingers place a sugar cube on her tongue. Finally I knew for certain that we'd been having the same dream. I took up position quite close to her, inconspicuously correcting my angle, for from this moment on every centimeter counted. I stood twice as high as Barbara, and if only for this reason, I had to make an extremely deep bow. My neck elongated from my shoulders, my tongue stretched out before me, and I took the sugar cube from Barbara's mouth. Barbara raised her arms in the air, and the audience roared.

We were able to repeat this scene many times during the following weeks, for scandalous as the kiss was, it wasn't censored. The circus adopted the name "Kiss of Death" after a newspaper used it as a headline. The tickets sold out every day, and we got invited to give guest performances in various cities in both East and West. To my astonishment we were even invited to tour the United States and Japan.

During our international tour, we were confronted with unexpected problems. In the United States, authorization for the kiss scene was refused on the grounds of hygiene and health. Jim, the booking agent who'd brought us to the New World, must have been shocked, because tickets had been sold out for weeks, and it was obvious that the Kiss of Death was the main draw. The agency responsible for hygiene and health standards claimed I had too many roundworms in my belly. When I heard this, I was so angry that I wanted to sue the agency for libel. Why should I allow some bureaucrat to determine my roundworm quotient? All animals should decide for themselves how many worms to keep in their bellies for optimal health.

Jim explained it all later. He said we shouldn't blame the hygiene authorities because pressure had been put on them by religious fundamentalists who refused to tolerate our kiss. One of the many threatening letters they received apparently said: "Sexual fantasies involving bears are a form of Teutonic barbarism." Another letter contained the remark: "The decadence of Communist culture is an affront to human dignity." I already knew by then that every country has its religious extremists whose immoderate imaginations often produce involuntary humor. But what a ridiculous exaggeration to speak of sexual fantasies. Barbara and I were just playing with a sugar cube and our tongues. Apparently it was true that for Homo sapiens, pornography had its seat in the heads of adults.

During the performance, I took great pleasure in watching the children in the audience. They stared at us open-mouthed and wide-eyed. In Japan we received a letter that said: "It must be exhausting to put on a bear costume in this heat and perform onstage. Please accept my heartfelt thanks for your wonderful performance! Our children were ecstatic." Apparently there were audience members who were incapable of believing I was really a bear. How fortunate that no one came into the dressing room and asked me to take off my bearskin.

An American newspaper published a large photograph of Barbara. We did well in West Germany too, though it disturbed me to see a few grim faces in the audience. When we returned home after touring the West, we were received with odd smiles. One colleague said: "So you didn't go into exile." Barbara put her arms around my head and said: "Do you think I could go into exile alone?" Barbara was expected to answer strange questions. Did you eat hamburgers? Sushi? Did you drink Coca-Cola? Did you see a geisha? Indifferent, Barbara replied: "The circus is an island, a floating island, and even when we're far away, we never leave our island." We never had any time and considered ourselves lucky if we got an hour off so we could buy a souvenir. Our appointment books were crammed full of rehearsals, performances, photo shoots, interviews, and travel from one place to the next.

In Japan, Barbara bought herself a bathrobe printed with cherry blossoms. I wanted to buy one too when we visited Asakusa together, but all the robes they had featured colorful prints, and I realized it made me feel panicky to abandon my white camouflage. I asked the saleswoman if she didn't have an all-white bathrobe. Surprised, she asked if I was intending to celebrate a ghost festival. In Japan, the ghosts of dead human beings dress all in white. The Japanese posters announced us as "The Bolshoi Circus of East Germany," which immediately spoiled my mood, since we certainly didn't want to figure as a secondhand copy of a Russian circus. The interpreter, Miss Kumagaya, reassured us, explaining that the Russian circus, which had enjoyed such great success in Japan in the 1960s, had remained fixed in people's memories as the "Bolshoi Circus." Emphatically she added that it was to our advantage to encourage the association. And after all, we represented a more evolved form of this circus, one suited to the 1970s, so there was nothing secondhand about it. "You were even born in Russia, weren't you?" she asked me. "No, I was born in Canada," someone answered in my place, which reminded me that I hardly had any connection to my native land anymore.

In Barbara's memory, two bears intermingled later—the older one was named Tosca, just like me, and Barbara had already kissed her in the 1960s. I too was born in Canada, but in 1986, and I came to Berlin just before the fall of the Wall. I am Old Tosca reborn and carry her memory within me. We look the same, and there is scarcely any difference in how we smell.

In the circus, none of the animals suspected the day of German Reunification was approaching. I saw something glittering in the air as if to foreshadow an unsettling spring. The soles of my feet itched unbearably. If human beings had taken seriously the wisdom of ancient peoples who entrusted bears with the task of predicting the future of the community, they would have been able to usefully diagnose the future in my itchy feet. And even if they hadn't managed to discern the concept "reunification," they'd have perhaps spotted some other words, like "abducted," "apartment share," and "adoption," that would have provided enough clues to let them approximately understand what lay in store.

During this time of upheaval, Barbara enjoyed the enthusiastic applause of enraptured crowds twice a day in a Berlin park. All the women of her generation were already retirees. Barbara, on the other hand, got up early each day, put on makeup, and transformed herself into the queen of the North Pole. The budget had been mercilessly cut, but thanks to her old connections, she had a top-notch costume. After the first performance of the day, she would fall sound asleep on an old sofa in her dressing room. After the second performance, she ate a mountain of spaghetti, then carefully washed her face and fell into bed. All that was left of our performance now was the kiss she and I shared. Back in the 1970s, the scenario had been more substantial: first the nine polar bears had danced on balls and pulled around a sled on which Barbara stood, followed by Barbara and me dancing a round of tango, with the finale of the Kiss of Death.

Now all we had left was the kiss.

When Barbara took up position in front of me, her body was taut and tense. Only her tongue was relaxed and soft when she reached it out to me with devotion. I saw her soul flickering in the depths of her dark throat. In the time since our first kiss, her human soul had passed bit by bit into my bear body. A human soul turned out to be less romantic than I'd imagined. It was made up primarily of languages—not just ordinary, comprehensible languages, but also many broken shards of language, the shadows of languages, and images that couldn't turn into words. Reunification was surely not to blame for all of this, but still I felt there was some inexplicable link between this political milestone and the fact that Markus was killed by a Kodiak bear before Barbara's eyes. Even after his death, Barbara and I continued to perform our kiss. In the first phase, she would splay her mouth wide open and stick her tongue out as far as she could. Later, all she had to do was part her lips slightly. Even through the narrowest crevice I could see the white gleam within the darkness of her mouth. I had to steal the bit of sweetness from her tongue quickly, otherwise it would melt. Barbara too seemed to enjoy the sweetness. Once I got confused because exhaustion had drawn the corners of her lips down in a grimace, and when Barbara was given a shiny new gold tooth by her dentist, my tongue was intimidated by the arrogantly glinting gold, but these minor disturbances were more a source of pleasure to me than true obstacles. I wanted to accompany Barbara in good times and in bad, and repeat our kiss millions more times, but in 1999 the Circus Union was dissolved, and Barbara—after almost fifty years of successful service in the circus world—was dismissed from her job. She took ill and was reluctant to leave her narrow bed. We heard

I was to be sold to the Berlin Zoo. I still felt young enough to adapt to these societal changes, so I bought a computer and suggested to Barbara that we keep in touch by e-mail if we really did have to live apart.

After her dismissal, Barbara lived another ten years. She was disappointed in mankind and didn't want to have to devote much thought to any human being, not even to herself. I hadn't completed the obligatory years of school but nonetheless took upon myself the task of committing Barbara's life to paper. What bear in the past had ever before succeeded in writing down the life of her human friend? It was only possible because her soul had flowed into me through our kiss.

Even during the period when I made the acquaintance of Lars in the Berlin Zoo, fell in love with him, and gave birth to Knut and his brother, I never allowed my pen to flag. I don't belong to the family of cats, who are so overprotective of their newborns. Knut's brother was born in delicate health and left us shortly after birth. I entrusted Knut's care to another animal. This wasn't an easy decision, but because of my literary work I didn't have enough time for him. Besides, he was destined for historical greatness. The brothers who founded the Roman Empire had been suckled with the breast milk of another mammal, a wolf. Knut, too, would be nursed by another mammal. My dream bore fruit, and Knut grew up to become a noteworthy environmental activist who made his mark on the global struggle for conservation. And not just that: Knut showed us that we no longer needed circus acts to draw the public's attention to us polar bears, to move human hearts, and awaken admiration and love. But all that is his story. I don't wish to write about the life of my son as if I could take credit for it. Among the mothers of Homo sapiens, there are some who treat their sons like capital. My task, on the other hand, is to narrate the magnificent life story of my friend Barbara, who otherwise would long since have vanished in Knut's shadow.

In March 2010, Barbara left our world. She was only eighty-three years old. For a bear, an unthinkably long lifetime, but she was a human being, and so I wished her an even longer life. I wanted to go on conversing with her at the North Pole of our dreams. I wanted to repeat our sugary kiss for another hundred years, another thousand.

I still hadn't adjusted to the system of time the humans had thought up, but I kept trying to calculate when the pinnacle of our happiness was reached. It had to be during the summer of 1995. We were performing the Kiss of Death twice a day. I would like to present my bear's-eye-view description of the kiss to conclude this biography.

I stand on two legs, my back slightly rounded, my shoulders relaxed. The tiny, adorable human woman standing before me smells sweet as honey. Very slowly, I move my face toward her blue eyes, she places a sugar cube on her short little tongue and holds up her mouth to me. I see the sugar gleaming in the cave of her mouth. Its color reminds me of snow, and I am filled with longing for the far-off North Pole. Then I insert my tongue efficiently but cautiously between the blood-red human lips and extract the radiant lump of sugar.

III

MEMORIES OF THE NORTH POLE

H E TURNED HIS HEAD AWAY, BUT THE NIPPLE CAME WITH it as if glued to his mouth. There was a seductively sweet odor, his brain could melt in it. While his mouth relented and opened, his nose twitched three times. Was the warm liquid running down his chin milk or saliva? He collected all his strength in his lips, swallowed, and felt the lukewarm sensation descend, landing in his stomach. His belly grew ever rounder, his shoulders lost their strength, and his four limbs hung heavy.

His ears picked out one voice amid a chorus of sounds. The voice awoke his vision. Gradually things assumed clearer forms. There were two arms with hair on them, milk flowed from one, while the other held the drinker's body in an advantageous position. Drinking, he forgot all else, and when his belly was full, sleep overcame him. Each time he woke, he was surrounded by four unfamiliar walls.

He looked up and noticed a small white piece of paper attached to the upper edge of a wall. He thought he could reach it, but it was hung too high. What is it? There were two black noses and four eyes, otherwise everything was white, snow white. There were ears too. A strange animal, or perhaps two animals, on a sheet of paper. Thinking was too much of an exertion, it cast him back into slumberous depths.

Soon he understood that he was not surrounded by walls but instead lay in a crate. All at once a floppy cloth animal sat beside him. How can you fend off the desire for sleep when you're wrapped in a wool blanket beside this soft companion, being gently squeezed?

As soon as he entered the sleepers' realm, the air around him grew sharply colder, with glittering silvery particles of light falling all around him. He watched the miniature flakes floating, they danced, liberated from gravity, yet still went on falling: falling ever farther until at last they alighted on the frozen earth and disappeared. The white, icy ground was full of cracks. With every step, the crack widened, and blue water showed through beneath the ice crust. When the dreamer placed all his weight on one foot, he saw circular waves expanding in the blue water. Surely it would feel pleasant to slide into these cold depths. But how to go on breathing if he could no longer climb back out?

He heard someone coming. The white world disappeared, and a hirsute, languid green rose up around him. This was the wool blanket that lacked all character and let itself be shaped into ever different forms. High walls made of wood were covered with a strange pattern of streamlines and circles. The prisoner already knew he couldn't climb the steep wooden wall, but nonetheless he found it impossible to keep still. He raised his right arm high and immediately fell over to the left. With his next attempt, he fell to the right, then again to the left.

High above him, someone was breathing in and out. His own breath and this other one refused to synchronize, they remained two separate entities. When one breathed in, the other breathed out. One mouth expelling breath was surrounded by a beard, and above this was a nose, and farther up, two eyes. Out of these eyes, two hairy arms grew. What existed in between couldn't yet be discerned. But gradually it became clear that all these parts belonged together and comprised a being: the source of milk. The inner wall of the crate was impatiently scratched.

"Aha, you're trying to climb over the Berlin Wall, but they've already torn it down," the strong, hairy arms said, lifting the wall-climber up toward the beard. In the middle of this bush of beard hair, two moist lips were gleaming. "You wanted to get out of your crate, and now you're out. How do you like being outside? Might I ask you to describe your first impressions, sir?" The milk-drinker was glad there was a place called "outside." Outside, he was given milk. But that wasn't the only reason he loved "outside." Even when he wasn't hungry, his hands still hankered to go out and scratched at the inside wall of his crate. His neck stretched long and high, trying to see what was out there, even if he could catch only the briefest glimpse. His life force wanted to leave this interior space.

His snout was the seat of the strength that bade him continue his efforts. His limbs were still too weak for walking. The impatient snout urged them on. His front legs kept sliding apart until his chin landed on the ground.

The man with the strong arms always excitedly called out the word "Knut!" to announce the milk. Desire for the white liquid acquired the name "Knut."

When he'd sucked in several mouthfuls of milk, the warmth began to make its way through his ribcage. The milk-lust named Knut reached his belly. He could feel his heart. Something warm fanned out from the center of his heart, arriving in the very tips of his fingers. His abdomen murmured melancholically, his anus itched, and just before he fell asleep, he was prepared to describe this entire well-warmed territory as Knut.

A new man appeared in the room. He gave the giver of milk with the strong arms the name "Matthias" and the milk-drinker the name "Knut." The new man placed a box on the table and said: "Matthias, this is the scale I've been going on about. Precise, reliable, easy to use. With equipment like this you can even weigh a flea." Knut looked at the apparatus. Perhaps it's to gnaw on or lick, he thought hopefully, but his new playmate soon proved a disappointment. It was plastic-white, smooth, and boring. On top of the box a small bathtub was mounted, but there was no water in it.

Knut was placed in this bathtub. He put his right paw on the edge of the tub and then his left paw, because he wanted to jump out. Matthias quickly pushed them back into the tub. This time Knut put not only his paws but also one of his back legs over the edge. The little bear, limber as an octopus, raised up his rear end to investigate the world tail-first. The new man patiently removed all of Knut's clutching limbs from the edge, gently pressing down on his white back. Then he quickly took his hands away, bent down, and looked at the scale from the side. After the weighing, he returned Knut to Matthias's hands and lengthened his fingers with a pencil before scratching on the surface of an open notebook. The fingers of this new man were already quite long. How long would they have to be before he was satisfied? Matthias too lengthened his fingers with a long stick made of metal when he stirred the milk. So both men belonged to a species with elongated fingers.

During the day, Knut saw no other species than these finger-lengtheners. At night he heard mice running around outside his walls. He imagined the mouse to be an animal with a tiny body and a mechanism for locomotion. Once, a mouse managed to scale the wall enclosing Knut's bed: she was almost about to cross over into Knut's private realm. She had many thin whiskers and two proudly displayed front teeth. Her little face was hairy and brown, while her paws, covered only with baby hair, displayed a glassy pink hue. Knut, who was bored to death in his isolation, snuffled with joy even though the mouse looked more ludicrous than affable. Apparently it was a mistake to snuffle so loudly. The mouse froze, then fell backward, returning to the outside, and he never again saw her little face, which, in retrospect, did have something amiable about it.

One day a young, courageous male mouse appeared. Knut wasn't alone, Matthias stood in the middle of the room. "A mouse!" he shouted, placing Knut carefully on the floor and raising his stick to attack the mouse, but he'd already slipped back into his hole in the wall. "Christian, a mouse just came out of this hole," he reported to the second man, who at that moment walked into the room. In this way Knut learned that the name of the second man was Christian.

Christian smiled, pressing his teeth together lightly and pulling his lips to both sides, and said: "It isn't just Homo sapiens taking an interest in the little polar bear, the mice are interested too." Knut understood that the species that lengthened its fingers referred to itself as "Homo sapiens."

Christian visited Knut every day and went through the medical examination checklist. First Knut was put on the scale, and his body weight was transformed into a number with a period in the middle that was recorded in a special notebook. Then Christian put his fingers into Knut's mouth and illuminated the interior with a small flashlight. Deep in Knut's throat lived an animal called "hiccup." Every time his mouth was opened too wide, this hiccup jumped out, tasting of milk, but without any trace of milk's usual sweet seductiveness. All that seduction had only produced something that tasted nasty. Christian stuck something cold in Knut's ear, used skillful fingers to pull back Knut's eyelids, open his anus, and inspect his paws and claws. "A Homo sapiens doesn't go for a daily medical checkup," Christian said with an ironic smile hovering around the corners of his lips.

"I haven't been for a checkup since I got hired at the zoo," Matthias admitted.

Everything Matthias did was easy for Knut to understand

and agreeable: he gave him pleasant-tasting milk, petted his belly, played with him. Christian, on the other hand, often did disagreeable things for obscure reasons. With Matthias, Knut was allowed to play with any object he liked, such as the spoon Matthias sometimes dropped on the floor by accident. Knut enveloped the spoon in a bear hug, and Matthias would let him wrestle for a while with his metallic playmate. Whereas Christian never let Knut touch any of his instruments. He never dropped anything, he never played; he just completed his tasks and left the room again.

But there were also similarities between Matthias and Christian. Both were tall and so thin that Knut could see the shape of their bones in their wrists. Because the arms of both men had hair on them, Knut believed for a long time that they must be hairy all over their bodies, but later he discovered that this was not the case.

Unlike Matthias, Christian didn't have a beard and always wore a white coat. But both always had on pants made of the same rough blue material that Knut's claw-nails often got caught in.

Matthias groaned. "I spilled milk on my jeans again."

"Your wife is going to scold you," Christian chuckled.

"I wash my own clothes. All my things are always covered with animal hair. You can't just put them in the washing machine with the children's clothes—that's what my wife says."

"Harsh!"

"Just kidding. She'd never say anything like that."

"True enough. I know her, remember? She's—how should I put it—not just beautiful—she's also tolerant."

Christian moved fast, but unlike a mouse he wasn't naturally quick. He was always under pressure, always having to finish all his tasks in a hurry, and tried to move more swiftly than he was able. Waiting was not his strong point. One day Knut was in a bad mood and grabbed on to the edge of the scale from the outside, refusing to let himself be weighed. Christian tugged at Knut's paws, and in a reflex Knut bit Christian's finger. Dropping Knut on the floor, Christian screamed, "He bit me!" His voice sounded higher than usual. "The crown prince is in a bad mood today," Matthias said calmly, petting Knut's head. "He won't let us have our way with him."

With a groan, Christian sat down on the chair—something he rarely did. He then chatted with Matthias about this and that, every now and then glancing over at Knut. It was Knut's first opportunity to observe Christian's face at leisure and consider what he saw. Christian's blond hair was cropped short, with hair that stood up like the bristles of the brush Matthias used to clean the floor. Christian's mouth above and below boasted gleaming white, rectangular teeth, but Knut never saw Christian eating anything. His skin was pristine and smooth, and his flesh was firm, though it was covered with a thin, attractive layer of fat. His lips burned red as fire when he spoke. The skin around his mouth displayed not a hair and no traces of a razor's passage.

Compared to Christian's freshness, Matthias's skin and hair looked dehydrated. His face seemed shadowy, as though he had poor circulation.

Eventually the epoch during which the two men were the only ones allowed to enter Knut's room came to an end. Day after day, additional new faces arrived, each accompanied by its own new sweat smell, or the scent of flowers, or the stink of cigarette smoke. Most of these new people barraged Knut and Matthias with questions and flashbulbs. Matthias was easily blinded; hence the look of suffering he displayed in all the photographs. Sometimes he raised a forearm to shield his face from this camera-wielding horde.

Answering questions was not Matthias's forte. When he tried to come up with an answer, his lips would move obligingly, but no sound came out. At such moments, Christian would step in front of the camera and rebuff the questioners with skillful words as if shielding his friend.

Christian, incidentally, was addressed as "Doctor."

Knut's body weighed more each day, and his hunger had grown along with him. "Development"—a word Christian uttered with pride—no doubt described these changes.

One day, after all the visitors and Christian too had left the room, Matthias sat down on the floor, exhausted, his head drooping and his arms around his knees, without first putting Knut back in his crate. Knut placed his paws on Matthias's knees, worriedly sniffing at his beard, lips, nostrils, and eyes. "Say, are you worried? I'm not a mother bear who's been shot, lying on the ground. Don't worry! I'm perfectly all right. No bullets, just flashbulbs—I'm not so easy to do in," Matthias said, his face filled with creases Knut was unable to interpret.

Knut grew more and more each day, while poor Matthias continued to shrink. Knut suddenly had the thought that perhaps the milk came from Matthias's body, that he was being painfully squeezed dry day after day. The more Knut drank, the smaller and more dehydrated Matthias became.

The number of visitors increased at an alarming rate, though not every journalist was granted an audience. Sometimes Matthias was nervous, seeking refuge in a corner of the room, where he would lean his shoulder against the wall, his head down. He'd have liked best to be invisible. Most of the visitors diligently jotted down Christian's words while casting expectant glances in Matthias's direction. Finally they would approach the recluse and beg him for permission to take his picture. For some reason, the media weren't satisfied with just photographing Christian. Matthias would listlessly pick up the milk bottle, cradle Knut against his chest with his other hand, and stare balefully into the camera lens. Knut would feel the trembling of these delicate human fingers, hear the oceanic sounds emanating from Matthias's entrails—and Knut's abdomen would take up the tune, rumbling in harmony.

Matthias's eyes were sensitive to light, even the gentlest flash-bulb set him blinking. Knut's eyes, on the other hand, were impervious to blinding flashes. Even when several rounds of flashbulbs were fired into them in quick succession, the soft darkness of his pupils remained unchanged.

The name of the first visitor was Journalist, and the second was called Journalist too. So it wasn't surprising when the third proved to be Journalist as well. Soon Knut understood that there were many journalists, while both Matthias and Christian were unique.

But what was behind this mysterious ritual of the photographs? One of the journalists spoke of the bear cult among the ethnic minority groups Ainu and Sami. When Knut thought of a bear cult, he imagined a ritual in which humans stood in a circle around a bear, photographing him with flash-bulbs to freeze the moment for all eternity.

"You've already been working all day long. You even spend the night with Knut. That would be too much for most people."

Matthias responded impassively to these words of praise spoken by Christian. "How can I give Knut milk every five hours if I don't spend the night here?"

"But what does your wife say? Mine starts threatening me with divorce if I so much as stay late every other day."

Knut thought Matthias was at his side day and night. But at some point the little bear realized that his two-legged companion would sometimes slip stealthily out of the room. First the evening milk was consumed, then the hour of sleep arrived, when no more Homo sapiens voices could be heard, but in their place, the voices of all the animals grew ever louder. As if emboldened by this animalistic atmosphere, Matthias removed his guitar from the black case that had waited beside his desk and took the instrument outside with him. Knut wanted to wake up and follow him, but sleep held him back. His little ursine ears remained awake while the rest of his body was in dreamland.

Knut heard the guitar strings being plucked. This reassured him: Matthias couldn't have gone very far off if he could still hear him.

When Matthias came back to the room and took Knut out of his crate, the guitar was nowhere to be seen, which was disappointing. "Even before you arrived, I couldn't go right home after work. I would play my guitar in front of the bear enclosure. At home, my family would be waiting for me, but I didn't want to go. Can you understand that? Probably not." Matthias didn't talk much when there was another human nearby, but alone with Knut, he would openly talk about himself.

One day Knut discovered the guitar case wedged between the desk and the wall, and scratched at it with his growing claws. Matthias always let Knut play with whatever he liked: spoons, buckets, brooms, dustpans. But he kept Knut away from this sacred musical instrument. No matter how zealously Knut attempted to insert his claws and fangs under the cover of the guitar case, the magic box refused to open. The small aluminum key required to open it lay in a drawer. If Knut had been given a chance to touch the guitar, he would surely have played the most enchanting music with his teeth. Even Matthias with his pathetically thin fingernails managed to make the notes ring out. How stunning the instrument would sound if Knut were to play it with his magnificent claws!

Knut couldn't remember when music had begun for him. By the time he realized that he could hear, he was already living amid an endless series of notes that went on without pause. This music, which had already begun before his birth, would not cease when he was dead. The guitar music was only part of the zoo's complex of sounds. At some point Knut came to recognize several sequences of notes that were repeated daily: the clatter with which Matthias removed a pot from the kitchen cupboard was followed by the sound of two rubber surfaces being pulled apart (the refrigerator door opening), and after this an ascending melody could be heard: the milk being poured into the pot. As the meal was prepared, ever more musicians joined in: powder was shaken into a bowl, a spoon stirred it, striking against the interior of the metal bowl with a clacking sound, and to conclude, the spoon struck three decisive beats against the edge of the bowl. Thus ended the little symphony entitled Baby Food for the Little Bear. Not tears but saliva bore witness to the audience's enthusiasm. He could remember a certain sequence of sounds if it was repeated often enough. There was a beginning and an end. Knut could distinguish Matthias's footsteps from those of everyone else. Whenever Matthias left the room, the bear metamorphosed into a listening ear. He couldn't settle down until Matthias returned.

Matthias began to spend the night out more and more often. A deplorable habit. In the evening, he would give Knut his last portion of milk, push him into a corner of the crate with his stuffed animal, cover him with a wool blanket, and then disappear, taking his guitar and leather shoulder bag with him. Only at dawn would he return.

During the Matthias-less nights, another man would be on milk duty. Knut was no longer a baby, the milk didn't have to come from his mother Matthias. This other man had fleshy cheeks and unusually warm hands. Knut liked the fact that this man smelled faintly of butter. Knut could eat his fill without Matthias; he could even pass a pleasant evening without him. But there was always a hint of fear. Really it ought to have been reassuring for Knut to have not just a single man but hundreds of them able to provide him with milk, but something in Knut was fixated on Matthias still. Whenever he heard Matthias coming, he would scratch the inside of his crate as if possessed.

"Hey, cut it out! What are you doing? You've ripped the photograph of your parents. I went to a lot of trouble to get you this picture of Tosca and Lars. It was hanging here even before you were able to see. Don't you understand? These are your parents!"

The photograph hung in shreds. Matthias had to throw it in the wastepaper basket. Knut was horrified, because he had never looked at the photograph properly. Too late. How could he know that this scrap of paper represented his parents? Christian noticed that Knut seemed more agitated than usual and said to Matthias: "Maybe Knut feels lonely because he misses the photograph. Why don't you have someone take a picture of you holding him in your arms, giving him milk from the bottle? I think foster parents are more important than biological parents, anyhow. I'm sure the journalists have already taken a picture of you holding Knut to your breast like the Madonna with the Christ child."

"Don't make fun of me. For the first time in months, I can permit myself to go home at night—my family is satisfied with me again," Matthias said, stroking Knut's head. The word "family" had an unsettling effect on the little bear, as if it would later bring him misfortune.

Every morning Knut heard the twittering of the birds who rejoiced as darkness withdrew and the sun arrived to start its shift. These winged beasts were harried, fearful of not finding any breakfast. Sometimes the weaker among them were attacked by stronger birds and fled shrieking across the sky. Knut couldn't see them, but their sounds were vivid enough that he could imagine their routine dramas.

Now and then, particularly cheeky birds came and looked right into Knut's room. All of them were referred to as birds, even though the only thing they had in common was wings.

The sparrow, a brown mixture of modesty and agitation, the blackbird with her unassuming humor, the magpie's painted mask, and the pigeon, who lost no opportunity to repeat her favorite motto: "Really? How interesting. I had no idea!" Knut heard countless avian voices and thought the world outside must be teeming with birds. Why didn't Knut, Matthias, and the mouse have wings? If there had been wings on Knut's back, he'd have flown straight to the window to look outside.

Knut felt liberated whenever Matthias plucked him from his crate. But he was no longer satisfied with the minor freedoms he experienced, for more and more he sensed the existence of "outside." He wanted to leave his room. "You're getting cheekier by the day," Matthias said, but that wasn't true. It was just that Knut couldn't keep his limbs still when the outside world was tugging at them. He scratched at the door as if he'd lost his mind—Matthias didn't know what to do, so he scolded. Knut tried to stop speculating about the world outside. But that wasn't really possible, without actually making its acquaintance and being disappointed by it.

One method that allowed his soul access to the outside did satisfy him: listening. The heard world was so commodious, so rich in colors, that the seen world was no match for it. This was perhaps the power of music of which the Homo sapiens sometimes proudly spoke. Christian revealed that at home he played the piano. A hobby, he called it. "But when I play for too long, my family puts in earplugs and hides in the farthest corners of the house. What about your family?" Christian addressed this question to his colleague with the guitar.

"I've never really felt like playing the guitar at home. I don't really think my family would mind, but I prefer to play alone. It's not so much about the music as a way of enjoying the solitude."

Knut almost choked when he heard the word "family."

Knut loved birdsong and guitar music, but there was one

sort of music he found intolerable: the church bells on Sunday. Already at the first stroke he would cover his head with his arms to protect himself. Holding his breath, he would wait for the last of the ringing to subside. "Are you a heathen?" Christian asked, and laughed with a sound like a coin striking a stone floor. Then with a more serious face, "Oh, of course—bears!" he added: "They were once worshipped by the Teutons, along with wolves, and to establish itself, the church was forced to combat them. Church bells still ring today to drive out the inner bears from our hearts."

"Is that true?" Matthias asked in a rather skeptical voice.

"I've read some articles on the subject," Christian replied offhandedly. His attention had already wandered off elsewhere and he quickly packed up his things to go home.

Matthias and Christian showed up for work on Sundays too, though the obligatory medical examination Christian performed on Knut always went much faster than usual. Matthias, too, would try to leave around lunchtime. After this, the new man who smelled faintly of butter was in charge. "Maurice, I'm leaving everything in your hands and going home. You know about giving Knut his milk in the late afternoon and then putting him to bed. After that you can go home or wherever else your heart desires, but you must return by 2:00 a.m. at the latest to be on time for the next feeding." Matthias spoke in an agreeably businesslike tone, while the new man, Maurice, gazed at him dreamily, almost as if infatuated. Apparently he found Matthias's face pleasing. But Maurice must not have listened carefully enough, for he never left the room, not even between the early-evening milk hour and the next feeding at two in the morning. Any time Knut woke up for a moment, he found Maurice in the room. Often he sat curled in a corner of the room reading a book. When Knut didn't want to go back to sleep, Maurice would lift him out of the crate to play-wrestle. Slowly, gently Maurice forced Knut to the ground and then petted his belly and ears so thoroughly that his entire body grew warm.

"Now we're tired. Enough sports. I'll read you something. What do you want to hear?" Maurice offered Knut the choice of Oscar Wilde, Jean Genet, and Yukio Mishima. Unfortunately Knut couldn't pronounce the names of any of these authors, but it didn't matter, for no matter which of the books Maurice read from, it always turned into a pleasant lullaby that tugged Knut back into slumber.

Maurice came ever more frequently, even on a non-Sunday he might show up in Matthias's place and stay until well past two in the morning. After even Maurice had gone home, and the room was free of Homo sapiens, Knut would suddenly hear animalistic, celebratory noises from outside, as if all the creatures had been waiting for just this moment.

Maurice came regularly, but sometimes it happened that instead of him an unfamiliar man would show up to look after Knut. This man smelled similar to Maurice. Knut was never able to find out his name.

When Knut listened closely to all the sounds of the night, he would feel sharp but beguiling stimuli in his body. Most of the night voices inspired not fear in him but a sort of respect. In each voice, he heard something like a tautly strung bow: every animal must constantly attend to his own life with the utmost care, making full use of all his abilities and intelligence, otherwise his chances for survival would be nil.

Once, Knut had the pleasure of hearing a series of lectures on the subject of darkness by Dr. Owl. Dr. Owl's rhetorical style was too abstract, too dispassionate, but Knut was nonetheless impressed by the wisdom of those creatures who have mastered the art of living in darkness. The nocturnal laments of a monkey who was being bullied by his fellow simians taught Knut the cruelty of animals who live in packs. Sometimes

Knut would hear the leader of the mice endlessly gossiping. What she had to say might have been summarized in a single sentence that went something like this: "When your attention flags, you will be caught and eaten." Was there an animal who could devour Knut? Knut listened attentively as two aroused tomcats fought over a female. Both of them wanted to have sex with her. Why were they fighting over this one female cat? Knut pondered whether it made any difference with whom one had sex. He didn't understand the animal world. The prickly monologue of the hedgehogs made an unapproachable impression, but they weren't trying to injure him, they just wanted to communicate their worldview. Knut always listened, regardless of what there was to hear. The subtle differences between the individual voices and the combination of these differences gave each night its own unique color, and to Knut this appeared magical.

Soon Knut could differentiate between the melodies that poured from the guitar in the evening. One was a composition that imitated a buzzing bee—as the little bear listened, his back itched. There was another piece of music in which Knut heard ice floes knocking against each other, followed by watery sounds like dripping and spraying. Matthias revealed to Christian that the itchy bee piece was called "El Abejorro" (bumblebee) and was composed by Emilio Pujol, while the ice floe music, "Miller's Dance," was by Manuel de Falla. Knut had no idea what sort of dance the Miller family liked best, but listening to the piece made him want to shake his hips.

Knut enjoyed these evening concerts, but he didn't like them to go on for too long, otherwise he got bored and just wanted Matthias to come back. This wasn't just out of a childish desire to have a playmate—Matthias's absence pierced him painfully.

The pain made it possible for him to remember the sequence of melodies. Matthias would always end by playing one particular sad tune. Then he would come back with a satisfied face, put his guitar away, pick up Knut and press the bear's cheek against his own.

"That sounded pretty sad—I mean, the music you just played. What was it?" Christian asked this question when he unexpectedly turned up one evening. Matthias didn't answer, he just grinned a little, like someone who has his reasons. The sadness in the music restored Matthias's joie de vivre. The melody made Knut euphoric too, because it signaled Matthias's imminent return.

Absence—an unendurable span of time—became ever more familiar to him. He pressed his body against the worn stuffed animal, because there was no one else anywhere near him. It was annoying that the cloth animal had only cotton in its head. It never reacted, no matter how hard Knut shoved it into the corner. Matthias would immediately shove him back, or else pretend he was about to toss the little bear up in the air. Even Christian, who was never really up for a game, would at least show some reaction: When Knut squeezed his hand, he would squeeze back. When Knut bit his hand, he would yell and screw up his lips and eyes. This drowsy stuffed animal, on the other hand, never showed any sort of reaction at all—it could bore you to tears. For Knut, boredom meant helplessness, tristesse, abandonment. You there, tedium personified, you just sit there with your boneless body and don't answer, no matter what I ask. Is there nothing in the world that interests you? Knut never received an answer. You really are good for nothing, you stuffed animal you!

When would Matthias show his face again? How unendurable Knut found this question, or maybe it wasn't the question, it was just the time he spent waiting, he thought. Once time began to exist, it was impossible for it to end on its own. It was intolerable how slowly the window recaptured the brightness it had lost at sundown. When with time his patience was at an end, Knut would finally hear the footsteps.

He heard the door of the room being opened. Matthias bent over the crate, picked Knut up with his hands, rubbed his human nose against the bear snout, and said, "Good morning, Knut!" At that moment, the thing Knut had been perceiving as "time" melted away. Because starting with this moment, he no longer had any time to think about time. He had to sniff everything in the room, ingest foodstuffs, busy himself with various games. Time didn't begin to exist again until Matthias left.

Time could not be compared with any sort of food: nibble at it as greedily as you liked, there was never any less of it. Knut felt powerless in the face of time. Time was a huge ice block made of loneliness. Knut gnawed and scratched at it, but without effect. When Christian complained of having no time, as he often did, Knut envied him.

Matthias loved to say hello to Knut "nose to nose," while Knut disliked it. Every time, he found himself worrying about Matthias, whose human nose lacked moisture. If an animal had a nose as dry as Matthias's it would probably be a sign of illness. Something had to be done for Matthias to keep him from dying young. Knut stuck his snout into Matthias's beard, which, smelling of cooked eggs and ham, made him feel calm again. From his mouth came the scent of that same toothpaste that had to be squeezed from its tube before every brushing. Knut didn't like this smell, he preferred the natural paste that came from Matthias's eyes and didn't hesitate to lick it up at every opportunity. Matthias would shout, "Cut it out!" and pull his face away, but there would be a happy note in his voice. His hair smelled of soap and cigarette smoke.

For a while, Matthias made his face available as an expedition territory, and squinted to observe the young explorer. "Do you know what never fails to surprise me? When I was first hired as a bear keeper, I began to read books about North Pole expeditions. I wanted to know more about bears. One explorer wrote that he once looked a polar bear in the eye and almost fainted. He couldn't forget this moment of terror—not because of any concrete danger, but because of the emptiness he found in the bear's eyes. They didn't reflect anything at all. A human who thinks he can discern malice in a wolf's eyes and devotion in the eyes of dogs discovers nothing at all in polar bear eyes, and this frightens him to death. You can't find yourself in the mirror. As if the polar bear had declared that human beings don't exist. Strangely, I felt the desire to experience this shocking gaze myself. But your eyes aren't empty mirrors—you reflect human beings. I hope this doesn't make you mortally unhappy."

Matthias drew his eyebrows together and looked penetratingly into the depths of polar bear eyes. But Knut wanted to be a wrestler, not a mirror, and attacked this boring man who was trying to be a philosopher for a little while.

One day after the obligatory examination, Christian set Knut down on the floor and opened his right hand in front of the bear snout. Full of delight, Knut pounced on the hand, was rebuffed by it, but refused to be intimidated. After a bit of back-and-forth shoving, Christian set Knut back at the starting point and held his open right hand before him like a wall. Knut stared at it and pounced at precisely the moment when his inner voice said: *Now!*

"Just as I thought!"

"What do you mean?" Matthias asked, bewildered.

Christian answered with paternal pride: "Knut goes to the right one instant before I think I'll move my hand to the right. In other words, Knut can read my thoughts faster than I can perceive them myself."

"That's nonsense!"

"No it's not. Try it yourself."

"Maybe later."

"What a fantastic discovery! I read something about it in a

natural sciences journal and wanted to try it out myself. Knut should become the captain of a soccer team, because he can read his opponent's movements even before the opponent is conscious of his own intentions. His team will win every game."

"Not so fast! Knut doesn't like soccer. You can't make him your fantasy soccer hero."

"How do you know he doesn't like soccer?"

"When there's boxing or wrestling on TV, he watches attentively until it's over, but not when they're playing soccer."

"And what about soap operas, your favorite programs?"

"Knut likes those shows."

"Only because of your influence—everyone knows you're Knut's mother."

"Why am I the mother and not a father?"

"Yes, that's just what you are: his male mother. You're a motherly man."

Matthias occasionally sat in front of the mouse-gray television set he'd brought in one day. Knut kept him company when he saw no prospect of more interesting games. Soccer bored him because all he could see on the screen were black dots moving around like ants. He loved wrestling matches, and also dramas with a lot of close-ups of women's faces. Although empathy meant nothing to him, sad faces were interesting to look at. Recently there was a scene in which a man said to a woman that he couldn't come to see her anymore. He slammed the door and went out into the street, where a large number of cars were parked. The woman had long hair. She wept in a kitchen in which delicious bananas were lying in a shallow bowl. The man had supposedly betrayed the woman, he had another wife and biological children in another city. Matthias forgot to blink as he stared at the screen. Suddenly Knut felt like wailing. What would he do if Matthias one day said that he could no longer come to see him? What about his wife and biological children outside the zoo?

The milk was increasingly being supplemented with solid food, and it took Matthias ever longer to prepare Knut's meals. "I don't have time right now. Can you watch TV on your own and wait for me?" Matthias said to Knut, but it wasn't possible to watch TV alone. Knut could feel the boxer's fighting spirit or the sadness of the abandoned woman only through Matthias's body. Without Matthias, the television set was just a dead box filled with tiny flickering particles of light. The box needed a human to animate it—and even then it would be far preferable if Matthias himself were to join Knut in a wrestling match. Any living creature, even the scrawniest little mouse or a nameless squirrel, would interest Knut more than the tube.

Every day now, Knut grew in both height and breadth. When he steadied himself against the wall and rose up on his hind legs, he could sometimes glimpse squirrels climbing the walnut tree outside the window. Birds and squirrels had almost weightless bodies and could effortlessly move in a vertical direction. Why was only Knut so plump and clumsy? He'd have loved to climb up the wall to see what everyone referred to as "outside."

While Matthias was preparing the complicated bear meals, Knut would be seized by the desire to climb up the legs of the cook, preferably so far up that he could sniff the cook's beard. But those human legs were so tall, and the beard was as high up as a squirrel in a tree. When the cooking time got to be too long, the waiting emptied out first Knut's stomach, then his chest, and finally his skull. "It won't be much longer now. You'll have to be patient. I still want to add many more healthy ingredients." Matthias pounded sesame seeds, squashed fresh oranges, boiled groats, mixed all of this with the contents of a can, added some walnut oil and stirred carefully.

Matthias once dropped the can, on which a cat was painted. Using his tongue as a rag, Knut wiped the floor clean in a flash. Ever since, he was of the opinion that Matthias should just serve him the contents of the can without mixing in so many other things. He couldn't understand why it was necessary to grind, squeeze, chop, and stir all that health.

Knut knew that the inhabitants of the North Pole required fat above all else. Christian had explained this to the journalists several times. Knut lived in Berlin, so he didn't need a layer of fat under his skin. There was a rumor going around that winter had arrived, but the heat wave refused to leave the city, and Knut couldn't imagine it.

It wasn't just about the fat: the fresh blood of a sea lion was apparently rich in vitamins. That's what Christian said when he was asked to explain the plan for Knut's nutrition. "The ideal thing would be sea lion meat, but of course that's out of the question. We give Knut beef, and add vegetables, fruit, nuts, and grain." A young journalist with glasses persevered: "There's a rumor that Knut is being fed a luxury brand of cat food that costs one hundred dollars per can. Supposedly this brand is popular among millionaires in the States. Is that true?" Christian laughed coldly and shot back: "How interesting! Do you have relatives in the U.S. who are millionaires? I'm hearing this rumor for the first time. It's very—shall we say—creative, as is often the case with rumors. In Brandenburg there's no doubt a rumor that Knut's favorite food is Spreewald pickles."

Matthias and Christian received an anonymous package in the mail. Inside the carefully packed box, they found two aprons, both of them printed with bears. Knut had to admit that they really were bears in the broadest sense, though to be sure bears of a peculiar sort. Their bodies were black except for their collars, which someone had forgotten to dye black. As soon as the two men tied these matching aprons around their waists, they began to be synchronized in their hip movements. On this day, it seemed, they took particular pleasure in preparing Knut's supper together. They ground, grated, and stirred the ingredients as a duo. Knut covered his head with his short, fluffy arms, sighed, and waited for the food to finally be ready to serve.

Knut wished he could stuff himself on a bratwurst like Matthias sometimes brought in from outside when hunger caught him unprepared. Knut would covetously beg for a bite, but the stingy Homo sapiens would resolutely reply: "No, sausage is only for the proletariat. You can't have any, crown prince." But once, Knut latched onto the proletarian trouser legs and climbed onto the lap using his strength and claws. Matthias stretched out his hand in all directions to keep the sausage away from the crown-princely nose, but eventually he gave up and surrendered the entire sausage to His Majesty the Crown Prince. Knut devoured it in just a few bites.

Christian read off Knut's weight from the scale and said, raising his voice a little: "The time for your stage debut will soon be here." Somber shadows gathered in Matthias's face. Christian went on encouragingly: "When the television shows how happy and sweet Knut looks running around outside, the viewers will start to think seriously about climate change. The ice floes at the North Pole can't keep melting like this, otherwise in the next fifty years the world's polar bear population will decrease by two-thirds."

Christian was confused because Matthias showed no reaction to his speech, so he turned instead to Knut and said: "On the day of your debut, you must sit on the wool blanket. I'll pull it behind me like a sled as I step proudly onto the stage. Can you wave regally with one hand like the Danish king?" Christian took Knut's right paw hand and held it up. Knut gave Christian's hand a gentle warning bite, but that only made him laugh. "Knut, you already have on elegant white gloves, but your manners are unseemly for a member of the royal house. For example, you aren't allowed to bite the hand of an emissary."

Knut didn't know whether a "debut" was a new sort of food or a new toy. But he knew at once when the day arrived that this was the day of the debut Christian had spoken of. Already the morning was filled with commotion and gaiety. The humans stank of phoniness and worries. It was a hybrid atmosphere of a sort Knut had never before encountered.

To be sure, Matthias appeared at his usual time, dressed as always, but his breathing was irregular. Christian wore a white suit and had a beautician with him whose name was "Rosa." Rosa looked at Knut and screeched in a sweet, shopworn voice: "Look how tiny! Like a stuffed animal!" Christian, annoyed, immediately set her straight: "Knut isn't tiny anymore. When he was born, he weighed only 800 grams. He spent forty-four days in an incubator. Now he's nice and big. Don't let me hear you calling him small!"

"Oh, pardon me." Rosa changed her tune at once: "What a big, strong bear!" She started to use moistened cotton to wipe the saliva from Knut's face and the mucus from around his eyes. At first he couldn't forget the insulting comparison to a stuffed animal, but his antipathy disappeared when he noticed the pleasant fragrance of Rosa's rear end. Unfortunately, she'd smeared some chemical with a strange, sour odor under her arms. Knut withdrew his snout, sneezed, and hid behind Matthias. Christian kept his eyes on Knut the entire time, now and then giving him an affectionate smile.

Rosa brought her face close to Knut's and tried to encourage him. "What Germany is really looking for is a star," she whispered. Knut remembered a TV show in which the people split into two groups: the first group was responsible for singing, the second for judging. A judgment might be, for example, that one person needed to stop holding back, whereas another was entirely lacking in talent. Knut had watched the show with Matthias, happy not to be a candidate himself. His debut today, he hoped, would have nothing to do with this show. The thought made him nervous.

Thanks to Rosa's presence, Christian's smell today was rather pleasant, whereas Knut found the tang of Matthias's fear sweat distressing. It occurred to Knut that Christian might like to mate with Rosa. But yesterday he'd said that slender women just looked scrawny and unerotic to him now that he was spending so much time with polar bears. Rosa was skinny—her wrist might break if a blackbird pecked at it. Was Christian really satisfied with this skin-and-bones woman?

"I hear your office is right next to the flamingos." With this pink sentence, Rosa's sweetened voice began a conversation with Christian. His own voice displayed naked delight as he replied: "I see you're well informed! Yes, I'm the flamingos' neighbor. Maybe that's why I stand on one leg when I'm working. Would you like to come visit me sometime?"

Knut envied Christian his tongue, so lithe and skillful in its movements. For Knut, the tongue was still a foreign instrument. Once, he tried to drink water from a deep bowl and got a cramp in his tongue and almost suffocated. Christian immediately flipped his small bear body upside down and gently pounded his back—and his breath returned. It was possible to be killed by one's own tongue.

Rosa was like a sparrow, unable to go even a minute without opening her beak. "Yang Yang was sick, and now she's dead. Could this have something to do with the fact that you now have eyes only for Knut and neglected her?" Rosa's voice was gooey.

"No." Christian's nostrils flared: "It's impossible to imagine Yang Yang suffering from lovesickness, much less dying of it. And if I may speak of my own inclinations, rest assured that I will only fall in love with a Homo sapiens, never with a she-bear." Christian delivered this statement with mock pride and a charming wink. What was the point of this exchange? And who was Yang Yang?

Matthias picked up Knut and asked in a whisper: "Have you practiced your songs? How's your dance number coming? The time for your debut has arrived." This gave Knut a shock. Songs? Dance? He hadn't prepared a thing. How stupid he was! Every time he'd heard "Miller's Dance," his hips had wanted to start dancing, but he always went right to bed rather than putting his predilections to use. When he heard all the lively twittering from outside, he always wished he could sing just like these winged creatures. But he never tried, fearing the birds' derision. When he kept silent, he felt safer and more valuable. Why should he try to wrench his voice into daredevil heights only to make a fool of himself? He was defiant, arrogant, lazy—and all because of fear. He felt ashamed. The day of his debut, he now realized, had arrived without his having learned to do anything but greedily devour his food and sleep like a log. Now he would have to go onstage utterly unprepared. "You can't do anything! This is giving me a headache. When I was your age ..." This was a sermon someone had addressed to Knut in a dream. When was that? The words came, but he couldn't listen—he was beside himself at the sight of the gigantic Snow Queen standing before him. She was ancient—so old that her age transcended years. Her body was ten times as tall as Matthias. Behind her stretched endless snowfields. Her snowy coat blinded him, he couldn't follow her sermon. When the old queen was about to leave, Knut recovered his faculties and said in a panic: "What's your name? I mean, what kind of animal are you?"

His questions horrified the Snow Queen: "You really don't know anything at all. No knowledge, no ability, no art. You can't even ride a bicycle. All you have to recommend you is your cuteness. Why are you always sitting in front of the boob tube?" This flood of words poured out of her, apparently against her will, since she'd been on the point of leaving. Knut was shocked to hear such critical remarks—Matthias and Christian had never reproached him for anything.

"Why should I ride a bicycle? What art do you mean?"

The old queen answered calmly: "By 'art,' I meant something that enlivens your audience."

"But people will be happy just looking at me. I don't have to put on a show for them."

"You are truly hopeless. I can't believe you're my progeny. Maybe you're popular at the moment, given that you're a healthy young tyke who happens to be cute. If I were you, I'd hide myself away in a cave—not to hibernate but out of shame. You have famous ancestors, you're waited on hand and foot, you live without cares—sure, if you were a human, they'd be grooming you to run a company or even lead a country. But in the polar bear world, we have other values."

Remembering this dream, Knut became even more nervous. He could no longer get around the fact that this debut marked his first appearance as an artist, and he was artless. He was learning what remorse feels like. Why had Matthias never taught him to dance or sing? Knut had a suspicion that the guitarist had practiced on his own so as to win all the applause for himself today, and there he'd be, the little bear standing beside the celebrated guitarist, artlessly sucking his thumb. No, Matthias couldn't possibly be so underhanded, but why hadn't he ever taught Knut to do anything?

Rosa, the beautician, now fixed her eyes on Matthias, who sat there with his head down, clearly wanting nothing to do with her. Rosa planted herself in front of him and asked: "How about you? Would you like some makeup? In the TV studio all the men have themselves made up too. At least some powder. But today the filming will take place outdoors. So it's up to you whether you'd like to be filmed with or without makeup." Rosa held up one of her small, cream-colored containers, but

Matthias looked in another direction and did not answer. "And you?" Rosa asked Christian in a seductive voice that was clearly out of place. He held out his cheek to her and said: "Please do powder me up. And Knut should have some powder too. The spectators of course expect a polar bear to be as white as snow, and as you see, Knut is unfortunately gray with dust."

Rosa applied powder to Christian's smooth skin and chattered away, repeating everything she'd heard: "They're saying there'll be more reporters than at a political summit." Threatened by the pointy sound of the word "summit," Knut hid behind the big cupboard, pressing his body against the wall. Christian got up and with his long arms extracted Knut, saying, "And then the star became a dust rag," and patted him, releasing a cloud of dust.

Several journalists had already found their way into the room and were snapping photographs before the main event. "We had an agreement that this room would be off-limits to the press," Matthias said indignantly, covering his face against the flashbulb attack. Knut had no fear of cameras, he gazed calmly at the lens a photographer was pointing at him. The photographer froze when he saw the two ripe, juicy blackberry eyes staring back at him. After a while the photographer recovered and asked: "Does Knut realize what a star he is?"

This question seemed to fray Christian's nerves all over again. "That's out of the question!"

Another photographer contradicted him, pursing his lips: "But just look how self-confidently he poses for the camera!"

"You're just projecting your own ideas onto Knut and seeing things. He isn't posing. Polar bears are generally uninterested in human beings."

"But Knut is interested in Matthias."

"Matthias isn't just any human, he's Knut's mother."

"Does Knut even care who his mother is? Whoever happens to be holding his milk bottle is no doubt important to him."

"Not at all!" Christian told the journalist the story of a far-sighted bear keeper named Susanna.

Susanna worked at a zoo in southern Germany, where she'd been given a newborn polar bear to look after and had successfully raised him. Jan (this was the bear's name) grew quickly. Soon after his body weight passed the 110-pound mark, he injured Susanna while they were playing. He hadn't meant any harm, he was still a child and in the excitement of the game forgot how thin human skin is. The experienced animal keeper was undaunted by the incident, but the zoo and the insurance company refused to allow her to touch Jan again.

Susanna couldn't get over the pain of this separation. She quit her job and married a man who had courted her indefatigably and unrequitedly since they were in school. Four years later she gave birth to a daughter and one day visited the zoo pushing a baby carriage. From relatively far away she recognized Jan. It wasn't the bear's body—which had grown enormously—but the expression on his face that Susanna recognized at once. She stopped short, nailed to the spot as memories of the baby bear assailed her: the weight of Jan's body wobbling in her arms in search of its center of gravity was there again. She felt the unexpected strength of his jaws as he bit firmly into the nipple of the milk bottle. She remembered the warmth of his body, and the ever-changing expression of his face between his gleaming eyes and the sucking mouth.

At just that moment a wind picked up the scent of her body and carried it over to Jan. He snapped to attention, sniffing at the air and climbing the slope of his enclosure with rapid steps to the topmost point of the rocky cliff. He extended his organ of smell as far as he could, longingly inhaling the wind. Since bears are nearsighted, he probably couldn't recognize Susanna's figure, but he was reunited with her scent. Christian's story came to an end, and Rosa wiped the tears from her eyes.

In the corridor, human sounds were percolating. Rosa

quickly took her leave, and in her place stood a man in a suit. Knut had seen him once before and remembered that this man was called "Director." And behind him was another man who had something bearlike about him. The director shook Christian's and Matthias's hands, glanced at his own wrist-watch, and said: "Knut will be made available to the public between ten-thirty and two o'clock, then there'll be a press conference. Correct?" His gaze wandered through the small, simply laid-out room. With surprise, he asked: "Where's our ambassador who's going to put a stop to climate change?" Matthias walked reluctantly over to the cupboard and called into the narrow space between cupboard and wall: "Knut, come out!" Knut had no desire to come out, and pressed his rear end against the wall. "Knut's all worked up," Matthias explained in a low voice, almost absentmindedly: "Let's leave him in peace."

The floor creaked beneath the director's every weighty step until he stopped, ready to probe the secret world behind the cupboard with his own eyes. His nasal cavities were overgrown with black hair, and this sight frightened the little bear. Did he need that much hair in his nose to protect himself from the dirt in city air? The director didn't notice that he was being perceived by Knut not as a person but as bunches of nose hair, and spoke in a gentlemanly voice: "I'm proud of you. The future of our institution rests on your shoulders." His bearish companion cast a glance behind the cupboard. His face crumpled, he was unable to keep his delight to himself and uttered a bit of superfluous commentary: "So *incredibly* adorable, this Knut. Almost as cute as my kid."

Christian stuck one arm behind the cupboard and with professional calm extracted Knut. He held up the bear at eye level for the two visitors and turned him around so he could be observed from every angle. Then the veterinarian in him withdrew the animal and turned his back on the visitors with the words: "We have to clean his ears." He pulled a blue handkerchief from his pocket and tried to clean the bear ears with it. Knut twisted his upper body around to box Christian's ears, but the doctor was quick: he got his face out of the way just in time. Then he commented on the attack just as charmingly as if Rosa had still been in the room: "I'm good at ducking when I'm about to get my face slapped, because I practice with my wife."

"Please let me take a photograph of the minister and Knut. Sir, would you mind holding Knut's hand?" Christian gently took Knut's paw-hand and gave it to the bearish man, who carefully took hold of it and smiled at his constituents through the camera's lens. The flashbulbs flashed and flashed without cease.

"We're ready. The team from the *New York Times* has arrived, as well as journalists from all over the world: Egypt, South Africa, Colombia, New Zealand, Australia, Japan, and so on." The excited voice of a young man slipped through the crack of the door. The two gentlemen left the room, followed by half the journalists. The other half stayed in the room and continued to take flashbulb photographs of Knut.

Raising both arms, Matthias shook his head and shouted: "I'm sorry, but you have to leave the room now! If Knut is stressed out, he won't want to play in front of the visitors later. He doesn't know the enclosure, everything's new and much too upsetting to him today." His voice was trembling faintly, and at once his eyes returned shyly to the floor. Why did he usually speak so softly, while other men bellowed? What was an enclosure? Knut's heart leapt at the thought of going outside, no matter where.

The last journalists left behind a "Good luck!" on their way out. Knut noted several odd gestures: One pressed all four fingers against the thumb of the same hand. Another pretended to spit on someone else's shoulder.

When silence returned to the room, Christian asked Matthias whether his wife and kids were coming. Matthias shook his head, or at least Knut thought that's what he saw and felt calmer.

Matthias snapped to when Christian tapped him on the shoulder. He wrapped Knut in the wool blanket and picked him up. In Matthias's arms, Knut left the familiar room, left the building, inhaled the smell of other animals, entered a strange building and then a room in which apparently he was to await his grand entrance. Matthias tried to peek outside, but the light was blinding. Knut stretched out his neck; his eyesight was only good enough for him to vaguely make out a large stone slab, and everything else was blurry. Knut heard a colorful mix of voices, there was probably a large crowd of people behind the slab of stone.

Matthias fashioned a sled out of the blanket, set Knut on it and pulled the bear behind him. Knut found this so entertaining that he forgot about the presence of the enormous audience. He also forgot that he hadn't mastered any art that might be presented on a stage. The sled was pulled to a slightly raised area of the rock where one could look out into the distance. A monstrous cry of delight rose up from far away, where a large number of Homo sapiens were gathered. The nearsighted bear was unable to make out the individual faces.

Matthias gently pushed Knut to the ground, raised his fluffy bear arms, and petted his exposed belly. Knut felt the desire to play rise up in him, he freed himself from Matthias's grasp, spun around and raised his rear end to get to his feet. He kept pouncing brashly on Matthias's hand. During one such offensive, his claws briefly sank into the back of Matthias's hand, and the delicate human skin bled a little. But Matthias gave no cry of pain, he just went on playing cheerfully. For a moment, Knut remembered Susanna's story, and felt frightened that he might lose Matthias. But he soon forgot these worries when he was wrapped tightly in the wool blanket and had to disentangle himself. Someone in the audience shouted: "He looks like a sausauge in a croissant!" Knut didn't want to be a sausage. For the moment his opponent was not Matthias but the blanket, whose strategies he had studied closely in recent days. Victory was just a snout's length away, and whether it was as a sausage or as some other species of buffoon, he would surely triumph. Knut gave the blanket a kick, bit into its fabric flesh and fought valiantly. Just as the blanket was about to concede defeat, Matthias picked it up and tried to wrap Knut up in it again. Matthias was apparently fighting on the blanket's side, and his betrayal was making it impossible for Knut to declare victory. It took a while before Knut was finally able to liberate himself from the blanket and run away. He stumbled, however, and spun once around like a wheel. The audience laughed in unison—Knut had brought people together by falling down. At this moment Knut understood something important, something a talented clown must grasp early in the course of his life. Or was this knowledge that had been inscribed in his genes?

The next day, the director of the zoo came into the room with a pile of newspapers, borne like a sacrificial offering on outstretched arms. "Yesterday more than five hundred journalists visited us. The minister said he was pleasantly surprised. Who'd have thought we'd get so much attention?"

The afternoon passed without Christian putting in an appearance, maybe he had the day off. Matthias sat on the chair, silent and withdrawn. He looked exhausted. As soon as the director left the room, Matthias wrapped himself in the blanket and lay down in a corner of the room as if he were sick. Knut took this as a declaration of war—after all, it was his blanket Matthias had commandeered. Joyfully he pounced on Matthias, opening his mouth wide to provoke him, pretending to bite his arms, and scratching at the fabric of his shirt, but Matthias did not respond. Worried, Knut stuck his snout into Matthias's beard to check whether the man underneath was still breathing. Finally his half-dead friend opened his mouth and said: "Don't worry. It'll take more than that to kill me."

Every day, Knut devoted two hours to public service. It was his responsibility to play with Matthias in the enclosure. Rapturous excitement kept bubbling up in the audience, whose faces formed a wall behind the moat. If there hadn't been a barrier, they would have thrown themselves at Knut. At first Knut felt pity for these poor humans who couldn't join in his games because they were trapped on the other side. In his body, he felt their burning desire to touch the little bear and hold him in their arms.

Knut soon ascertained that it was his own movements eliciting the audience's joyful exclamations. By experimenting a little, he discovered which poses particularly delighted the human beings and which did not. The crowd's raucous cheers grated on his nerves; its thunderous roars gave him an earache. For this reason, he learned to manipulate the audience's excitement level. He would gradually allow the crowd's enthusiasm to increase and then, just before the climax, let it sink again, postponing the shrieks of delight. Then he would start from the bottom again, elevating the mood in increments. The little bear began to enjoy this divine omnipotence. The ebb and flow of the audience's excitement was in his hands.

Although the morning sun had not yet cleared away the darkness, Matthias was there already, wearing a new jacket. Out of breath, he said: "Knut, starting today, we can go for walks in the zoo. We've been given official permission." Knut didn't know what sort of game "walks" were that Matthias was so looking forward to. The door was opened, the bear legs followed Matthias's heels, which strode outside with long steps. It wasn't the public enclosure he was already familiar with. From all directions, the wind brought unknown smells, but there wasn't anyone about.

Behind wire netting, tiny birds flew back and forth, wearing jackets the color of egg yolk. Knut already knew their voices, and their smell too, but this was the first time he was seeing them. In front of the mesh, sparrows landed. They pecked at the grains lying scattered on the ground. Then they flew off again. The sparrows were free, they could go wherever they wanted. But the beauties in the aviary had no freedom at all.

"Birds from the African continent live here. Look! Aren't they pretty? In countries where red and yellow flowers bloom all year round, bright colors like this count as camouflage. The residents of industrial nations, on the other hand, all wear gray, which," Matthias explained, "is also a sort of camouflage."

Knut took a better look at the birds. His own coloration struck him as out of place. He felt ashamed. Matthias wasn't brightly dressed either, but at least he was wearing blue, green, and brown. Only his underwear was white. But Knut was dressed in white from head to toe. The tropical birds would think he was only wearing underwear, and for this they would despise him. Knut would have liked to have on a brown sweater and blue jeans.

They twittered without pause, these saucy little birds. It sounded like: "Little bear, little bear, taking a walk in his underwear!" Maybe Knut was just imagining it. He rolled on the ground to give some color to his arms and shoulders. Then he lay on his back and rubbed an itchy spot against the ground, which felt incredibly good. "What are you doing?" Matthias shouted, picking Knut up. "Look how dirty you are. We haven't even visited the hippopotamus yet, and already you've perfected your mud technique? How did that happen?"

Knut suddenly saw the familiar stone slab before him. "That's the enclosure where you always play." Marveling, Knut stared at this familiar place that he was seeing from a new angle. The cheers of the visitors were activated in his memory. So this was the other side, the reverse of the stage. But what did that mean, the reverse? Knut felt his brain cells begin to twitch. The gray matter revolved slowly around its axis and something from the middle flew out. What was that just now? Knut gazed up at the sky, something was different from before. If he could just view everything from above, he would never again be startled by a change in perspective. "Knut, what are you looking for? Polaris? Soon the sun will rise higher. Then there won't be any stars left in the sky, just the sun. Let's keep going."

Knut followed Matthias, walking along a fence that soon came to an end. In its place was a dividing wall made of wooden poles and straw. Behind it, wire netting was stretched, and through this Knut saw white dogs sitting in a circle. Their narrow faces had an aristocratic plasticity, and their bony, thin legs gave a somewhat weak impression. Just like Knut, they were dressed all in white, so they too were members of a species that ran around in underwear. "Come over here, Knut, from here you can see better: it's the Wolf family from Canada." Knut ran over to Matthias, who was beckoning. A glass wall separated the wolves from the visitors. One of the wolves, apparently the head of the family, immediately bared his teeth when he saw Knut. The skin around his nose drew back in sharp folds. He growled, got up, and came closer. The female lying beside him rose and followed, and then came the rest of the family. They formed a triangle as if they wanted to become a single gigantic animal. With this method, even though no individual among them looked particularly imposing, they could bring down a giant. Knut was covered with gooseflesh at this thought and retreated between Matthias's pant legs. "Don't worry! Behind the glass wall is a deep moat you can't see from here," Matthias said. And indeed they stopped, probably at the moat that Knut couldn't see. "The wolf isn't your favorite, is he? I can see that. Wolves always stick together. If you aren't part of their clan, they immediately see you as the enemy. They'll kill you just for not being one of them. It's not that they have bad intentions, it's just a habitual behavior pattern. Polar bears are strong enough to be loners, you won't understand the wolf mentality."

A bit farther ahead, Knut discovered an empty enclosure with a terrace made of stone slabs. "This is the domain of the moon bear. She's still asleep. Maybe she's jet-lagged. She's an Asian bear, just like that one over there, the Malayan sun bear." In Africa, elegantly dressed birds sing songs, in Asia the bears are asleep, and in Canada dangerous wolves lead peaceful family lives: this was Knut's modest takeaway from his morning walk.

Knut went home, feeling extremely hungry. He stuck his snout deep in his bowl and ate too quickly, choking on his food. "Chew first and then swallow," Matthias helpfully advised, but this mushy breakfast contained nothing that could actually be chewed. The humans wanted the little bear to eat only food that was easily digestible, to help him grow as fast as possible. Most bears—not just polar bears—are relatively small at birth. Christian said it was beneficial for the newborns not to weigh too much, since the mother animal gave birth while hibernating. But large, deep-seated worries about the tiny infant still filled Christian's head. At every opportunity he emphasized how much weight Knut was putting on. Meanwhile the journalists with their questions often touched his sore spot: "Childhood mortality is said to be particularly high among polar bears, especially for a cub separated from its mother. Is it correct to say that Knut's case is still quite risky?" Knut sighed in relief when he heard Christian's nonchalant response: "No, he's out of danger."

"Regardless of the risk factors? He's truly out of danger?"

"Absolutely."

"One hundred percent?"

A few of the journalists secretly seemed to be hoping Knut would die.

"Knut is not one hundred percent safe. You or I could die tomorrow too," Christian answered irritably.

The director had once sighed as he said to Christian: "It's a miracle Knut is still alive." Knut felt as if someone had just whacked him on the head. A miracle he hadn't died yet?

Christian had just nodded slightly in response: "But an astonishing number of polar bears are raised by humans. I looked it up. In the last twenty-five years, there have been seventy such cases in Germany alone."

The director cleared his throat. "But it's not a good idea to tell the journalists things like that. Even if Knut isn't unique, he's still one of a kind, because he's been attracting so much attention. Just like Jesus. Lots of people were resurrected, but Jesus is the only one who is famous. That's what makes him one of a kind. Knut was born beneath a very special star. It's his responsibility to bear all our hopes upon his shoulders." The director's casual comment had led to this whole pathos-laden speech.

Matthias beamed with pleasure when he was allowed to take Knut out for a "pre-opening-time walk." Opening time meant the opening of the main gate, which neither he himself nor Christian nor the director nor Knut ever used. The main gate was for humans who bought admission tickets. Sparrows, rats, ravens, and cats paid no attention to opening hours and visited the zoo whenever they liked without paying a fee.

The hordes of visitors who wanted to see Knut formed an infinitely long line. After opening, the line became a river flowing toward the enclosure where Knut played every day. Matthias called these games their "show," pronouncing the word with irony. The journalists, on the other hand, called it "recreation." Once, Christian said to Matthias: "This recreation is really forced labor, and in the evening, the workers are locked back up in their cells. The term 'show' is actually more appropriate."

For Knut, the show was fun, but he soon became aware that it wasn't teaching him anything new, whereas his morning walks were highly instructive. The zoo offered almost more educational material than he could process. He walked past many of the enclosures without speaking to their occupants. He hadn't once spoken, for example, with the elephants or giraffes. These were enormous figures swaying in the distance like fata morganas. The tiger in his nicely manicured green garden was unapproachable, mechanically pacing from one corner to the other without a pause, whereas the black seal gleamed so attractively that Knut almost pounced on him. Matthias held him back at the last moment. After that, Matthias stopped taking him to see the seal. There were also animals that differed only slightly from Homo sapiens.

Taking a walk in the early-morning hours soon became an indispensable part of Knut's routine. The director asked Matthias and Christian if it would be all right for a journalist to accompany Knut on his morning walk. "Knut is a major presence in the press. I have you two to thank for that. I even found a website devoted exclusively to Knut reports. If we don't keep feeding them news items, they'll stop talking about him. That's why I thought that maybe we could offer them something new every week: next week the morning walk, the week after swimming lessons, and so forth." Matthias swallowed hard while Christian took a step forward and said: "It's still too soon. Let's ask the press to be patient. It would be awful if Knut were to be frightened by a camera on his morning walk and leap into the black bears' enclosure. Besides, what would we do if his fans found out about his walks and started trying to sneak into the zoo early in the morning? We've known ever since John Lennon's death that there is nothing more dangerous than fanatical fans." The director made a fanning gesture with his left hand in front of his nose and left the room.

Every morning on his walk, Knut made the acquaintance of new species. One fellow was nonchalantly sitting high up on a branch in a tight-fitting shirt that made him look sexy. "Have a chat with the Malayan sun bear!" Knut took this suggestion, since the sun bear looked neither arrogant nor mean. "It seems we're going to have another hot day. It's already so warm at this hour."

The sun bear responded offhandedly to Knut's cautious icebreaker: "It's not warm at all. I find it chilly."

"You aren't dressed warmly enough. Just look at Knut. He's wearing a nice sweater."

When the sun bear heard these words, innumerable laugh lines appeared on his face. "You call yourself Knut? A bear speaking in the third person? I haven't heard anything that hilarious in a long time. Are you still a baby?"

In the brief fit of rage that followed, Knut vowed to avoid all contact with sun bears in the future. Knut was Knut. Why shouldn't Knut say "Knut"? But he found it impossible to get the sun bear's remark out of his head. Listening carefully to the conversations between Matthias and Christian, it was immediately clear that Matthias never referred to himself as Matthias. He didn't use his own name—as if his name had nothing to do with him—and left its use up to the other humans. What a strange phenomenon! And what did Matthias call himself? "I." What was even stranger was that Christian too referred to himself as "I." Why didn't they get confused if they all kept using the same name?

The next morning, "I" went back to the sun bear's enclosure, but unfortunately he wasn't there. Maybe he was still asleep in his cave. I discovered the moon bear in an enclosure nearby. Clearing my throat, I spoke the word "I" for the first time: "I am Knut, in case you don't know." The moon bear stared at me, narrowed her little eyes until they were even littler, and murmured: "Kawaii."

This was a word I'd heard many times before, but only ever on the lips of skinny, immature girls. "What language does that word come from?"

"From the language in Sasebo, where my grandmother was born. The word has spread like the plague recently. You can often hear international visitors saying it here in the zoo."

"I know. And what does it mean exactly?"

"That someone looks so cute that I'd like to put my arms around him and eat him right up."

I didn't want to wind up on her menu, so I withdrew without saying goodbye. Matthias, who hadn't understood our conversation, lobbed a question at my back: "What's wrong? What's the hurry? Don't you think someone ought to send the moon bear's grimy moon to the cleaners? But first I should pop you in the washing machine. Why do you keep rolling around on the sandy ground? Do you think you need to camouflage yourself? Berlin's winter is gray, so you want to be gray too. Winter at the North Pole is probably as white as snow and incredibly beautiful."

But what did it mean that the moon bear would want to devour something she found cute? Was this the custom in her hometown? I'd never considered any sort of food to be kawaii. Admittedly I'd always found Matthias sweet. But I'd never want to eat him. I tried in vain to find some connection between the lovableness of a creature and the desire to eat it.

My education as a walker was continuing apace, but this schooling left deep wounds. Speaking of oneself in the third person meant one was a baby: with this statement, the sun bear had wounded my pride. Since I was cute, I'd get eaten up: the moon bear had turned me into a fraidy-cat. Once I started using the word "I," the words spoken by others struck me like stones. I would flop down on the bed, exhausted and wrung-out, thinking how nice it would be if I could spend my time only with Matthias. Alone with him: that must be just as nice as being all alone, or even better, since I could then take this new burden called "I" from my shoulders and relax as Knut. But after a restful sleep I was once more curious about the outside world.

One day a photographer accompanied us on our walk. He didn't bother me. Christian insisted that no more than one be allowed, because a large number of journalists might constitute a mortal danger for me. The video of my walk was broadcast that same night on the evening news, and I too saw myself on TV. Christian said to Matthias: "How can you act so natural the whole time when you know you're being filmed? Hordes of nervous wrecks are sitting on their sofas worrying about— or at least eagerly waiting to see—whether Knut will survive. And you just go out for a stroll with him as calmly as you please, as if he were some mongrel you'd found on the street."

"I wish Knut really were a street dog. Especially a mixed-breed dog."

"You shouldn't underestimate the power of a star. A star can influence society, maybe even more than a politician. I dream that one day Knut will be like Joan of Arc, holding a huge SAVE THE EARTH banner in his hand and leading a massive demonstration."

Our morning walk was comparable to an academic education, while the show was like a day job. To make our task easier, I tried to determine under what circumstances and on what occasions human joy was produced and what made it vanish again. The more I thought about it, the more complicated it seemed to me. When I did something on purpose, the audience didn't like it. I couldn't plan anything in advance. The audience got bored when I repeated myself too often, but also was soon overwhelmed when too many ingenious new ideas came in rapid succession. Then the viewers would stop laughing and retreat into their own narrow minds. I staged their excitement like ocean waves. When I heard their enthusiasm increasing, I would briefly cut back on my offerings. When the reaction was too muted, I would turn toward my audience once more.

I dubbed the street where the brown bear, the moon bear, the sun bear, and the sloth bear lived with their families Bear Street. I was gradually coming to understand why Matthias considered all these completely different animals members of the "bear group."

Most of the bears slept at night in a bedroom you couldn't see from outside, and in the morning they would step out onto a terrace made of a stone slab augmented with a swimming pool.

Only the panda bears lived on another street, although they too were members of the bear family. They lived not in an open pen but in an enormous cage. They didn't have a terrace either, though they did have a bamboo garden right next door. Matthias said to me: "Christian took really excellent care of Yang Yang. When she died, he was devastated—for months he was in mourning. Then you came along and got him back on his feet again." I tried to imagine what it must feel like to lose a protégé, to be deeply saddened, and then to get back on one's four or two legs with the help of a new protégé. My train of thought was interrupted when a panda bear who until then had been nibbling on rustling leaves looked me up and down and dryly remarked: "You're pretty cute. But don't let your guard down! It's the animals who look the cutest that are dying out." Horrified, I asked what he meant by this. "You look adorable. So do I. Since we're in danger of becoming extinct, we have no choice but to activate the Homo sapiens' protective instincts. To this end, Nature is doing its best to deform our faces in such a way as to make them ever more pleasing to human tastes. Just look at the rats. They couldn't care less whether or not human beings find them cute. Their species is in no danger whatsoever of dying out."

I was tense before each of these walks, not knowing what new insight would appall me this time. Matthias, on the other hand, appeared relaxed before and during the walks, nonchalantly letting his shoulders and back be borne along by his strong calves. But as the hour of our show approached, he would become distracted, and if I jumped on his back shortly beforehand, his shoulder blades were as hard as a cliff face. As for me, I felt no anxiety before the show, I felt confident it would be successful. Matthias believed that we shouldn't allow ourselves even a moment's pause—he would challenge me again and again, but I could tell he didn't really feel like playing. When we were wrestling, it didn't bother me so much, since I could feel him in the warmth of his hands, but the ball game became problematic. I couldn't manage to take an interest in all the balls he tossed to me, and there was one ball I didn't even want to touch. It was the color of a gold coin and stank of rubber boots. Three words were written on it: Globalization, Innovation, Communication. When I appeared distrustful and ignored this ball, Matthias became nervous. I sensed that this ball was a gift from an important sponsor, so I pounced on the ball, but couldn't bring myself to embrace it. I was trying to be cooperative, but simulating love for a ball was too difficult for me. So I threw it away from me as hard as I could. The ball flew high up into the sky, and the audience cheered.

The next ball Matthias threw me was a small, unostentatious red one. I pressed it to my heart, lay down on my back and gave it a few gentle kicks. With bated breath, the audience waited to see what would happen next. The spectating heart beat ever faster, the anticipation grew by the second, but I didn't know how to fulfill the audience's desires. I remained lying there on the ground with the ball obediently resting on my belly. "How much longer are you on break for? Are you ever going to shoot a goal?" This heckler from the crowd made all the spectators laugh, filling my ears with a dull roar.

I knew I had to offer something new to keep the show going. But since I couldn't think of anything, I kept kicking away at the ball I was holding on my belly. For a second, my attention wandered and I kicked too hard. At once the ball was launched from my arms, it rolled down the rocky slope and fell into the water of the swimming pool. Delighted, the humans burst into deafening laughter. Sometimes it's quite easy to make even a full-grown Homo sapiens happy, since he is childish by nature.

The unexpected is always the most interesting: this is a lesson I learned all over again that day. It hadn't even occurred to me that the ball might fall in the water, and that was a good thing. A little girl cried out in a pleading voice: "Knut, please go in the water! Get the ball for me!" But I didn't want to go in, since I hadn't yet had any swimming lessons.

In a dream, the beautiful aged queen appeared to me once more, wearing a gleaming white fur coat. She praised me: "You weren't half bad. I underestimated you." I hadn't seen her in quite some time and noticed that I'd grown taller by a head. "You discover how the stage you perform on should appear without anyone teaching you. You perform nothing out of the ordinary, instead you try to show how interesting an ordinary child's game is. Perhaps this is a new art I knew nothing of."

"Who are you? Are you my grandmother?"

"I'm not only your grandmother, I'm also your great-grandmother and your great-great-grandmother. I am the superimposition of numerous ancestors. From the front you see only a single figure, but behind me is an infinitely long line of ancestors. I am not one, I am many."

"Are you my mother too?"

"No, I only represent the dead. Your mother, after all, is still alive. Why don't you go visit her?"

For Matthias, the end of the show always meant the beginning of relaxation. Back in the room, he made coffee and flipped through a tabloid. For a long time I believed that newspaper pages existed only to be crumpled, crinkled, and torn up. In other words, to be a toy. But now that Matthias read me an article every morning, the conviction that newspapers were there to be read was becoming ever firmer in me.

There were strange stories in the newspaper, for example: A zoo supposedly sold the meat of dead kangaroos and crocodiles to fancy restaurants to get through the financial crisis. The meat was advertised as a delicacy and eaten by customers who wished to partake of something unusual. A cold shiver ran down my spine as I recalled the words addressed to me by the moon bear, who'd said that an animal could be so adorable that everyone would want to devour him. Matthias groaned and said: "I feel sorry for them." I thought he was feeling sorry for the kangaroos being roasted as steaks, but no, Matthias added: "Other zoos are suffering from a lack of funding too." It became my habit to study the printed letters while Matthias was reading me the articles. The first letter I learned to recognize was O, which appeared twice in the word "Zoo." After a while, I was no longer illiterate.

Every day letters and packages reached us from outside. Matthias tore open the envelopes in a fury, read the fan letters, and fed them to the new extra-large wastepaper basket. We also received packages of various shapes and sizes. "Knut, this is a present for you from a fan: chocolate, which is bad for your health. I'm going to donate it to a charity organization. Any objections?" Matthias never let me taste chocolate.

One day Matthias came into the room carrying a large box. "Knut, you know what this is?" The package looked like a gigantic cube of chocolate, but what he pulled out of the box looked more like our television set.

"You have to type in your name and click here. Do you see? These are all photographs of you. You can see yourself on the Internet." Matthias went on tapping at the keys, and I saw something white lying on the stone slab. "Do you recognize yourself? That's you! How adorable!" Matthias stared at the other Knut like a man in love, apparently forgetting that the real Knut was sitting right next to him. If the picture is Knut, I'm not Knut anymore.

Christian came into the room, bearing traces of exhaustion around his eyes. "Well, here's something I never would have expected from you. A computer on bear turf!"

Matthias frowned. "The press department asked me to answer as much fan mail as I possibly can. The fans are different than before. Their infatuations are no longer enough for them. Now they want to be noticed. Some fans would even kill their idol if he ignores them. Every day we get more than one hundred fan letters. It's impossible to answer all of them, but I have to respond to as many as I can. Here's an example for you," Matthias said and read out a few of the letters lying before him.

"Dear little bear, my name is Melissa, I am three years old. I think about you all the time, especially when I go to bed."

"Dear Mr. Knut, I've made up my mind to purchase an electric car. It's important to me to do something to stop the ice at the North Pole from melting. Yours sincerely, Frank."

"Dear Knut, this week I turned seventy, and I still love to go hiking in the snow. I always keep your picture with me as a talisman. Yours, Günter."

"Dear Knut, my hobby is knitting. I would like to knit a

sweater for you as a present. What is your size, and what is your favorite color? All my best, Maria."

Some of the emails were written in English, and Matthias translated them as he read. "Sorry that I'm writing in English. Or do you speak English? I often wonder what language the inhabitants of the North Pole speak at home. English, no? Love, John."

Matthias found all this entertaining, but Knut couldn't understand what was supposed to be so funny about these fan letters.

Apparently many of the animals had no difficulty at all ignoring my interest in them. The birds from Africa, for instance, found me completely unremarkable, whereas I never tired of looking at them. I'd stand before the aviary until Matthias lost his patience. The muddy, ponderous gait of the hippopotami was equally mesmerizing, but they never turned their heads in my direction. I, in turn, took no interest in either the moon bear or the brown bear, though each dolled herself up for me and glanced over flirtatiously.

Thanks to Christian, I'd been well informed at an early age about the dangers of the female sex. I didn't miss a word when the all-knowing animal doctor conversed with journalists. "There's a case study involving a young bear that was raised not by his biological mother but with a milk bottle and never learned to communicate with other members of his species. In his post-adolescent years, he tried to declare his love to a female bear, but she took a swipe at him, and he was injured."

Christian answered conscientiously: "Not to worry! We won't introduce Knut to any female bears until he's strong enough to protect himself from womanly aggressions." In other words, the human milk bottle that nourished me would be to blame if women didn't understand me. And being misunderstood could lead to serious physical injuries.

On my walk the next morning, the brown bear started flirting again: "Wait a sec, will you? Why are you afraid of me?" I wanted to ignore her, but Matthias wouldn't let me. "You polar bears will die out if you keep committing incest," the brown bear declared. I was never sure how well Matthias understood bear language. His thoughts, at least, swam on the same wavelength as bear thoughts, otherwise he wouldn't have picked this very moment to remark that there were ever more biracial cubs born of polar bears and brown bears.

"Of course, in the zoo we don't want to encourage these unions. But out in nature, this happens as a matter of course, since there's ever less viable territory for the polar bears. They're being forced to emigrate ever further south."

I didn't want to move south under any circumstances, I thought. The brown bear persisted, sticking her snout in my direction: "International marriages are coming into fashion. Pure breeds are dying out. Don't you even want to see what it's like to have sex with a brown bear?"

Matthias's gaze was wandering back and forth between the brown bear and me. "Knut, can you sense what a near relative the brown bear is to you? You can marry her if you want. A sun bear, on the other hand, wouldn't be close enough."

I didn't want to marry anyone from the sun bear family anyhow—I found scrawny bodies unattractive. When I grew up, I wanted to marry Matthias and live with him until death did us part. But he wasn't saying anything about the genetic link between Homo sapiens and polar bears. In front of the sun bear's enclosure, I compared myself, Matthias, and the sun bear. Regardless from what angle I looked at it, the similarity between Matthias and me was greater than the similarity between me and the sun bear.

"How is our little bear doing today, the one who speaks of himself in the third person? Or is his problem now the love triangle and no longer the third person?" The sun bear knew that I was secretly watching him even though I pretended to be in a hurry. His words annoyed me.

"What's that wisecrack supposed to mean? Whom are you referring to?"

Around his nose, arrogant, disdainful folds gathered. "Why, you, Matthias, and Christian."

"The three of us work together in harmony."

"But you don't have the slightest idea with whom Matthias and Christian have relationships. Outside the zoo, I mean."

His words struck me like a blow, but he paid no attention to my reaction. Instead he remarked, his eyes glazed over: "Next month I'm getting married to a woman."

"Is she from Malaysia too?"

"Whatever gave you that idea? She's from Munich."

When I was alone again, I started thinking. What did Matthias do when he wasn't working at the zoo? I felt endlessly liberated the first time I was allowed to leave my four walls and go for a walk in the zoo, but every outside world had yet another world outside it that filled me once more with unease. What was outside the zoo? And when would I finally be able to reach the outermost outside world?

During the night, rain washed the air clean. I filled my lungs, and as if in response a lizard slipped out of a bush. She stopped abruptly, crept bowleggedly forward, then stopped again. She described a half circle and then disappeared back into the bush. "That was a descendant of the dinosaurs," Matthias explained. "Its ancestors were gigantic, even bigger than today's elephant. We mammals were so afraid of the reptiles' ancestors that we didn't even venture outside during the day." To my astonishment, I could immediately imagine the figure of the dinosaur even though I'd never seen anything of the sort. Not only that: several days later, as another lizard crossed my path on my morning walk, she suddenly appeared in my retinas the size of an elephant. In terror I jumped back. Matthias didn't laugh, he asked if I was frightened. "Fear is proof of imagination. A rusty head knows no fear." What head did Matthias mean when he said "rusty"?

Matthias and I watched the lizard, not letting her out of our sight for a moment until the tip of her tail had been sucked entirely into a bush. I was relieved. "We mammals always have a ton of worries," Matthias said, sighing.

One day Christian asked Matthias how his family was doing. "My family is doing splendidly, but sometimes I can't understand what my own children are thinking. Probably it's because I'm too exhausted."

"But you understand perfectly well what bears are thinking. Am I right?"

"You can't compare the bears to your own children."

"No. But you discuss everything with Knut. Do you do that with your wife, too, or are you hiding something from her?"

"No."

"You're happy with your wonderful wife and children, right?"

"So are you."

I pretended to understand nothing of this conversation.

When I went straight down Bear Street, at the end a bridge would appear that crossed a pond. We stood for a while on the bridge, and then a duck swam up with three ducklings behind her. I could sense that Matthias wanted to say something to me. "A duckling can swim as soon as it's born. That means that ducklings are born as ducks already and can't grow up to be something else instead. But you, Knut, have to have swimming lessons. You've splashed around in a tub often enough, but you've never swum properly in a real swimming pool." The ducklings were moving their swimming feet hectically beneath the water, hurrying as though they were afraid their mother might swim out of sight.

"In Nature, a newborn bear spends two winters under his mother's supervision. There are so many things the cub must learn in order to survive in the wild. In Russia there was a professor who put on a bearskin and spent two years in the wilderness with two baby bears whose mother had been shot by a hunter. He became a mother bear. It's still too cold for me to go swimming outside, but if I too want to be a proper bear mother, I'll have to pull myself together and teach you to swim."

The next morning, Matthias put on bathing trunks and before my eyes jumped into the little swimming pool. The liquid mirror shattered, integrated the human body, and grew calm again. Matthias had to exert effort to keep his head above water, since it wasn't attached in a convenient place like the head of a duck. He had to keep his skinny arms constantly in motion so as to not drown. He put a smile on his face to reassure me, but it was clear to me that he could never grow up to be a duck. In a panic, I ran back and forth on solid ground. Matthias beckoned to me with his hand, which he quickly plucked out of the water to wave again and again, but I didn't have the courage to jump in. I could only breathe freely again when Matthias, shaking his head, finally got out of the water. He didn't stay beside me on dry land for long, however: his eyes were fixed on me as his body disappeared backward into the water. Something was wrong with him. After long hesitation, I jumped into the water. Surprisingly, the water gave me a friendly welcome, it embraced me and held me up. What wonderful water! My body already knew it.

How I frolicked! Shrieking with delight, I pretended to be drowning. Once it did hurt—the formless water can sting the mucous membrane inside your nose if you inhale at the wrong moment. By the end, the muscles in my arms were like stretched-out rubber bands, but I didn't want to stop, even after Matthias told me several times that the end of today's water game had come. I would have fallen asleep in the water's arms if Matthias hadn't forced me to take my leave of my new beloved, the water. Back on solid ground, I gave my body a good shake, and right away my fur was dry again.

"Swimming is a pleasure." I couldn't keep my mouth shut the next morning when I saw the sun bear. He scratched his belly with his thin fingers and turned away from me before replying: "Swimming is a senseless activity. I have no time for silly little games. A grand new project is calling me. I shall write the glorious history of the Malaysian peninsula from the sun bear perspective." It would never have occurred to me that this sun bear might scratch not just his belly but also manuscript paper. He unhesitatingly referred to this as "writing." When I asked whether this peninsula was far away, he replied, making use of the folds around his nose to show his disdain for me: "Far away, of course, though I don't know how far it would have to be for you to think it far enough to be considered far away. You've never even been to the North Pole, have you?"

"Why would I have gone to the North Pole?"

"Aha, I see you're now using the first person like a champ. I'm already starting to miss the baby bear who talked about himself in the third person. There's nothing more boring than a civilized polar bear. Never mind, just a joke. You don't have to travel to the Pole. But doesn't it worry you that the North Pole is in danger of disappearing? I wasn't born on the Malaysian peninsula, but I do feel concerned about the future of the region where my ancestors lived. That's why I'm researching the history of the peninsula and thinking about possibilities for the coexistence of cultures. You ought to give some thought to the North Pole too, instead of just occupying yourself with walks, swimming, and playing ball."

"My ancestors are all from the GDR, not the North Pole!"

"Oh, really? Even the ones who lived one thousand years ago? Seriously, you're hopeless."

Unlike the unkind sun bear, the sloth bear was perfectly amiable when I addressed him for the first time.

"It's the perfect weather for a nap."

"Yes, the weather is quite pleasant."

That was our first conversation. But this same bear criticized me harshly the second time we met: "You run around in this zoo without purpose or goal. You sell yourself to the audience with your show. Does your life have any meaning at all?"

"And you? What do you do all day long?" I shot back.

"Me? I loaf," he replied calmly. "Loafing is a dignified labor. It requires courage. The audience expects you to perform something interesting, to entertain it. Do you have the courage to refuse to play any game at all and to disappoint the audience? Every day you go for a walk because it's fun for you. Can you renounce fun, or don't you have the nerve for that?" He was right: I didn't have the courage to disappoint my audience and Matthias. I was incapable of loafing.

It was disconcerting to speak with the other animals about our lifestyles. The Canadian wolves had frightened me right from the start, and I tried to keep away from them, but one day I accidentally passed close by their compound and realized it too late. The head wolf immediately addressed me. "You there, always running around all by yourself. Don't you have a family?"

"No."

"What about your mother?"

"My mother is Matthias. He's right here. He always goes walking with me."

"But there's no resemblance at all between you and Matthias. He must have kidnapped you as a baby. Just look at my big family. All its members resemble one another like peas in a pod."

Matthias came back to get me and delivered his commentary as if he'd overheard our conversation. "Wolves have a slender, elegant, aristocratic figure. But I prefer bears. Do you know why? Male wolves fight each other until they've established who's the strongest in the group. Then the strongest male produces offspring with his mate. The rest of the wolves in the pack don't have pups. That gives me the creeps." Just as Matthias couldn't understand the wolves' speech, the opposite was fortunately true as well.

I didn't like the wolves and tried to ignore their opinions. But I couldn't get what the wolves' leader had said to me out of my head. Didn't Matthias and I look alike? Had I been kidnapped as a baby? All day long this thought turned over and over in my head.

The press often wrote about me. When Christian brought us an article, Matthias would read it aloud, then I would study every sentence on my own that evening. "First Swimming Lesson for Knut." They took a piece of my life away and locked it up in newsprint. When I went swimming, Knut should have stayed contained within this swimming "I" rather than being consigned to newsprint one day later. Perhaps I should have kept so many people from learning that my name was Knut. They used my name whenever they felt like it, to amuse themselves.

One article made a particularly strong impression on me and refused to give me peace even weeks later. Not a day passed now without my reading some article about myself. I no longer read out of curiosity, it was more out of worry. "Knut was rejected by his mother immediately after birth and was raised by a human being. Now he is learning to swim and other survival techniques, all taught to him by humans." What did it mean that my mother had rejected me? This was news to me. I dug around in the stack of old articles, searching for clues. Somewhere there had to be a master article that explained the circumstances under which I came into human hands. At the end of my search, I still hadn't learned anything else about my biological mother, though I did perfect the art of reading. Among other articles, I found one that said: "After the birth of Knut and his brother, the mother animal, Tosca, showed no interest in her brood. After several hours, specialists determined that the newborn cubs were in mortal danger, so they were removed from Tosca. Normally a mother bear displays aggression when an attempt is made to remove her offspring, even if she doesn't intend to raise them, and for this reason, she must be tranquilized beforehand. But Tosca, astonishingly, showed no reaction at all when the zookeepers removed the cubs. The specialists conjectured that Tosca's stressful circus life had made her lose her maternal instincts. It's well known that circus animals under Socialism were overworked and under a great deal of pressure."

The day I was scared to death of overtook me without any warning. I injured Matthias while we were playing. His thin skin ripped, and in no time he was red with blood. Matthias didn't even raise his voice, but the incident took place during our show, and many of the audience members were horrified at the sight of the blood and began to shriek hysterically. We returned to our room, and Christian treated the wound. He applied the bandage while I tried to lick the bottle of disinfectant. The bottle fell over, and Christian scolded me.

We returned to the play area. For the first time, I felt on my skin an audience's corrosive hostility and trembled. "Dear visitors," Matthias shouted at the top of his lungs, "the injury was completely minor, nothing of any importance!" Shouting was not typical of him. The audience applauded enthusiastically.

With great effort, we continued the show until it was time for it to end. Christian looked at us pensively when we returned, and said: "If things continue at this rate, Knut's body weight will reach 110 pounds by next week already." Since Matthias didn't respond, he continued: "We agreed on 110 pounds as the upper limit a long time ago. Yesterday I was thinking that possibly we could raise the limit to 130. But now the audience has seen you bleed. Besides, it'll be no time at all before Knut weighs 130 pounds. Sooner or later, you'll have to say goodbye. Maybe this is exactly the right moment."

Christian spoke calmly, but in the end his voice cracked despite his best efforts, and he wiped moisture from his eyes with the back of his hand. Matthias placed his arm on Christian's shoulder. "If it were death separating us, that would be bad. But it's not death driving us apart, it's life. I'm happy that we were able to get this far together."

Then he turned to me and asked: "You'll write me an email now and then, right?" At that moment I heard a monstrous voice and was terrified until I realized the voice was coming from Christian. He was sobbing.

That same day, I moved into a cell. There was a bed of straw in the middle, and next to it Matthias installed our old computer. Then he patted the bed all over to make sure it was all right. Through the bars of the gate in front, I could see the stone slab where our daily show took place. At the back of the cell was a small hatch through which my food could be passed to me. Matthias checked the doors and gave detailed instructions to the humans standing by silently. Then he himself lay down in my future bed, shut his eyes and lay there like a dead man. After ten seconds he leapt to his feet and left the room without looking at me.

After that day, Matthias never came to see me again. In the morning and at night, my food was served to me through the hatch. The staff taking care of me changed often, as I could tell by the smell, but neither Matthias nor Christian was ever among them.

Every morning when the gate was opened, I would go out into the enclosure, where, off in the distance, I could see the audience, now much smaller than before. At night, when I smelled food, I would withdraw to my room. The computer still stood beside my bed, but I couldn't remember how to turn it on. In one corner of the bed sat that boring stuffed animal that had accompanied me ever since I was an infant. It looked depressed.

I lost all desire to entertain the visitors by playing for them. The only advantage of being outside was that the sun, when it was shining, would clear my head and warm my back. It soothed the pain. I would tuck all four limbs under my belly and not move from the spot. "Knut looks sad." A small girl's voice rode a wind horse to reach my eardrum. "He doesn't have anyone to play with." Children recognized my condition at a glance, while any number of adults thoughtlessly wisecracked. Their statements reeked of their cynical entrails; their humanity was deployed only when discussing their fellow Homo sapiens.

"Just look at those terrifying claws. He injured a zookeeper with them."

"Full-grown, even Knut is dangerous. He's a wild animal, not a dog."

"He doesn't look cute anymore."

My mother left me in the lurch right after I was born: I thought up this phrasing after Matthias abandoned me. As long as he was with me, I didn't feel the urge to probe the secret of my birth.

It was a male Homo sapiens who raised me, and it's rare for such a thing to work, it was almost a miracle. It was a while before I understood this miracle to be my own life story. Matthias was a true mammal, far more so than many of his sort, because he gave me suck: he fed me not only milk but part of his own life. He was the pride of all mammals.

Matthias wasn't even a distant relative, let alone my biological father. As the white wolf had once pointed out, Matthias and I bore no resemblance to one another. From our buttocks to our faces, we were different. The wolf was proud of the fact that the members of his family looked as alike as photocopies. But I revere Matthias for having suckled and cared for a creature like me who was not at all similar to him. The wolf devoted himself only to the expansion of his own family. Matthias, on the other hand, gazed far into the distance, all the way to the North Pole.

Matthias was always beside me, devoting his days to my care even though he had a charming wife at home, and even though his own adorable children—to whom he had given his genes—were waiting for him. He didn't do it because I was cute. Billions of worried eyes were watching me in those days. If I had died, the greenhouse gasses in the sky would have formed a giant, steel-hard layer that would have lowered itself upon the city like a lid on a pot, and then, what with the boiling steam, the temperature would have drastically risen, and all the inhabitants of the city would have quickly been cooked through. At the North Pole, all the ice floes would have melted, the polar bears would have drowned, and the green meadows would have vanished beneath the rising sea. But because the miracle worker Matthias had succeeded in making milk flow from his fingertips to feed the wunderkind, the North Pole was saved and thus the rest of the world as well. The little bear was saved, and so it became his duty to save the North Pole from further dangers. He would have to pore over all the philosophical and holy writings, which human beings in the past had indefatigably produced, to find an answer. He would have to swim, crossing the icy sea with its floes to reach the answer. An expectation as huge as the sky lay upon his shoulders, weighing many tons.

It sounded like a heroic tale, but I was nothing more than a helpless creature. I lay there, pathetic as a skinned rabbit. On TV I saw myself as a newborn. My eyes were still squeezed shut, my ears, not yet able to hear, hung down limply, and my four unstable limbs couldn't even lift my belly off the ground. Why had this child been sent into the world? Wouldn't it have been better if he had stayed on in his mother's womb? The TV viewers must have asked themselves this question. If it had been possible, I'd have denied that this was me.

The question of why Tosca refused to nurse me did not occur to me so clearly formulated for a long time. My mother no doubt had her reasons, incomprehensible to me. Children in general cannot understand what goes on in their parents' heads. It's pointless to speculate. This is one of the basic principles of Nature. What I wondered instead was why mammals were created in such a way that they cannot survive without their mothers' milk. A newborn bird, for example, can survive without his mother if his father brings him tasty worms to eat. But mammal children must drink milk. That's what defines a mammal. No substance other than milk can nourish them. This is one reason, perhaps, why we're always forced to remember our milky pasts and can never be as free as the birds.

The other thing I couldn't understand was why only females could produce milk. If my father Lars could have suckled me, my life would have gone in a different direction. As it was, Tosca was forced to assume all the responsibility.

The circus protests against every injustice in Nature. The magician makes his bowler hats give birth to doves. The acrobat leaps from one branch to the next even though he wasn't born a monkey. The wild-animal tamer forces creatures afraid of fire to jump through a flaming ring. And Matthias made milk flow from his fingers. At some point I watched the performance of an East Asian circus on television. Water sprayed from the fingertips of the women, who were dressed up as pheasants, just like a fountain. What a glorious theatrical accomplishment! And Matthias achieved at least that much. To be sure, it wasn't long before I saw through his trick with the milk bottle, but my astonishment and respect for him remained undiminished. There can be no magic without tricks. And Matthias did not merely provide me with milk. Ceaselessly he worried about me, asking himself whether I wasn't too cold or too hot, or whether I might injure my head on the sharp corner of some object. He stopped going home and for a while spent every night with me, providing round-the-clock care. When I was being weaned, he prepared complicated weaning meals day after day.

He gave me the feeling that I could never be abandoned. He washed my body in a tub and dried me with a towel. After the time-consuming cooking process, he would patiently wait until I'd finished my meal. He never rushed me. He collected the scraps of food I scattered everywhere, and cleaned the floor. He sat beside me when I watched TV and explained to me about the humans who turned up in the programs. He jumped into the cold water to teach me how to swim. He read to me from the newspaper every day, and one day he disappeared without saying goodbye.

Newspapers kept being delivered to my cell. Matthias had no doubt arranged for this. For the most part, it would be one of those free Berlin city papers with lots of photos and not much text. Most of the articles were incomprehensible in terms of content, while others were heartrendingly sad. I never found an article that made me happy. Nonetheless, I couldn't stop reading once I'd stuck my snout into a piece of printed matter.

And this news too reached me in the form of a newspaper article: Matthias is dead. He died of a heart attack. At first I didn't understand what that meant. I read the article through several times. Suddenly a thought struck me like a stone: I can never see him again. Of course it was perfectly possible that I'd never have been able to see him again even if he'd remained alive. But I would have gone on thinking now and then: Maybe

I'll see him again after all. This "maybe" is what human beings call hope. My "maybe" was dead.

Matthias had first fallen ill with renal cancer, I read, and then had suffered a heart attack. He died instantly, even though the heart attack was his first. Why hadn't he come to visit me before his heart was fatally attacked? He could have mixed some of his saliva into my food as a sign—that would have meant a lot to me. He could have hidden amid the throng of visitors and called out my name—I would have heard him.

The newspaper offered a hodgepodge of tidbits. None of them could nourish me, but since I had no other source of information, I nibbled my way through them day after day down to the last corner.

One day I read the opinion that Matthias's death was all my fault. I was a changeling, this human wrote: the devil had replaced a proper child with me. There were people who tried to open his eyes, but he refused to return to his own proper child and instead stayed with Knut, whom he took for his one true child. Matthias, the writer said, had been possessed by the devil.

I didn't know of any animal called Devil, since this species was not represented at the zoo.

In another article, a journalist claimed I'd sucked out Matthias's life force. Possibly he was referring to the milk I'd imbibed each day.

Matthias's funeral was said to have been a private, closed ceremony for family and friends. I wasn't invited. I don't know what exactly humans do at a funeral ceremony. Maybe the humans who were close to the deceased are able to feel his presence once more during the ceremony. No one had been closer to Matthias than me, but I wasn't invited, and the reasons for this remained forever obscure to me.

I read an interview with Christian, who said: "Matthias had a lot of stress." Once again, the humans were talking about stress. Stress was the explanation they gave for why my mother rejected me and also for Matthias's death, but I didn't know of any animal called Stress. At least not at our zoo. This must have been an imaginary animal the humans thought up, as if there weren't enough real animals. I felt a need to discuss this with the sun bear, but ever since my separation from Matthias, I was no longer allowed to go for walks in the zoo and I no longer spoke with anyone.

Since I was being kept away from the other animals, I paid ever more attention to the sounds made by plants. The rustling leaves of the trees, for example, calmed me, although I couldn't interpret their language.

Outside in the play area, hot air shimmered even in the shade. Every movement, no matter how slight, made my temperature rise, and I was about to explode. So I had no choice but to go swimming. When I got into the water, the spectators shouted in delight and pointed their cameras at me. I still didn't know why. In the water, I soon felt bored again. Apparently the visitors also found it less than thrilling to observe my boredom. The number of visitors had fallen off dramatically in recent weeks.

One rainy morning, my unpopularity had grown to such an extent that only a single visitor stood behind the fence watching me. He stared at me without once averting his gaze, even when he clumsily opened a black umbrella. A faint breeze brought his smell to me—a smell I knew. Who was this man? I stretched my nose out as far as I could, eagerly sniffing, and inhaled the odor deeply. It was Maurice, the night shift substitute. Back then, he'd read a bit to me from his collection of books. I waved my snout in the air, and he raised his hand and waved back.

After Matthias's death, a whole series of disruptive events followed. I wanted to wrap myself in the black woolen blanket of grief and brood over my clutch of sorrows until they hatched and flew away, but it wasn't possible. Instead I had to defend myself tooth and claw against the world's malice. One of the main problems concerned inheritance—not that I believed I had any claim at all to Matthias's estate. How could I be entitled to someone else's money if I didn't even receive a share of the profits I generated for the zoo? The dispute was not between the zoo and me, but between two zoos. They were feuding over me, but I wasn't even called to testify. All I could do was follow the trial in the newspaper and hang my head lower each day. The zoo in Neumünster, to which my father Lars belonged, had sued the Berlin Zoo, which was making a pretty penny off me. The Berlin Zoo, the suit charged, should pay the Neumünster Zoo 700,000 euros of its profits. I lost my appetite when I saw a caricature in which my body was drawn in the shape of a euro sign. Another article reported on the toxic chocolate that had been sent to me as a gift.

Whoever owns the father also owns the son and thus also the son's property: one newspaper claimed there was a law establishing this ownership structure. In another paper, a journalist wrote that modern society must reject so outdated a law. However that might be—whether in truth or allegedly—the Neumünster Zoo claimed that I was in fact its property. The Berlin Zoo relented and offered to pay the Neumünster Zoo 350,000 euros, but not a cent more. At least, this was the state of affairs as best as I could tell from these various reports.

Though it would never have occurred to me to consider myself a source of financial gain, not only had more tickets been sold for admission to the zoo, but the Knut merchandise had proved quite profitable as well. Untold thousands of stuffed animals with my face on them had been sold as sacrificial stand-ins. There was a tiny Knut made of hard material, a middle-sized Knut, a fluffy Knut, and even a Knut of exaggerated proportions. Apparently every time the shelves of stuffed animals were emptied, a truck would drive up to the rear entrance to deliver a fresh load of these clones, and they were all called Knut. Imagining this huge pile of Knuts, I wanted to shout at the top of my lungs: "There's only one real Knut here—me!" But no one was listening. Knut was for sale not only as a stuffed animal, but also as a keychain, coffee mug, t-shirt, polo shirt, sweater, and DVD. On TV I learned there was even a CD of Knut songs. There were decks of playing cards—my head replaced that of the king—and even a teapot with a handle shaped like me. Notebooks, pencils, tote bags, backpacks, plastic cell phone cases, wallets: I was everywhere.

All the tabloids reported on humans steadily increasing their wealth, building magnificent villas, going to parties dressed all in black, red, and gold velvet and silk, and being photographed with jewels in their ears. I wasn't interested in money, but there was one article that shook me awake: a man had been arrested on suspicion of corruption, but had then paid 100,000 euros in bail and was temporarily released. I vaguely remembered something Matthias had once explained to me: you could buy your freedom, at least for a certain length of time. Could I too pay to leave my cell and experience freedom?

Early in the morning, it was still reasonably cool outside in the play area, but after the sun had reached its peak, the cruel heat grew more intense by the minute, tormenting me. Thinking about the Knut merchandise and the court cases involving me caused my organ of cognition to overheat until it hurt. I covered my head with my arms and tried to breathe quietly. Behind the fence I heard someone say: "Look! The financial crisis has gotten so desperate that it's even giving Knut a headache."

One day the playing card of my morale was finally turned over, and a lucky number appeared. During breakfast I suddenly caught the scent of a familiar man, it was Maurice again, and I discovered a letter on my breakfast tray. Impatiently I opened the envelope and read that a mayor was inviting me to a private reception. Maurice would come the next evening to pick me up. The zoo was making an exception in allowing me to go on this outing because the invitation had been extended by a person of importance to the zoo, but still this was a private event and as such had to be treated confidentially. The reception was to take place in a suite in a luxury hotel that stood directly on the shore of one of Berlin's lakes. The spacious terrace on the seventh floor afforded a lovely view of the water. A limousine would pick up first Maurice and then me from the zoo and bring us directly to the reception.

Maurice and I got out of the limousine. I don't know whether it was the sight of the lake nestled in its green surrounds or the already setting sun, but for the first time in ages I felt I was finally breathing fresh air again, cooling and refreshing me. In front of the hotel entrance, two doormen stood in fir-needle-green uniforms. They had playfully wrapped and decorated their torsos with strips of leather. I almost smiled at them, but their eyes, observing us, were stern and forbidding. Otherwise I might have asked: Are you real policemen or actors?

Maurice took my right paw and led me through the empty vestibule. A monstrous chandelier hung from the ceiling, bathing the room in yellow light.

Thanks to television, I was already familiar with the elevator as a device, but it was my first time riding in one. When its metal doors opened again before me, I was standing before another world—and didn't know if it was real or a projection.

The room was already crammed with guests, who were chatting with one another. Their voices buzzed around my brain like swarms of bees. The sweet smell of charred meat streamed through the room. I couldn't see through the crowd. Everywhere, packed into shirts and trousers, were backs, bellies, and buttocks! Maurice pulled me through the crowd, making for an unknown destination. All at once a man was standing in front of us. His face was flushed, his suit elegant and cold. I tried to find out what made this man so interesting. His smile drilled itself into my eyes, and he kissed me on the cheek. The guests around us applauded—apparently I was being observed. Maurice wished him a happy birthday and handed him a box with a big ribbon fluttering on top. There was a photograph on the wrapping paper, a picture of me! The man thanked us, hastily kissed our cheeks again, and entrusted the present, still wrapped, to a young man who stood beside him ready for service. Then I was given a glass two-thirds full of a yellowish liquid. The birthday boy clicked glasses with me, there was a glass-clear ringing in the air. All the men in the room abruptly raised their glasses and shouted "Prost!"

I gazed deep into the liquid. Tiny bubbles clung to the inner wall of the glass, gradually pulling away from it and rising to the surface until they reached the outside air and burst, disappearing. I wanted to go on watching the bubbles, but Maurice took the glass away from me, whispering that it was better I didn't drink the champagne. He went and got a different glass for me. I took a sip and was satisfied with the apple I tasted in it.

The man had neither a robust loudspeaker body nor an especially powerful voice, but every time he opened his mouth, all the other mouths in the room closed, and all the ears listened attentively. The man must be a star, I thought, and felt envy creeping up within me. I too had been a star once and each day had a large audience cheering on my every move, no matter how small. At the time, calling forth the attention of a million humans, I felt strong enough to blow away the clouds, or make a rainstorm pour down on the entire globe, or summon the sun with a wave of my hand, or rebuff a stormy wind. I wanted to turn back time and have that power in my grasp again.

At some point the esteemed gentleman disappeared in the press of people, but focusing my ears, I was able to hear exactly where in the crowd he stood. Around him, the guests formed several circular waves. The innermost circle listened to him in silence, while the wider circles distorted his words and transported them ever further out from the center.

Making his way behind me, a man pushed me a little, causing my nose to briefly press against Maurice's chest. I smelled his butter scent from back in the old days. Suddenly the joy of being reunited with him took hold of me—somewhat belatedly but still with tremendous force. Spontaneously I licked his cheek. He pulled his face aside for show, but in reality he was enjoying the situation, otherwise he wouldn't have explained to the man watching us enviously: "Different species, different customs. There are many ways to kiss."

The smell of roasted meat drifted from the direction from which humans were now streaming, each with a plate containing a minuscule bit of food. Maurice read my face and whispered: "Wait just a little while longer. We can go get some food too, but not just yet." I waited for a very long time, then could no longer endure it and inconspicuously took a step in the direction in which my sense of smell was leading me. Maurice stopped me, looking worried. "I'll go get food for you. Wait for me here." I couldn't understand why he was so worried.

While I was waiting, several men came up to me and said they'd seen me on TV. One of them cautiously touched my fur.

Finally Maurice returned with a plate on which a piece of meat—as puny as half a dead mouse—was arranged beside three little potatoes and a dollop of applesauce. In the newspapers I'd often enough read about the city's precarious financial situation. To be sure, the zoo also suffered from shortages, but this appalling poverty that we were invited to taste here with our own tongues quite surpassed my idea of hard times.

When I looked down at my plate, it was already empty. "You can't gorge yourself here," Maurice whispered to me. Insulted, I went out on the terrace alone and looked at the black watery surface of the big lake. The moon trembled between the waves.

Among the men standing in a circle on the terrace was one who spoke uninterruptedly in a clear voice. I gathered that he was discussing a television talk show that had been broadcast the day before. Jokingly, the man imitated one of the participants, though at first I thought he was trying to impersonate a falcon. "I just can't accept the way every married couple keeps adopting children. Like it or not, today we have same-sex couples too. So far so good. But if they too adopt children and exert influence over them, these children will later adopt children of their own, and someday not a single child will be born in this country. There will only be adopted children." Laughter. The expression on the performer's face shifted back from professionally mimed grotesquerie to his own: "I couldn't believe it. The person who'd been saying this was still young but already had a chair-of-the-department haircut. But wait, here's the best part: A gray-haired, elegant lady got up. She was probably in her early eighties. She said in a calm voice: 'But almost all the parents whose children go on to live in same-sex partnerships are heterosexual. They're the ones who produced these homosexual children. So if you want to prevent this, you should outlaw straight marriage.'" A few of the men trumpeted with laughter, others grinned. "But I'm not sure how many in the audience understood the lady's words. So many people are blockheads, impervious to irony, humor, and innuendo. And yet it's so important for minds to constantly be stretched and turned in all directions. I started clapping right in front of my TV screen, I wanted to show what respect I had for her. It was the author of that book ... What was the title again?"

I didn't have the courage to join their circle, so I stayed where

I was, in an armchair off to one side. From there I observed all these unfamiliar buttocks in their snug-fitting trousers. They were firm and toned. Nothing at all like my own posterior, as saggy as worn-out overalls. I felt too ashamed to get up again. The armchair next to mine was free, but no one wanted to sit down. So I sat there, slowly slipping down into my fur, until a stranger wearing a snow-white sweater approached: "Are you okay?" he asked in a gentle voice. Unfortunately there was something catlike about his face, but it was nonetheless quite handsome. I stared at him, enchanted, while he introduced himself: "Michael." It wasn't entirely clear to me whether I should also say my name or perhaps instead tell him what I'd like to eat. I decided on the latter course of action: "Boiled potatoes with parsley would be good, but mashed potatoes with lots of butter would be even better." Michael laughed, and a deep shadow appeared between his long lashes and the relatively high cheekbones. "I can't tolerate most foods, so usually I avoid eating anything at parties. Even at home I find it difficult to eat. I know this makes me look unattractively gaunt. When I was little, people were constantly telling me how cute I was. Then came puberty, my body shot up explosively, and I was horrified when people told me I'd lost my charm. I no longer had an appetite, I lost weight, and had no way of returning to what I'd been." His cheeks were like deep troughs, while his full lips still gleamed as red as blood.

"Were you sad when they said you were no longer cute?"

"I felt lonely and abandoned. All I could think of were cheap phrases from TV soap operas, like: 'No one loves me!' And during the worst of it, my mother left us."

"Did she die?"

"No. She ran away."

Maurice returned, his cheeks red. "It's time to go home." It wasn't a suggestion, it was an order. Maurice ignored Michael as if he weren't even there, he didn't even say hello. When I looked back longingly, Michael replied in a consoling voice: "I'll visit you soon. I know where to find you." His voice had a quality only a bee can achieve with her honey. I was salivating.

Maurice took me by the paw and dragged me through the crowd, out of the suite, out of the hotel. In the elevator, he placed his arm around my shoulder. I didn't want to go home. In the limousine I said to Maurice: "I'd like to go to another party with you soon." He gazed at me with pity and stroked the fur on my chest.

The next day, the sunlight rebounded off the stone slab more brightly than usual, almost blinding me. I stretched, taking my time, consciously positioned myself in the light, stuck out both my arms in front of me like an Olympic swimmer, and dove into the water. There were only three people in the audience, but they applauded enthusiastically. At first I swam on my back, then I flipped over and switched to a breaststroke. A branch was floating on the water in front of me. I tested its consistency with my teeth. Then I held it in my mouth and started swimming in earnest. Shaking my head, I observed how the branch disturbed the water. Slowly the audience grew. Already there were ten humans standing there pointing cameras at me. Suddenly seized by a burning desire to play, I whipped the branch back and forth, and with a whooshing sound, glass-clear drops of water struck round holes in the air. I whirled the branch around, dove underwater with it, held my breath and stayed there until I couldn't possibly stand it any longer. Then with a great flourish I popped to the surface again. Jubilant applause. I dove down again, this time trying to swim as far as I could while still holding my breath, then emerged in a far-distant spot, shaking my head so hard the water flew in all directions. There were already more than thirty humans standing behind the fence. I floated on my back, my sky covered with camera lenses.

When dusk fell, the voices of the visitors became ever fainter, and soon birds were supervising the zoo's acoustic design with their twittering. At this hour, human voices could be heard only in isolation, and by the time the sun had set behind the high-rise, all beaks had fallen silent. Around midnight I would sometimes hear the old wolf howling. He wasn't my best friend, but on lonely nights I'd have been glad for the chance to converse even with him.

The night grew deeper, without musical accompaniment. Something sent a shiver down my spine, I turned around and saw that the dusty screen of the computer was glowing from the inside. From the beginning that piece of equipment had stood there like a family altar, but I'd long since forgotten its existence. I almost collapsed when Michael appeared on the screen. "You had a good day today, didn't you?" he asked casually, as if there were nothing to be surprised about. But I couldn't manage to conceal my stupefaction.

"Have you been watching me all this time?"

"Yes."

"Where were you? Hidden among the visitors? Unfortunately I can't distinguish the faces of individual people behind the fence. They're too far away. I can try to discern if a person is a man, a woman, or a child—but it's only guesswork, based on the general mood and blurry outlines."

"I wasn't with the visitors. I was standing on a cloud watching you."

"You're nuts!"

"Have you read today's newspaper? They're planning a meeting between you and your mother."

"My mother? Matthias?"

"No, Tosca."

For a moment I tried to imagine a conversation with my biological mother, but my attempt was instantly derailed: instead of Tosca, all I could think of was a child's drawing of two silent snowmen standing side by side.

"Michael, since you know so much, I'd like to ask you something. Why do people think my mother was neurotic?"

Michael stroked his smooth chin, on which not even the shadowy trace of a razor could be seen. "That's not an easy question. I'm not sure if my answer is right, but what I think is that zoo people consider the circus something unnatural. In the circus, dolphins and orcas turn somersaults and toss balls back and forth, and that might still be acceptable, but it goes too far when a bear rides a bicycle. A bear doing a thing like that suggests that she's emotionally disturbed. That's how these people think, based on their quite particular notion of freedom."

"Did my mother ride a bicycle?"

"I'm not exactly sure. Maybe she danced on a ball, or walked a tightrope. In any case, she did appear onstage in an act that wouldn't have been possible without rigorous training. I don't know if they forced Tosca to do this, or if she just inherited something her ancestors had learned. Like I did."

"Did you work in a circus too?"

"No, not a circus, but something not so different either: I started performing onstage—singing and dancing—at the age of five. When I was barely able to stand on two legs, already I was training hard. I sang love songs without knowing what they meant. I quickly rose to stardom, and then my star just kept rising. When I entered puberty, people suddenly stopped finding me attractive. One friend told me that I'd been robbed of my real childhood and that I should fight to get it back."

"Did they force you to dance and sing?"

"In the beginning, yes. But after a while it was me putting myself under pressure, and I couldn't help it, because I liked performing so much—it was like being high every time I went onstage."

"Was it the same for my mother? Is that what made her ill?"

"I don't think so. When you see her, you can ask her yourself. Now I have to go home."

After Michael's visit, I fell into a deep, carefree sleep. When I woke up again, the inside of my eyelids was a luminous pink. After breakfast I ran out to the play area, as thoughtless and gay as a child. Matthias was no longer here, but his smile still shimmered in my brain. On the other side of the fence, a large number of visitors were already awaiting me with their cameras at the ready. The wind brought me the scent of the director. I used my right hand to steady myself against the naked tree—the only tree in the enclosure, growing out of a crack in the rocky ground—and with my left, I waved to my old acquaintance. He waved back. Then it started. Like an athlete doing warm-up exercises, I moved my shoulders up and down and turned my head to both sides. In the course of the afternoon, the number of visitors increased. During the hottest part of the day it sank somewhat, but in the late afternoon the audience grew again. The humans stood pressed tightly together, two or three rows deep, staring fixedly at me.

It wasn't easy to keep thinking up new games. I throttled my brain, hoping to squeeze new ideas out of it, but this made my body temperature rise unpleasantly. My desire to show the audience a new game was impertinently strong, as were the expectations of the viewers, especially the children. The adults weren't always curious right from the start, I had to coax the interest out of them. When I succeeded, I observed with satisfaction how these stiff human bodies softened, their faces glowing.

On this day I had only a single crackpot idea—in any case, better than having no idea at all: I imagined what it would be like if the stone slab were covered with a layer of ice, and I went sliding across it. "Oh, look, Knut's practicing walking on ice!" a small boy shouted. "Maybe he's homesick for the North Pole," a male, grown-up voice replied.

"Will Knut go back to the North Pole someday?" a girl's voice asked, sounding sad. I thought of the figure skaters I'd seen and admired on television. I wanted to be like them, to wear a short skirt and perform an icy dance. I wanted my chest to glitter with jewel dust like theirs. Or was it just ice splinters and water vapor? Ice dancers can glide forward while sliding back. I wanted to try that too, but for some reason it didn't work. I fell on my backside and heard the audience roar with laughter. Practice makes perfect. I decided to work more on this the next morning.

The summer with its tormentingly hot days—on which I couldn't really do anything but sit in the shade waiting for sundown—dragged on and on. I closed my eyes three-quarters of the way, hoping to see a snowfield if only in my brain. Instead, an expanse of water there began to swell. I could smell that the water was made of melted ice. There wasn't a single tiny ice floe upon this water, which glittered blue blue blue all the way to the horizon. "Oh no, Knut is drowning!" a child screamed. Horrified, I abruptly returned to my senses and quickly breast-stroked back to terra firma. It had been a long time now since my grandmother had appeared in my dreams.

Michael's visit was soon a regular part of the evening routine I spent all day looking forward to. "You give your audience pleasure." He seemed to be watching me all day long.

"I enjoy it."

"I used to enjoy being onstage too, even though at the beginning I was forced to perform. As a child, I thought it was normal not to get any dinner if I didn't do well in my song and dance training."

"Matthias never forced me to do anything."

"I know. When I look at you, I'm glad there's a new generation now. But you still aren't free. And you don't have any human rights. Any moment they feel like it, human beings can kill you."

Michael told me about a certain Mr. Meier who specialized in animal law. He sued the director of a zoo in Saxony for putting a newborn sloth bear to sleep after his mother refused to nurse him. The regional public prosecutor's office rejected the claim on the grounds that a bear raised by humans could later develop a personality disorder, the disastrous consequences of which could be only be averted by prophylactic euthanasia. After this decision, all the humans involved considered the issue settled. It wasn't yet clear that Mr. Meier loved not animals but animal rights. There are men who catch fish as a hobby. There are men whose hobby it is to hunt deer. Mr. Meier was after a very different sort of quarry: he hunted laws. He sued the Berlin Zoo for not putting their baby polar bear to sleep after he was rejected by his mother. A bear raised by humans, he argued, would lack the ability to find his way in bear society. It would be better if a problem bear of this sort did not exist. When it came right down to it, a bear in this situation should be shot to avert disastrous consequences. If the zoo in Saxony was innocent, it meant the Berlin Zoo must be guilty. It was illogical to declare both zoos innocent. This was Mr. Meier's line of argument. I felt frost skittering down my spine, then a commotion tumbled through my brain, and a column of heat rose from the top of my head. "Human beings hate everything that is unnatural," Michael explained. "They think that bears must remain bears. It's just the same way some people think that the lower classes must remain poor. They would consider anything else unnatural."

"If that's true, why did they build a zoo?"

"Ah, that is indeed a contradiction. But inconsistency is mankind's very nature."

"Now you're fudging."

"You don't have to worry about what's natural and unnatural. Just live your life as you please."

This question of what was natural robbed me of my natural ability to fall and remain asleep throughout the night. Would it have been natural if I had blindly taken Tosca's teat into my mouth and sucked on it with all my strength? If warm fur without beginning or end had enveloped and never left me? Then I would have spent the first weeks of my life in a cave of maternal odors until the harshness of winter had passed. Ever since my birth, I'd had little to do with Nature. But was this reason enough to consider my life unnatural? I survived because Matthias gave me milk in a plastic bottle. Was that too not part of Nature in the broader sense? Homo sapiens is the result of a mutation, a monster. And just such a creature took it into his head to save an outcast baby polar bear. Was this not one of Nature's marvels?

If everything had proceeded according to the natural order, I'd have found a maternal body at the center of our den. But at the center of the crate I grew up in, there was nothing. In front of my nose was a wall. Was my longing for the world beyond the wall not in and of itself proof that I was a Berliner? When I was born, the Berlin Wall was already part of history, but many Berliners still carried a wall around with them in their brains, separating the right and left halves.

There are people who feel contempt for a polar bear who's never been to the North Pole. But the Malayan sun bear never visited the Malaysian Peninsula either, and the moon bear was never in Sasebo, where the soldiers wear collars just like hers. All of us know only Berlin, and this is no cause to despise us. We're Berliners, that's all. "Michael, what about you? Are you a Berliner like the rest of us?"

He smiled in embarrassment. "Actually I'm just a visitor here. Now that I've turned my back on life as a performer, I'm free to travel as I please. So I'm always on the road."

"Where do you live?"

"Have you ever walked around on the moon?"

"Not yet. It must be delightfully cool there."

"It's too warm for you in Berlin. You might be tempted to complain about not having an air conditioner, but actually that's for the best."

"Why?"

"If it were as cool in your room as inside a refrigerator, and as hot outdoors as a desert at noon, you'd never be able to go outside again. You like to go outside, don't you?"

"Yes, I love the outside air. There's nothing better than outside," I replied in a loud voice.

"One day you'll be able to go all the way outside, just like me," Michael said with a smile and disappeared. As always, he left without saying goodbye. Matthias too had disappeared one day without saying goodbye. I can't remember any parting words from my mother Tosca either.

The next time he visited, Michael told me they were planning a meeting between me and a young female bear, assuming that the meeting with Tosca went well. Then I would see my father Lars as well. I wasn't reading the newspaper as regularly as before. Michael said: "I don't know what to think of this meeting with a potential partner. It's actually rather impertinent of them to be testing your ability to integrate. That's the main reason for the meeting. You aren't emotionally disturbed!"

I sighed, and Michael stroked my shoulder consolingly. "Don't think about it too much. They constantly feel as if they need to be keeping tabs on all the other animals."

Michael was looking pale, much paler than Matthias at the end. Worried, I asked: "You aren't sick, are you?"

"No, it's only because something very unpleasant just occurred to me. My blood refuses to circulate in my body when my thoughts get stuck somewhere. My problem wasn't the female sex, I never took much interest in it, but I wanted to have children and be very very close to them, and no one could understand this. And even before my punishment, I'm being tormented by all possible means."

I was able to find words for everything, but the heat wave that summer left me mute. Each afternoon, I thought that finally the summer's heat had reached its peak, but then the next day would be even hotter. When would the sun be satisfied with its accomplishments and stop plugging away? Michael now visited me only at night, when the temperature would have fallen slightly.

I asked Michael if he had come by bus or bicycle, since he'd once remarked that he hated sitting in cars. He shook his slightly lowered head and did not answer. I noticed that his pants pocket were flat, there couldn't be even the tiniest wallet inside. He wasn't wearing a watch either. From the top of his head to the tip of his toes, he was as smooth and elegant as a black panther.

Apparently the heat didn't bother the zoo's visitors. Day after day, ever more spectators gathered before my enclosure. Not just on weekends—even during the week, these human bodies formed a double wall without a single gap. Since I made an effort every day to look attentively at their faces, I gradually became farsighted. I saw very small children stuffed into their strollers. They stuck their hands out in front of them and cried with the voice of a cat in heat. The faces of the mothers standing behind the strollers taught me how many different sorts of mothers there could be: one looked exhausted and severe, another as empty as a blue sky, and a third clung to her own gaiety.

On that day, I saw four strollers standing side by side. The four mothers were equal in height, as if all stamped out with the same template, and the cheerfulness in their faces appeared copied from one another. Suddenly I realized that there were only three living children and that the fourth stroller held only a stuffed animal with my face. Where was the child? I shuddered and couldn't tear my eyes away from the mother with the stuffed animal. Atop her head, a tuft of hair stuck up like an antenna. The collar of her blouse was crumpled. She was beaming just as I'd imagine a happy mother would. Did she know her child was just a stuffed animal? Was that all right with her?

The stuffed animal in the stroller could be my departed twin brother. I couldn't remember him, but I'd read in the paper that my brother had died four days after we were born. Since that day, my dead brother had ceased to grow. Perhaps he'd remained a baby and was now wandering around the zoo in the form of a stuffed animal in a stroller. Would he go on roaming around like this for years or even decades?

Finally the heat let up a little, and the word "autumn" even occurred to me. At breakfast I accidentally spilled some milk. The staff placed old newspapers on the floor. Right in front, I saw a large photograph of Michael. Because of my farsightedness, I could no longer read the tiny print of the newspaper very well. With effort I made out the words beneath the photo. Michael was dead. The date was too small to decipher.

But that evening he visited me again, as if nothing had happened. I must have misunderstood the newspaper article. It's always best to pose a dicey question directly to the person involved, but in this case I didn't know how to formulate it. Michael asked whether I'd met my mother yet.

"No, not yet. But there are rumors that the meeting will take place soon."

"You'd better decide in advance what you'd like to ask her. During the meeting itself, you'll probably be too excited to know what to ask. That would be a shame."

"What would you ask your mother if that were possible?"

"Hmm, probably I'd ask how she'd have raised us if our father hadn't been there. He was very poor and forced us to become successful pop musicians. I thought he was only thinking of the money, but that wasn't the most important thing to him. When he was young, he wanted to be a musician too, he even played several instruments. His older brother had made fun of him. To the brother, it was clear that my father could never be a musician. The hatred between the brothers drove my father mad."

"Why did you say goodbye to the stage?"

"I thought we could survive all the changes in our environment if we'd only change our bodies and our thoughts. But I don't have an environment anymore. So there's nothing left to do."

I asked myself whether I still had an environment. No one visited me in person any longer except Michael. I was the only one who made use of the large terrace with its swimming pool, but it didn't really constitute an environment for me. When I looked up at the sky, I was overcome by a desire to travel far away. I had never been properly outside, but I was nonetheless convinced that our earth is enormous—otherwise the sky wouldn't be so large.

Winter approached from far away with slow, heavy boot-soles. If there were no far away, the winter would lose all its cold in the Berlin heat. One day a cold wind would finally blow even here where I was. There must be a distant place where the cold can protect itself from the city's heat and survive. That's where I want to be.

The visitors to the zoo turned up in wool coats, and some of them wrapped thick scarves around their necks and even put on gloves. They stood patiently behind the fence, watching me, their noses red with cold.

Recently a visitor tossed a pumpkin into my enclosure. It was an amusing present. It rolled across the stone and fell into the water, but it didn't drown: to my astonishment, it knew how to swim. I jumped into the water after it and pushed it around with my snout. After a while I started nibbling at it, feeling a mild hunger, and discovered that it didn't taste half bad. Then I went on playing with the pumpkin, which now was missing a chunk.

"Isn't Knut cold? He's taking a bath outside!" a child said in surprise.

"He's never cold. He comes from the North Pole."

That adult voice was lying. I don't come from the North Pole. I've read several times in the newspaper that I was born in Berlin. I also often read that my mother was born in Canada and raised in the GDR. Still, people kept saying I was from the North Pole, probably because of my snow-white fur.

During the night, the temperature plummeted. Michael never wore a coat when he came to see me, perhaps he didn't own one. This night he wore, as always, a white blouse with a lace-trimmed collar beneath a black, skintight suit. His socks were white, his shoes black leather. "You look so gorgeous with your black hair," I said.

"I have a hankering for white fur, that's why I came to visit," he replied in a jesting voice. "But you mustn't tell anyone I visit you. Wouldn't want to tip off the paparazzi."

"I don't read the newspaper anymore. It's full of lies."

"Some of the things they've written about you are degrading," Michael said indignantly.

I nodded and said: "They write horrible things about you too!" I hadn't meant to say that to him, but it was too late. Michael's face froze. It was a long time before he could respond to me.

"I'm sure there wasn't anything about me in the paper."

"Yes there was. They said you were dead."

The yellowish-green hues of the pumpkin resembled the autumn leaves the wind had brought to my terrace. How many days had passed since Michael's last visit? He'd stopped coming, and I didn't know how to measure the time. Since it grew colder every day, I was relieved at the thought of having survived the summer. But this relief scarcely alleviated my pain and sorrow. I didn't know what I still had to look forward to. The day when I would see my parents again? The day I would meet my future wife? I'd have far preferred to go to another party with Maurice rather than get married. I didn't want to have a girlfriend, start a family. I wanted to go out again!

I was waiting for the day when winter would so intensify that I could plunge into the season of ice. Winter was the reward for all those who'd survived the purgatory of summer. I wanted to lie dreaming of the North Pole in chilly air, wanted to see a snowfield before me, a field that—unlike newsprint covered with gossip and lies—would gleam an immaculate white. The North Pole had to be as sweet and nourishing as mother's milk.

The damp air hung so heavy in the sky that I didn't know whether to cry or laugh aloud. I noticed a disturbance in my throat. Also, my spinal chord felt strangely cold and sodden. I thought I was about to faint. My mood was moist and dark, but with a coating of euphoria. This feeling had weighed on me all day long, and in the course of the afternoon it grew unbearably thick. A wet wind licked my skin, wanting to taste the flesh and then the marrow in my bones. Behind the sky's gray membrane, a fluorescent lamp gleamed. The weak light confused all of us: me and the objects around me. The fence and the stone slab displayed the wrong colors, as though they no longer knew if they were experiencing a dawn or a dusk. I looked up. Something darker than the air was fluttering in between. It was a snowflake. It's snowing! Another flake. Snowing! And another. Snow! The flakes danced here and there. Snow! At first the snow looked surprisingly dark, despite the fact that it was just a white crystallization. It's snowing! How wondrous it was, the way this brightness in motion instantly appeared dark. Snowing! The flakes spin as they fall. Snowing! One more flake. Snow! And another. Snow! There was no end to it. I couldn't stop looking up. To either side of me, the little white leaves flew past like autumn leaves in a storm. The snow was a spaceship, it lifted me up and flew off as fast as it could in the direction of the skull—the cranium of our earth.